SLUGGING IT OUT IN JAPAN

SLUGGING IT OUT IN JAPAN

An American Major Leaguer in the Tokyo Outfield

Warren Cromartie with Robert Whiting

KODANSHA INTERNATIONAL
Tokyo • New York • London

Distributed in the United States by Kodansha America, Inc., 114 Fifth Avenue, New York, NY 10011, and in the United Kingdom and continental Europe by Kodansha Europe Ltd., Gillingham House, 38-44 Gillingham Street, London SWIV 1HU.
Published by Kodansha International Ltd., 1-17-14 Otowa, Bunkyo-ku, Tokyo 112, and Kodansha America, Inc.

First edition, 1991.
91 92 93 10 9 8 7 6 5 4 3 2 1

Library of Congress Cataloging-in-Publication Data
Cromartie, Warren, 1953-
Slugging it out in Japan : an American major leaguer in the Tokyo outfield / Warren Cromartie with Robert Whiting.—1st ed.
p.   cm.
ISBN 4-7700-1423-6
1. Cromartie, Warren, 1953-   2. Baseball players—United States—Biography. 3. Baseball—Japan. I. Whiting, Robert. II. Title.
GV865.C68C76 1991
796.357'092—dc20
[B]
90-26956
CIP

Grateful acknowledgment is made to *M Inc.*, where portions of this work first appeared, and to the *Weekly Asahi*, from which the article "Learn From The Major Leaguers Who Have Changed Japanese Baseball" was translated.

To my father
who taught me the game of baseball—
Thanks, Pop

Acknowledgments

I'd like to acknowledge the people and institutions that have had something to do with my successes. They are all part of a part of my life: Chris, Candice, Cody, and Carole Cromartie; Marjorie Welbon, Gladys Walker, LeRoy Cromartie, Mary Keaton, Lulabell and Charles Brown, Wendell Welbon, Lenny Booth, Miami Parks and Recreation Dept., North West Boys' Club of Miami, Gordon Whitehurst, Buster Zeigler, Doug Cooper, Ray Granda, Joe Miranda, Miami Jackson Senior High School, Miami Dade North Junior College, Anchorage Glacier Pilots, Ora Bendross, Andre Dawson, Tim Raines, Pete Rose, Rod Carew, Tony Perez, Mickey Rivers, Dick Williams, Lance Nichols, Sadaharu Oh, Hiroaki Hirano, Ichi Tanuma, Toshio Shinozuka, Kiyoshi Nakahata, Larry Sazant, Hank Blieir, Nick Buonaconti, Barry Garber, Jason Berkman, Geddy Lee, Jim Mansilla, Bruce Davison, Joe Gardner.

—*W.C.*

Also, the authors wish to thank Elmer Luke for his support, encouragement, and astute editing—which helped make this a better book.

CONTENTS

SLUGGING IT OUT IN JAPAN

1984

THE MESSIAH

Tokyo was a long way from Montreal. Fourteen hours, ten thousand miles, half the world away. My Japan Air Lines flight had just landed, and I was waiting, as ordered, to be the last one off. I was exhausted from the long haul.

A stewardess finally approached me in the first class section. "You can deplane now, Mr. Cromartie," she chirped, beaming down at me. She looked happy enough for both of us.

I picked up my flight bag, straightened my tie, and stepped out of the plane and into the terminal at Narita Airport. Although it was a freezing cold February night, a huge crowd had shown up. There was an instant of quiet, and then the flashes started going off like crazy.

I stood there blinking, disoriented, feeling slightly embarrassed. Then a man stepped forward and introduced himself as the general manager of the Tokyo Giants, the team I had recently signed to play for. He shook my hand vigorously, at the same time bowing from the waist.

"Welcome to Japan, Mr. Cromartie," he said, "You are our messiah."

In a daze, I mumbled, "Hello"—and bowed back.

Then it dawned on me what he had just said.

The flashes kept going off every second. I forced a smile, bowed some more, and followed my new GM through immigration and customs, to a hastily assembled press conference. There, in front of more reporters than I'd ever seen in any one place in my life—more even than at a White House press conference, it seemed—I fielded questions through an interpreter.

How did I like Japan? How many home runs would I smack? Could I eat Japanese food? Could I guarantee the Giants a pennant?

I was beginning to feel a little silly.

I'd been called a lot of things in my life—some good, some not, some downright nasty. But the last time I was called a messiah was never. Then again, I'd never played for a Japanese baseball team before. For eight years, I'd been a Montreal Expo, and I'd had a pretty decent career. I'd been a .300 hitter on a team of superstars that included Andre Dawson, Gary Carter, Steve Rogers, and Tim Raines. When I became eligible for free agency in the winter of 1983, I put myself out for the highest bidder—like everyone else. Little did I expect the Tokyo Giants to outbid the San Francisco Giants and make me an offer I couldn't refuse. It was a three-year contract to the tune of $600,000 per. I would be the first starting level major-leaguer to play in Japan while still in his prime.

Japan wasn't the States. But as a 29-year-old black dude from Miami who'd been playing in a white city like Montreal while married to a French-Canadian woman, I was used to doing things differently. I talked it over with my wife Carole, the mother of my two children, and when she said *oui*, I signed.

The Tokyo Giants were a Japanese institution. Owned by the *Yomiuri Shimbun*—the largest newspaper in the world with a circulation several times that of *USA Today* or the *New York Times*. They were Japan's premier team, with thirty-three league pennants and a stack of Japan Series championships to their credit. They were like the Yankees, and the Dodgers, and the Mets—all put together. And then some.

Nineteen eighty-four was the fiftieth anniversary of the Giants and big things were expected. Sadaharu Oh, the team's former great batting star—the man who had hit a record 868 home runs in a long, spectacular career—was the new manager. The *Yomiuri Shimbun,* on a gamble, had invited the Baltimore Orioles, winner of the 1983 World Series, to play the Japan Series champion at the end of the season, fully expecting, of course, that the Tokyo Giants would be doing the honors.

I, Warren Cromartie, had been hired to make certain that would happen, which explained the reception accorded me that chilly evening at Narita.

"Will you win the triple crown?" a reporter was now asking me.

I was careful how I phrased my answers. I hadn't walked on water lately. Besides, I'd been warned about the Japanese press: Another American, upon his arrival in Japan, said in answer to a similar question that he would hit anywhere between five and fifty home runs. Safe enough, one would think. The next morning, many of Japan's sports dailies, which have huge readerships, headlined the new American's vow to hit fifty out of the park.

With that kind of reporting, I wondered, why have a press conference?

So I just kept repeating that I would do my best to help the team win until the thing was finally over and I was ushered into a limousine for the long ride into town.

The apartment that was to be my new home was an ordinary three-bedroom unit on the twelfth floor of a fifteen-floor apartment building in the center of Tokyo. It wasn't bad. There was a balcony, sliding glass doors, a washer and dryer, a toilet I could sit down on. But it was nothing that would appear in *House Beautiful,* which should have been the case given the five-thousand-dollar rent per month the Giants were paying for it. You could walk across the living room in four steps. I later discovered, though, it was a palace compared to what the average Japanese lives in.

I walked out on the balcony and looked out at the winking

lights of the city, then stared down at the street below. A detachment of press cars had camped there after following me in from the airport. Now, to be perfectly honest, I didn't mind a little bit of attention. In fact, I didn't even mind a lot of attention. The more the better I'd always thought. But already I was beginning to have my doubts about the Japanese media. With a security guard downstairs, I felt as if I had some privacy. But how much, I asked myself, as a photographer below pointed his zoom lens camera up at me.

I awoke at 5:00 A.M. Jet lag. I was dying for a cup of coffee. I padded to the kitchen and flicked on the light. No such luck. The cupboards were bare. The refrigerator was empty. I had to settle for a glass of water. Then I took a long hot bath and stepped out onto the balcony to watch the winter sun come up. The morning was cold, and I shivered as I took in my new surroundings.

A couple of press cars were still there, parked next to a row of spindly trees, propped up by sticks. Beyond them lay a vast ocean of gray concrete buildings and telephone lines. It extended into the distance as far as I could see. Haze hung over the city.

It was grim. Soulless. Possibly the most depressing sight I had ever seen in my life. I groaned. What had I gotten myself into? What had I left behind?

Two days later—lonely, depressed, in a Japanese daze—I received a phone call from my wife in Miami. The news was not good: my grandmother, whom I loved a lot, had just died at age 66. I'd seen her the day before I came to Japan, and she looked well enough even though her health was failing. She suffered from bad blood circulation and had had a leg amputated, but I never thought she'd die.

She was my mother's mother, and we'd been very close all my life. She understood me, and she was like me—or rather, I was like her. I was left with the emptiest feeling—like there was a hole inside me. With her dying and me half the world away from everyone who was family, I really felt isolated.

THE VIEW FROM MIYAZAKI

I had heard of the famed Japanese work ethic—company men and factory workers going twelve to fourteen hours every day, hardly ever taking vacations. And I had heard that the same philosophy carried over into baseball.

Bump Wills, an old friend of mine who'd played the previous year for the Hankyu Braves of Osaka, had filled me in. He hated it. He'd had bad vibes right off the bat. He didn't like his manager, who was known for being very strict. He didn't like the hard work, and he didn't like the long hours. In fact, he didn't like anything about Japanese baseball except the money they were paying him—which was considerable.

I had also talked to Reggie Smith, the other American on the Tokyo Giants that year. League rules allowed two foreigners—the word is *gaijin*—per team. Reggie wasn't too encouraging either. "Camp is going to be hell," he told me over the phone before I arrived, "pure hell."

With all this good news, what I did was to go out and get into the best shape of my life. I had vowed to myself that the Japanese weren't going to show me up. So there I was, 6', 185 pounds of rock hard muscle, ready to play. But I still wasn't emotionally prepared for the scene that greeted me at the Giants' training facility in Miyazaki, on the southern coast of Kyushu.

Although it was only the middle of February, my teammates had already been practicing for a month. They had started after New Year's with "voluntary" group training. Then, at the end of January, they had gone to Guam for two weeks of tough workouts. Now it was time to get serious, and the guys already looked in better shape than any group of athletes I'd ever seen.

Their schedule was baseball all their waking hours, literally—from stretching exercises in the morning to shadow swings in the evening. By comparison, it made major league camp—with its leisurely 10–2 routine beginning in March in sunny Florida or Arizona—seem like a vacation.

All the teams in Japan trained like the Giants. Management wanted you to concentrate on baseball constantly, to think about baseball all the while you were awake, and to dream about it when you weren't. But on the Giants, it was especially bad. Of course, everybody wants to win, but here the pressure was intense and unrelenting. I found that out the first time I met the Giants' manager, the legendary Sadaharu Oh.

Oh was a dignified man in his forties, of medium weight and build, but with the biggest calves I'd ever seen on anyone in baseball. They were the result, I was told, of all the running he had once done. Oh was half-Chinese, half-Japanese, and well-educated; you could see right off that he was a bright man. But already he was experiencing the strain of his job. There were small worry lines on his brow and his hair had traces of gray.

"Hello," he said, greeting me in English, "how are you? Welcome to Japan." Then he smiled and said, "We must win."

"We must win?"

He nodded and repeated more firmly this time: "We must win."

Speaking through the interpreter assigned to me, Oh made it clear how vital it was that the Giants capture the pennant that year and how important my role was. Then, as he posed with me for the photographers who had surrounded us, he spoke again in English.

"We must win, Cromartie-*san*. We must win."

It was a phrase I would hear over and over in the following months.

Despite all my preparation, I found I still had to bust my ass to keep up with the regimen in Miyazaki. We awoke at 7:30 every day for a "morning walk" and other exercises on the beach behind our hotel. Although the sun was usually shining, there was an icy wind that whipped in off the Pacific Ocean, and it was always freezing cold. After breakfast, we put on our uniforms, took a fifteen-minute ride to our seaside practice stadium—a small, rusting structure with a grassless infield and seats for about 12,000—and began work in earnest.

Starting at 10:00, we did forty-five minutes of jogging and calisthenics—leapfrog drills, agility drills, carrying a guy on your back, stretching, and a lot of other excruciating stuff that didn't have anything to do with baseball. Then we worked on cutoff and relay plays.

At 11:00, we changed shirts. Outfielders would chase fly balls for half an hour, then hit until noon when it was time to break for lunch—which usually consisted of rice balls, sandwiches, and green tea, served right there on the field. We'd stand huddled around the dugout *hibachi*, the smell of burning coal in the air, wolfing down our food. We had fifteen minutes. To the second.

After lunch, we did what the Japanese call "sheet batting," which was to hit in a simulated game versus different pitchers, and work on running the bases in different situations—first to second, first to third, first to home. Then it was time for a practice game. When that was over, we ran laps around a nearby track. We did this until we couldn't see straight.

Some of the players—usually the pitchers—also ran the several miles back to the hotel.

When I saw the work the pitchers had to do, I couldn't believe my eyes. They'd have to throw 200 to 300 pitches every day, even the pitchers with sore arms, and they had to run 50-meter sprints twenty-five times on the day they were scheduled to pitch in a practice game. It was nuts!

Then there was the thousand-fungo drill. The coaches would take a guy out and hit ground balls to him until he collapsed. Every day it was a different guy. One coach, two buckets of balls, about an hour and a half. And when it was all over, the guy would be flat on his back, and the coaches would praise him for his fighting spirit. "*Naisu gattsu,*" they would say, nice guts. Then the trainer would come out and give the poor bastard a massage.

It was a conditioning drill and a mental drill rolled into one, they told me. The Japanese believe that if you don't have the proper spirit, then you can't be a good baseball player. One way to develop the proper spirit is to go through exercises like the thousand-fungo drill. Getting through it makes you tough, or so they said.

Back at the hotel, in the evening, we still weren't finished. We had after-dinner lectures and night practice indoors until lights out at 10:00. Then the next morning we had to get up and do it all over again.

Our routine went on like this for twenty straight days, with minor variations. You could compare it to marine basic training at Parris Island, I guess, except there you don't have to train as hard and you also don't have several hundred reporters and photographers monitoring your every move.

Our hotel, the Miyazaki Grand, was known as a Western-style hotel, but the only thing Western about it was that we didn't have to sleep on the floor. We stayed in tiny rooms that weren't much bigger than jail cells. You could lie in bed and touch both walls, turn on the TV, and write a letter on the desk next to it without ever getting up.

The food was fish and rice and bean curd soup, with an occasional steak. It wasn't great but it was OK. My teammates preferred to eat out, on the rare evening off, in nearby Miyazaki city—a little metropolis of narrow streets, shops selling *tofu* and fish, old wooden houses with sliding doors, and rice fields on the outskirts.

But from the time they stepped out of the hotel, they were hounded by fans. That was more celebrity than I liked. As a result, most of the Giants hung around the hotel and spent time in the bar in the lobby, which was always packed with reporters.

I spent a lot of time each evening alone—in my little cell, lying on an undersized bed, feet sticking off the end, watching television in a language I couldn't understand. I did a lot of talking on the phone to my wife and the people back home in Florida. I also did a lot of thinking. And what I was thinking was, I'm not going to go through this for three years in a row.

"It will be a miracle if I last through this season," I said to Carole one bleak night.

Reggie Smith did not make life any easier. On our first day on the field, the press wanted Reggie and me to pose for photos. Just the two of us. I said sure, nice idea, but Reggie flat out refused. He walked off without a word, and I was left standing there—alone and not a little embarrassed.

Negative vibes flowed from him all the time. During practice, Reggie kept his distance. He had his own routine, and he didn't have to train the way everyone else did. At one stretch, Reggie wouldn't even eat with the rest of us. He holed up in his room and ate peanuts for a week, losing five pounds in the process.

At first, I couldn't figure it out. Reggie was a big powerful guy who had had a fantastic major league career. He was a switch hitter, had hit over 300 home runs, and he'd been one of the best defensive outfielders of his time. He had led the Los Angeles Dodgers to the World Series more than once. The year before, his first in Japan, Reggie hit 28 homers for the Tokyo Giants and had helped take them all the way to the seventh game of the Japan Series, before they lost to the Seibu Lions.

He was a proud man—and he had reason to be—but I couldn't understand his moodiness and his negativity. So one night I asked him, "What's going on, Reggie? Why are you pissed off all the time?"

There was a moment of silence, and then, in a rare burst of communication, he blurted out: "Because I can't hit the fucking fastball anymore, Cro."

Ah. So that was it.

The injuries he had suffered over the years had worn him down, he said. His body wouldn't work like he wanted it to. He couldn't run or throw like he used to. He couldn't get around on the fastball. He was losing it, facing the end of his career, and he was having a very hard time dealing with it, which is why he didn't feel like talking—to anybody.

I sympathized. And I stayed away. The day would come when I couldn't hit the fucking fastball anymore either.

Reggie's aloofness was pretty much the start of my trying to mingle with the other players—in bits and pieces, step by step—out of sheer loneliness.

The guy who broke the ice for me was a rail-thin, sleepy-eyed second baseman named Shinozuka. A lifetime .300 hitter and one hell of a nice guy, he was the first one to come up and introduce himself to me at Miyazaki. All the guys had introduced themselves in the beginning, but Shinozuka had been the first and he'd done it in English, too.

"My name is Shinozuka," he'd said, removing his cap, bowing, and shaking my hand. "Nice to meet you."

I'm sure he had practiced saying that before he

approached me, because the guy was not exactly bilingual. It made me appreciate him all the more. But whereas Shinozuka made me feel comfortable, it took a while with the rest.

In time, I got the feeling that the Giant front office didn't want their guys to mix with the *gaijin* too much. I think they were afraid the players would learn bad habits from us. Perhaps it was paranoia. Perhaps it wasn't. That was one of the things about Japan I was beginning to discover. You never really knew where you stood, because the Japanese were reluctant to tell you. It was easy to be paranoid in that environment. Culture shock was setting in.

If we were pursued like rock stars outside camp, we were treated like prisoners of war inside. On the team, there was no such thing as a star, with the exception of Reggie, and his was fading. Everyone, from our most popular player, third baseman and cleanup hitter Tatsunori Hara, down to the rawest rookie, went through the same hard schedule. No one was exempt, because team harmony was of utmost importance. So in good Japanese fashion, I tried to do everything that everyone else did. Almost everything, that is.

I caught fly balls until I couldn't stand up, and I ran until my tongue hung out. Fortunately, the coaches in their wisdom did not demand my participation in the thousand-fungo drill and the ten-mile marathon that everyone else was required to run one day. And thank god for that. But otherwise, I did the work and I made it through. And when I finished, I felt as if I deserved a medal—or at least a stripe on my sleeve.

THE ROAD TO KORAKUEN

Japan consists of four main islands and a population of one hundred twenty million people. Most of them, it seemed, were Giants' fans. After we broke camp at the end of February to begin playing exhibition games around the country, everywhere we went we were mobbed.

We played in places like Kagoshima, Fukuoka, and Kokura—drab, colorless cities of ferroconcrete buildings—as well as Kyoto with its weird mix of ancient temples and neon signs. Wherever it was, when the team bus pulled up to our hotel, the fans would be out there in the thousands, screaming and cheering. I couldn't believe it. I began to understand how Michael Jackson must have felt while on tour.

The Giants drew more people for an exhibition game than most major league teams in the States could hope to attract for a regular season contest. The pregame ticket lines always went around the block. The smallest crowd we played before was 25,000, and that was because the stadium couldn't hold any more. Hell, even our practice sessions were standing room only.

We played in freezing cold, rain showers, even snow, and still the fans came. We were an all-weather baseball team. The umpires would never call a game off because they were afraid the fans might riot.

The nation had grown up watching the Giants. The team had been formed in 1935 and was Japan's first pro club. The Giants had dominated baseball in the postwar era, including one stretch in 1964–73 when they won nine Japan Series championships in a row. There were two leaguess: the Central and the Pacific. But the CL, you might say, was the Gucci bag league because the Giants were in it. The PL, in contrast, was plain canvas bag; it got far less attention.

Every Giants' game was telecast nationwide, and the ratings were always sky-high. They were on the front page of the many national sports dailies every morning, and quite often, I noticed, there was a picture of me. Japan was paying particularly close attention to my activities.

Many of the parks we played in were worse than the ones I'd seen in the minor leagues back in the States. They were dark, aging, prewar horrors with cramped clubhouses and smelly communal toilets. The locker rooms were so jammed with equipment, trunks, suitcases, and whatnot that there was no room to change our clothes. We dressed in the hotel, took the bus to the park, then after the game we went back to the hotel to shower. We carried our own bats and bags.

You had to "small up" in Japan. It was a land of volcanic mountains and little open area. Every available inch of space was used, if not for construction, then for farming. Rice paddies dotted the hillsides. Everywhere you looked you saw TV antennas and power lines. If there was a wilderness in Japan, I certainly hadn't seen it yet.

Japan was crowded. But it wasn't until we got back to Tokyo and I settled in that I got a sense of just how much. It was overwhelming—tiny houses and apartments jammed together, dense traffic all the time, neon signs stacked one on the other in the entertainment areas, and so many people that when you walked down a main street, you had to be as alert as if you were driving an automobile. If you stopped suddenly, you might cause a chain of pedestrians to smash into each other.

Reggie and I lived in the same building, in an area named Hiroo which Reggie liked to call the Beverly Hills of Tokyo because it was filled with outrageously priced boutiques and antique shops and expensive French restaurants. It was also Americanized—fast-food joints like McDonald's, Kentucky Fried Chicken, Wendy's, and Shakey's Pizza stood next to *sushi* and noodle shops.

Reggie had begun to loosen up toward me. He taught me how to use the subway system to get to the park, which was a lot faster than going by car. The subways were clean and safe and bright—not like in New York—but they were also a lot less private, especially if you happened to play for the Tokyo Giants. We'd stand in the car and everyone would gawk as if we'd just landed from outer space.

Once, the train stopped at a station on the way to the park, the door opened and a hundred kids, all wearing Giants' baseball caps, came dashing in. They surrounded us, touched us, felt our hair, and begged us for autographs.

On Spring Equinox Day, a national holiday in Japan, it was worse. All the kids were out of school, and with no one working, the train was jam-packed. We were sandwiched in there tighter than sardines in a can, people pushing and shoving. The train would stop, thirty people in our car would get off and forty more would crowd in. Passengers would literally get stuck in the doors, and the platform conductor would push them in.

I stood there, shoved up against a wall, the breath squeezed out of me, smelling the hair tonic of the guy next to me. I glanced at Reggie. He looked homicidal. Still he was adamant that this was the best way to get to the park. And when Reggie made his mind up about something, he didn't change it easily.

Korakuen Stadium, the Giants' home ground for 40 years, was as bad as the subway—shoulder to shoulder with people. Reserved seats for the Giants' games were always sold out, and lines for the bleacher non-reserved seat tickets started forming twenty-four hours in advance. You could see people outside the center field gate with sleeping bags and pup tents.

The stadium itself had a major league air to it—with a huge electronic scoreboard, artificial grass, and seats for 45,000. It also had beautifully short fences, like most parks in Japan, measuring about 300 feet down the lines and about 380 feet to center. By game time the place was overflowing with people sitting in the aisles and standing in the back rows.

Add to this the fact that the stadium was part of an amusement park complex, and you begin to picture the setting when I made my debut on Opening Day...and began the long process of humiliating myself.

THE EDUCATION OF WARREN CROMARTIE

Opening Day itself wasn't bad (it was what came later that blew my mind). It started with a lavish ceremony, where I was introduced and presented with flowers, a band played the Japanese national anthem, "Kimigayo," and the mayor of Tokyo threw out the first ball.

To tell the truth, it was great. It was playing baseball in Japan just as I imagined. White clouds floated in the blue sky above. A pleasant warm sun shone down. On the center field flagpole above our million-dollar scoreboard the Giants' team flag rippled in the wind.

I stepped up to bat in the fourth inning, after grounding out in my first time up, to face a heavy-lidded, stone-faced fastballer named Komatsu, of the Chunichi Dragons. From out in right field came the roar of the Giants' cheering section: thousands of fans in orange and black *happi* coats banging drums, blowing trumpets and whistles, and screaming my name in unison, madly: "*Ku-ro-ma-tei, Ku-ro-ma-tei, Ku-ro-ma-tei.*"

Komatsu threw me heat, a 90-mile-per-hour fastball off the

outside corner. "*Sutoraikku!*" yelled the umpire. Komatsu wound up and threw another, a curve that backed me off the plate. "*Sutoraikku tsu!*" His next pitch, another heater, came sailing in, but I was waiting for it. I didn't breathe. I slugged it—far into the right center field stands for a home run. The roar of the crowd was now deafening, and it was wonderful. I felt like a billion yen. After I rounded the bases, Oh and my teammates were standing in line before the dugout, huge smiles written on their faces. They pumped my hands and pounded my back. It was intoxicating.

I should have savored the moment more, because it was the last such experience I would have for a long, long time. It was also the last fastball I'd see for a while. In the next two games against the Dragons, their pitchers threw me nothing but breaking stuff. So did the Hanshin Tigers' pitching staff on our subsequent road trip to Osaka. And the Carp and the Whales after that.

At the Tigers' home field, Koshien Stadium, an aging barn of a place with a brand new scoreboard that lit up in purple, the color of the Imperial Court, I made an error that caused us to lose a game, sending the 58,000 fans there into spasms of delight. In Hiroshima, playing against the Carp in their creaking old park just a few yards from the Peace Dome, I got two hits in twelve at-bats, and repeated that performance in Yokohama against the Taiyo Whales. I was seeing lots and lots of curves and sliders and fork balls and *shooto* balls (which in the States are known as running fastballs).

Some of them were nowhere near the strike zone, but they were called strikes anyway.

A month into the season, I was really getting my lunch. My batting average was somewhere around .260, and home runs had all but disappeared from my repertory. Photos of me appeared regularly in the sports dailies still, but now they were shots of me striking out or popping up—portraits of a *gaijin* as a failure. I couldn't understand the articles, but it was obvious they weren't saying what a great hitter I was. According to people who could read Japanese, the press was ripping my ass blind.

Reggie told me the same thing had happened to him. He

hit only eight home runs the first half of 1983, his first season in Japan, and had missed several games with injuries. To hear him tell it, they were ready to deport him. But then he got his bearings and was able to redeem himself.

Reggie also warned me to control my emotions. No haranguing the umpire, no bat throwing. The Japanese thought that it was bad manners to lose your temper. It was bad for team harmony—*and* a sign of a weak character. After striking out, the correct thing to do—the Japanese thing to do—was to run back to the bench with a tight smile on your face, your anger kept firmly under lock and key.

The style of baseball in Japan was better than good, but it was a notch or two below the level of the major leagues. The players were excellent in fundamentals—they did the bunt, the hit and run, hitting to the opposite field, and such—better than Americans. In the field, they were very sure-handed and made fewer errors in general. But the players weren't that big—5'9" or 5'10", 165–170 pounds on the average—and they did not have a great deal of power. Although the pitchers had good control of their breaking pitches, in general they didn't dazzle you with their fast stuff. They just finessed you to death.

I knew in time I would get the hang of things—or rather I hoped I would get the hang of things—after I learned the strike zone, which was bigger and wider than it was in the States, and memorized the pitchers and their names. It wasn't like the States where you had a Smith or a Jones coming in. In Japan, you had a Watanabe, a Kobayashi, a Suzuki, and so forth. It was like being back in elementary school when you had to learn the states and their strange-sounding capitals.

Outwardly at least, I was confident, but everyone around me was uptight as hell. It was the first time the Giants had ever paid anybody the kind of money they paid me. Reggie was making a million dollars, but he only had a one-year contract. Mine was guaranteed for three years. That meant no matter what happened, they had to pay—all of it. The man who had scouted me and recommended me to the Giants, Iwamoto, a team official, was worried sick. I was doing so bad, he thought he was going to get fired.

Oh looked worried too. So did the two Giants' batting coaches, who were casting disapproving looks at my Pete Rose–style batting crouch. The coaches were fanatics about proper form, which is to say Japanese form. Every batter on the Giants hit the same way: semi-closed stance, hands in close to the body, compact swing. That was how you could hit to all fields and handle any type of pitch, they said. My crouching style of hitting was a sacrilege. One batting instructor told me flat out the reason I was not hitting was because of incorrect form. It was *dame,* he said, no good.

Well, I could see that I would have to shorten my stroke somewhat, and learn to hold back and wait a little longer because of the slower breaking pitches. But I'd be damned if I would let them force me into their mold. Good reflexes and knowledge of the pitchers were what made a good hitter in my opinion. Form was important, but it should be something you felt comfortable with. I wasn't about to change the way I'd been hitting all my career.

Someone explained to me that the emphasis on form was a throwback to the country's feudal history. For centuries, daily life had been tightly controlled. There was a right way to pour tea, to hold a sword, and, here in the twentieth century, to swing a baseball bat. The same with driving a car. In order to get a driver's license, you were required to attend a driving school which taught you driving by the numbers. Starting from the basics. If you unlocked the car door on the street side, for example, you were allowed to open it six inches, and six inches only. Then you checked for traffic. You looked first to the right, then left, and never ever the reverse. Only then could you get into the car. While you were measuring the inches, you could get run over.

But I didn't have much room to argue about the way I swung. By mid-May I was down to about .230, and I'd been dropped to seventh in the batting order. Iwamoto looked ready to commit *hara-kiri.*

SMALLING UP

My batting form aside, I was getting better at "smalling up."

But not entirely. There was the matter of the Giants clubhouse in Korakuen. It was smaller than anything I'd experienced thus far in Japan, and it was always cluttered with gear.

My locker was a wire mesh affair, one of many rows of such lockers, which I was happy with in one sense because, as I found out, it had belonged to Oh before me. The one nearby, over in the corner by the window, had been Shigeo Nagashima's. Nagashima was the third baseman and batting star who had teamed with Oh to win all those pennants for the Giants back in the sixties. I had yet to prove that I belonged in such exalted company.

Even so, it was too small. I had a little chair in front of my little locker which I could scarcely sit on. Guys were taking off their clothes a few inches away from my nose. A guy named Komada, a 6'4" outfielder, had the next locker. He would be standing next to me, changing into his uniform; then all of a sudden he would bend over and moon me unintentionally. I'd be putting on my socks and there would be his big rear end six inches from my nose.

"Turn your fucking ass around," I'd say.

"*Gomen nasai*," he'd say, "*gomen ne.*"

"*Gomen*" meant "I'm sorry." It was an expression you learned fast.

If the locker room was small, the trainer's room was microscopic. And so was the sauna—a tiny box you had to jackknife your body to get into. All the doorjambs in the clubhouse were so low, I kept banging my head.

There was a constant flow of people in and out—like ants at a picnic table. I was continually getting whacked in the face by doors opening into me, and doing the same to my teammates. I'd open the clubhouse door and find out I'd knocked somebody on his ass.

"*Gomen nasai, ne.*"

No shoes were allowed inside the clubhouse. Everyone had to wear slippers. That was the rule. The slippers made this horrible sound: "Phee...phee...phee."

The only place you went barefoot was in the shower room. That was another rule—which was bad because the guys would piss in the shower all the time. Everyone pissed in the shower.

Shinozuka, our second baseman, pissed in it. So did Egawa, our ace pitcher. Even our star cleanup batter, the heartthrob of millions of girls, Hara, pissed there. You *had* to piss in the shower because we didn't have a lavatory in the locker room. There was no room for one.

If you didn't want to piss in the shower, you had to dry off, get dressed, and go out by the main entrance to the clubhouse where the press congregated. That was where the toilet was.

So everybody pissed in the shower.

In the beginning, it was hard not to feel self-conscious when I took off my clothes in the clubhouse. I was certainly different from everyone else, and while I didn't especially feel that my teammates were checking me out to see how I measured up against them, I'm sure they took a peek when I wasn't looking.

Athletes in the States are used to other guys walking around naked in front of them, but the Japanese are a little shy about their bodies. They'd undress and then cover up their privates with a small towel. They didn't just let it all hang out.

Another thing that was different was that we'd sit down to shower—on a small plastic stool—and even wash each other's back. Guys in the States might get nervous about this, but in time I got used to it. It beat doing it yourself.

After we showered and rinsed off the soap, *then* we'd proceed to the bath—a big, communal tile bath the size of a small swimming pool. It was hot, real hot, and we'd sit and soak, the water up to our necks, for as long as we could, which in my case was not long at all.

It was more than just a way of getting clean. It was a kind of ritual, a way of relieving stress and hanging out with your teammates at the same time. Too bad that other aspects of life on a Japanese ball team weren't as easy to adjust to.

THE ROAD TO OBLIVION

Reggie and I weren't the only *gaijin* players with problems. Three other Americans, including Don Money, had left their teams that spring with various complaints over the way they were treated, and now it looked as if Bump Wills wasn't going to make it either. Bump was hitting about .217 for the Hankyu Braves, and his relationship with his manager wasn't any better than his average. They'd had one big argument when Bump missed a sign. His manager blasted him in the press, and eventually shipped him off to the farm team.

Playing ball in Japan was a hazardous occupation. Over 250 Americans had tried their luck in Japan since the end of the war; few of them lasted. One who did was Leron Lee, a former St. Louis Cardinal, who had played for seven years with the Lotte Orions of the Pacific League, and had a career average of .320 with about 30 homers a season. Lee had married a Japanese woman and understood the country—sort of. His first words of advice to me were, "Don't expect to have everything you had in the major leagues. Don't complain about the little things. If you learn to give a little, you'll be much better off."

Leron's brother Leon, a former Cardinal minor leaguer, played for the Taiyo Whales. He was a .300 hitter too, with a 41-homer-season in 1981. Then there was an American named Randy Bass, who played for the Hanshin Tigers, who had similar stats, and Gregory "Boomer" Wells, Bump's 6'7", 220-pound teammate who'd hit .304 with 17 home runs the year before.

Success was certainly possible, which is why I wasn't overly worried—even if everyone else was. I was confident I'd make it. If they'd just be patient and leave me alone.

But that was a very big *if.*

With June approaching and the Giants second in the division, seven games out of first place and two games under .500, everyone was pointing his finger at you-know-who. And at Reggie too, who was out with an injury.

And then Oh benched me.

Me. His multi-million dollar *gaijin* star. The messiah. On the bench along with the other Giant subs. It was outrageous. It was also embarrassing. I felt like crawling into a hole.

It wasn't just my disappearing batting average that had prompted Oh to erase my name from the lineup. It was my refusal one afternoon to watch films of opposing pitchers we were likely to face that night. This was a daily exercise the Giants went through, and it was regarded as necessary because Japanese teams always kept the starting pitcher's identity secret until game time. You might think: Well, Cromartie, what's so bad about watching films. Why make such a big deal about it? And I'd say to you: It's not such a big deal unless you have to watch those same films day in and day out, ad infinitum, ad nauseam, with no possibility of parole.

There were only five other teams in the Central League, and we faced the same guys time and time again. Still, we had to study the films. In my two months in the league, I had seen the pitchers enough to know what they were going to throw. If I was familiar enough with them, my teammates, who'd seen them the year before, and the year before that, and the year before that, should have had every pitcher in the league memorized—what he could throw, what mannerisms he had, even what way he combed his hair. But still they had to watch the films every day. What were they going to learn that was new? I didn't see any point to it. Not every goddamn day anyway. I was sick of watching the things.

The problem with my hitting, or non-hitting, I thought, was concentration. It was a problem that no amount of film viewing was going to cure. But when I didn't show up at the daily matinee this one time, Oh got pissed. And to teach me a lesson, the son of a bitch benched me.

The Japanese press had a field day with that. One paper did my astrological chart and concluded that my moons were out of sync with those of my teammates. Another paper did a study of my character by analyzing my facial features. Because my ears were small and my nostrils not very prominent, my character, according to the paper, was feeble. Furthermore, I was supposed to be stingy!

Was there no end to this degradation?

I tried to ignore all the bullshit, but still it got on my nerves. The day after my benching, on my way to the park, I spied a man lurking outside the apartment building, camera in hand. I recognized him as a photographer from one of the magazines—in quest of a candid shot of the now-disgraced foreigner. He was trying to hide behind a tree in front of the main entrance, which was not a very good idea because the trees were so scrawny. When I saw him, I flashed. I snuck up behind him, grabbed the camera cord and twisted it around his neck, as hard as I could.

That was me, Mr. International Goodwill.

A LESSON FROM THE MASTER

"*Irasshaimase! Irasshaimase!*" Welcome, welcome.

Oh slid back the door and led me through the entrance of a smoke-filled *yakitori* restaurant in the Aoyama district of Tokyo.

"*Irasshaimase!*" A collective hush fell over the room as everyone recognized who we were. Patrons turned to gape, chopsticks frozen in midair. They cast a brief glance of contempt at me, the Fallen Gaijin, then resumed their reverential stares at the man whose face and name, according to one survey, were better known than the prime minister of Japan or the president of the United States.

A waiter ushered us past a long counter—stacked with every imaginable kind of grilled chicken on a stick—to a private VIP room in the rear, where we were seated at a low table. The clean, grassy, sweet smell of fresh *tatami* mats filled the room.

"*Irasshaimase, Oh-san,*" beamed the proprietor, bowing several times, "*konban, zannen deshita.*" Wasn't this evening a disappointment.

The "*zannen deshita*" was a reference to our unfortunate loss earlier that evening at Korakuen. But then again it might have also been a reference to Oh's choice of American players.

The proprietor took our order as men scurried in to serve us beer and jugs of *Nihon-shu*, otherwise known as *sake*. And then we were left alone—Oh, me, and an interpreter—behind *shoji* screen doors which were slid firmly shut. The room was simplicity itself—the black lacquered table, three *zabuton* cushions, an alcove with a flower display, and a framed, hand-painted Chinese character on the wall. Oh poured for me as I held my glass. Then I poured for him, as per custom in Japan.

Then we toasted each other with a little bow of the head and the word *kampai.*

Oh had invited me out that night, I suspect, to help lift my spirits. He'd put me back in the starting lineup, after a couple of days on the bench. But I still wasn't hitting. It was mid-June, my average was .250, with 11 home runs and 24 RBIs, and I'd failed to come through in many key situations. "*Dame Kuromatei*" the papers were calling me. No Good Cromartie. And with Reggie missing games because of injuries, the press was now saying that the Giants would be better off without any foreigners at all. "*Gaijin,* Go Home," screamed the daily *Sports Nippon.*

Oh understood how the *gaijin* felt, I thought. Though he was born in Japan, he was a *gaijin* himself. His father, a restaurant owner, had emigrated from Taiwan as a cook, and Oh had suffered from discrimination growing up in Tokyo. Oh had been unable to play in one big baseball tournament simply because he wasn't a Japanese citizen. So he knew what prejudice was, and he was able to understand the world from both sides.

He tried to help put my mind at ease by not putting pressure on me. So far, aside from the video incident, he had let me practice as I wished. He just said, "Take your time and get used to the game."

If I had a problem, we'd talk about it, he'd listen. Like tonight. He spoke English somewhat. He had been very good in school from what I understand, but when he just barely failed the entrance exam to Waseda University, one of Japan's top colleges, he went straight to the Tokyo Giants.

I had really gotten to like the man. He didn't seem to have a harsh bone in his body. With his soft voice, ready smile, and big merry eyes, he was one of the friendliest people I'd ever known. I'd never seen him complain to an umpire, or lose his temper, or raise his voice in anger. He was decent to everyone. I had heard about the time he went to New York for a luncheon in his honor. There were maybe a thousand people there, and about five hundred of them asked for his autograph. He stood there for two hours and signed for every damn one of them.

Sitting across the table in his coat and tie, pouring *sake,* Oh looked more like a businessman than an athlete. He'd developed a bit of a paunch, but you could still see the power in his shoulders. He told me that in his playing days, before going to bed each night, he would swing a bat in front of a mirror five hundred times.

I'd seen him step into the batting cage and take a few practice swings with that foot-in-the air stance of his. He still had it. This was the man who hit 868 home runs in a 22-year career. That's an average of 40 per year. Sure, you could say that the parks were smaller and the pitching inferior to the States', but that man could hit. Nobody could deny that.

As soon as he stepped up to bat, he took on a commanding presence. He seemed to magnify to twice his size. He had concentration that was unbelievable. He'd lock on to the pitcher with an intensity that was scary. *He* was challenging the pitcher.

His attitude was that there wasn't a pitcher alive who could get him out. And to be sure, there hadn't been many. Oh had faced the best America had to offer in postseason and preseason exhibition play: Seaver, Koufax, Palmer. He'd hit them all. Hell, even then, at 45, the guy looked like he could still bat cleanup for us.

We discussed my batting difficulties. Unlike the other Giant coaches, he had no objection to my style of hitting. He knew that I was a different type of batter. My problem—one of my problems—was that sometimes I'd get off the rocker and swing too hard or swing under the ball. I was uppercutting too much.

"Think about hitting ground balls, Cro," Oh said. "Hit the ball down, down on the ground, to counter what you're doing wrong."

When he was playing, Oh said he liked to hit in a downward motion, as if swinging a sword—like a *samurai.* He practiced swinging that way. Sometimes he would go out in his backyard with his sword, throw a piece of paper up in the air, and try to cut it in half, swinging the sword like a bat. There is a way that you can actually do that, he told me, but it had to be precisely the correct swing and motion and it required absolute concentration. If you did everything right, all in one step, then you would slice the paper in half. But if you did something wrong, if something was out of sync, you wouldn't succeed because the paper was so light.

"Same as your hitting, Cro," he told me. "Same motion—whoof!—sword cuts paper. You hit the ball."

Oh stood up on the *tatami*, imitated my left-handed batting stance, and showed me how I had been lifting my shoulder when I swung. Then he picked up the magazine he had brought with him and stuck it under his left arm.

"When hitting," he said, "pretend you have a book under your left arm. Try to keep it there when you swing. If you open your shoulder, the book will fall down."

He opened his back shoulder as he swung, the magazine fell. Then he tried it again. This time, his shoulder stayed in place, and so did the magazine. It was amazingly simple.

"When you hit," Oh continued, "use a motion as if you were going to punch somebody. When you punch somebody, you don't punch flat-footed. You come back. You move your body and you cock your fist. Same thing with hitting. You get a thrust going. You rev it up."

I was dazzled. A batting lesson from the master. And a lesson that was easy to understand and easy to remember. If the people out there only knew what was going on inside this room. I sat there and soaked it up and thought to myself how lucky I was. I was sitting in a restaurant halfway around the world from the States, with one of the greatest hitters of all time, getting a private behind-closed-doors batting seminar. It was an experience worth coming to Japan for.

REGGIE'S COMPLAINT

The rainy season had arrived and the streets of Tokyo were one big sea of umbrellas. If you walked down the street in some crowded areas, you had to wear glasses or risk losing an eye. It wasn't the most pleasant time of the year. Five straight weeks of rain, temperatures that bounced around, and mold everywhere. They weren't the most ideal conditions to play baseball.

My wife and children had arrived from Miami for the summer vacation, having waited until the school year ended. Carole walked into our apartment in the Beverly Hills of Tokyo and said, "The whole place is only a little bigger than our living room back home!" But she took that, and the rain, and Tokyo, in what might loosely be described as good cheer. At least she didn't pack up and leave right away like some guys' wives did.

It was great to be a family man again. Christopher was seven, and Candice was four, and they really liked Tokyo, which was like a huge carnival to them. Everything was new and different and kind of cute in a Japanese way. The language was a barrier, of course, but the place was utterly safe and clean, and Carole and I never had to worry about anybody hurting them or ripping them off.

Carole's presence was a godsend besides because my social life was almost zero, and I was beginning to go crazy. I had tried to mix more with my teammates. I'd pat them on the shoulders and try to get them to laugh. I'd remember words I heard on the bench and try to speak their language. But while they seemed nice enough, they were always a bit reserved and restrained toward me.

Reggie and I were not exactly glued together either. During games, we did not always sit next to each other on the bench, and this raised a lot of eyebrows in the Japanese media. Normally, if there were two *gaijin* on a team, they were like Siamese twins. But Reggie went his own way, on and off the field. And I was forced to go mine.

We just had different personalities. He was into jazz. I liked rock. He played the saxophone. I loved the drums. I was still trying to get it together adjusting to Japan, while he was working on where his next stop was.

The only times Reggie and I saw each other were at the park or in taxis going home together after games. We never had dinner together, and only a couple of times did we have a drink on the road, during which he would clam up. Reggie was pretty much of a loner.

But as far as baseball was concerned, he was there when I needed him. "You don't have anyone but me to talk to. And vice versa," he said. "So we've got to support each other."

He filled me in on various pitchers, and he warned me never to get complacent about my play, no matter how well I eventually did in Japan. "They'll always find something wrong with you," he said, "and they'll never give you the credit you deserve.

"The Japanese teams look to the American players to come through in tough spots," he went on, "because they don't really want to have to come through on their own. They're too nervous and scared. Last year, they were calling my name out in pressure situations. 'Come on, Reggie,' they'd say. 'Home run, Reggie,' '*Gambare*, Reggie.' They always look to the *gaijin* to do it, and they love you if you do do it. But when time comes to give out credit, you might as well forget it."

Reggie thought that ball players in Japan were all wimps and pussies. "They don't play hard ball," he said. And after watching the game for a while in Japan, I began to see that it was true. They didn't slide hard. They didn't throw brushback pitches. They didn't play a balls-out style of baseball. "Soft baseball" is what he called it.

Reggie used to sit on the bench and laugh at the guys on the field, and so would I. We would watch how the runner would tiptoe into second base, how the batter would get hit by a pitch and do nothing about it. All they'd do is hide in the dugout across the way and yell insults out.

We would laugh at what they called strategy. We couldn't help it. We'd never seen anything like it before. One team would have runners on second and third in the early or middle innings of a close game, and the pitcher would intentionally walk the batter to load up the bases for a possible double play. You'd never dream of doing that in the States. That would be giving the other team too much.

Or the number eight hitter in the batting order would sacrifice bunt, letting the pitcher hit. Or a hit and run would be called on a count of 3–2. Or a squeeze. The batter would strike out and the runner would be thrown out. It was unbelievable.

I'd look over at Reggie and he'd be dying laughing. He'd look back at me and say, "Tell me, Cro, what the fuck is going on?"

Our laughter would extend even to our own team. It wasn't Oh we were making fun of. It was the coaches—they were the ones advising Oh. They'd look over at us cracking up, and they knew we were laughing at them. It was rude of us, but we just couldn't control ourselves.

It seemed that confrontations like this were inevitable as far as Japanese and Americans went, because the psychologies were so different. Their style of play—to say nothing of their way of life—was so much more cautious and conservative than anything we were used to. They were much less confident, at least outwardly. In the game, for example, they'd sacrifice bunt in the first inning. The leadoff batter would get on base, and the next batter would bunt him to second. It was automatic. Americans would rarely do something like that. Not in the early part of the game. You went for the big score. Or you tried to advance the runner by some other means. That was the American way. The Japanese thought they were playing it safe. But, to the American way of thinking, you weren't supposed to give away outs—the other team was supposed to earn them.

Reggie was having it worse than me. He was hitting about .230 with 10 home runs over the first three months of the season. He had a bad knee, a bad arm, and now his eyes were bothering him. The media was eating him up, calling him a broken down jalopy. The fans and the opposing players were starting to screw with him too, which bothered him a lot because he was such a proud man.

The fact that the pitchers wouldn't challenge him annoyed him no end. They were scared of his power, so they always gave him dinky shit outside the plate. Numerous times I saw him yell at the mound on his way back to the bench: "Challenge me, you motherfucker!"

Then there was his arm. He had hurt his shoulder with the Dodgers and had undergone a big operation. He couldn't throw anymore. Guys would take second and third base on him. Once, a player singled to right and went into second standing up. He stood there on the base and grinned out at Reggie.

Reggie started yelling at him from right field. He came back to the dugout at the end of that inning and kept yelling at him from the bench. "The next time I get a chance to break up a double play," he shouted, "I'll knock your little squirmy ass all the way into left field."

Reggie got mad a lot that year. Another time, he popped out and walked back to the dugout, screaming in frustration. "Motherfucker! Motherfucker! Motherfucker! Motherfucker!" About a half-dozen players who had been sitting on Reggie's end of the bench shifted to the other side; they wanted to stay out of his way. I stayed where I was, and he came down to my end. He kicked the bench as hard as he could, sat down, and swore a blue streak for about fifteen minutes. I was the one who had to listen to it, because I was the only one who could understand what he was saying. Not that it required a great deal of linguistic ability.

This was the guy who had told me what to expect and how to behave and keep my temper under control, and here he was, doing exactly what he had warned me not to. It wasn't hard to sympathize with what he was going through, though. He had been a major league star, top of the line, and now he was unable to cut it in even a Japanese league anymore.

I think the other Giants understood what he was feeling. They certainly knew who Reggie was and what his career represented. I don't think Oh really minded Reggie's outbursts, either. He was philosophical about it. He just shrugged and said, "The pride finally got to Reggie."

Oh once told me that he wished his players would show more balls. He said that there were times in his playing days when he came back into the dugout and wanted to tear everything up, but *he* could never allow himself to do that. He had to wait until he was away from everyone. He had to show *samurai* discipline, he said. He couldn't reveal weaknesses for other people to see and pick apart. Because he was not a pure-blooded Japanese, he had to be doubly careful how he behaved.

But I know he liked it when, on those rare occasions, players showed some raw aggressiveness. He wanted you to show the pitcher who fanned you that you were angry. He wanted the attitude that told the pitcher, "Next time I'm going to get your ass," instead of the usual Japanese way of coming back with a smile on your face, trying to show how cool you are by not showing any emotion.

That behavior—that type of Japanese macho—was OK, I guess, if you were in the martial arts. But baseball is a highly emotional game, and losing your temper is a way of venting pressure. It can be a release, as long as it is done in a way that doesn't hurt anyone else. The problem in Japan was that even talking in a loud voice was enough to affect the people around you.

INDEPENDENCE DAY

Toward the end of June, my game finally started to click. My lesson from Oh had begun to pay dividends. I hit a homer here, a game-winning extra-base hit there. Then, on the Fourth of July, I really exploded, hitting three home runs in one game. Talk about symbolism.

Prewar Jingu Stadium was the home of the Giants' crosstown rivals, the Yakult Swallows, who were owned by a health drink company. Set in the western part of the city, the stadium was surrounded by a small forest and, having been just renovated, boasted the largest, most expensive electronic scoreboard probably in the world. It lit up with a bewildering array of Chinese characters and inspiring slogans, like "*Rettsu Go!*" And the night of the fourth, the name *Kuromatei*, was all over it. In the second inning, with a light mist falling, I came up against a hard-throwing right-hander named Obana and whacked an inside curve into the right-field stands. I did it again in the fourth. And I did it in the fifth too—with the bases loaded—against a reliever named Nakamoto. I slammed the ball 400 feet into the center field stands, exactly to the spot where my son Chris and his friends were sitting.

I was off and running. In my next six games, I hit eight more home runs, and by the third week of July, when we broke for three all-star games, I had 24 home runs. I was second in the league. What's more, my average stood at a semi-respectable .266.

Oh was ecstatic. So was Iwamoto, the man who had scouted me. He would not be losing his job after all, and he would not be commiting *hara-kiri* after all. What's more, the press started running favorable pieces about me again.

A reporter came up to me and asked how many times a day I brushed my teeth. Three, I replied. He asked when. In the morning, after a game, and before I go to bed, I replied. Somehow, with that juicy bit of information, he managed to write a feature story in a sports daily.

I wasn't voted into the all-star games by the fans, but six other players on our team were, despite the fact we were eleven games behind the league-leading Chunichi Dragons of Nagoya and struggling to play .500 ball. Hara, our golden boy, was the overwhelming choice at third despite an average of .250 and 15 home runs. Our good-looking catcher Yamakura was also voted in even though he was barely hitting .200. They were the Japanese Giants—and to most of the fans, that was all that mattered.

THE LONG HOT NATSU

Splatt! Crackk! Whapp!

Splatt! Crackk! Whapp!

Komada, our lanky outfielder, my occasional mooner, was taking batting practice. The sweat was flying off his brow like a geyser; his uniform was soaked clear through.

It was 2:30 in the afternoon, and the sun was white hot, beating down hard. The dugout temperature at Korakuen was 90 degrees, but out on the artificial surface, it was much, much higher. It was like a sauna bath. A frying pan inside a sauna bath would be more like it. The heat was coming off the turf like it was a radiator. It was so intense we couldn't touch the metal ball rings or the batting cage poles with our bare hands.

And we were having special practice. The team hadn't been winning, so this was our punishment. For a solid week during the all-star break, we had been out at our practice field on the Tama River, on the outskirts of Tokyo, an hour by train from where I lived. We had gone through three-to-four-hour work-outs every day in the blistering heat—stretching, running, batting, fielding. Everybody on the team had lost ten pounds, it seemed, and we were all dragging our asses.

Then when the second half of the season began and we kept on losing, we had these intensified pregame drills at the park.

Americans would have eased up in weather like that. Conserve your energy for the game, they'd say. Do ten minutes of batting and ten minutes of fielding in pregame workouts. Run a few sprints and that's it. Head back into the cool of the clubhouse. Sometimes in places like New York, Atlanta, and Chicago, it got so hot the players wouldn't have warm-ups at all.

But not in Japan. If anything, we worked even harder. That was why we were there at 2:00, instead of our usual 3:00 practice time, for a game scheduled to begin at 6:00. Komada had been at the park since 12:30, along with a few others, for special hitting. He was still swinging away—like a *kendo* student working on his *kata*, his form.

Splatt! Crackk! Whapp!

We had a game that night, and Komada would have nothing left. Neither would anybody else. All I can say is, thank god they didn't include Reggie and me in the drill. Why, I don't know—perhaps they figured there were some things *gaijin* just couldn't take.

The fellows who did have to undergo this martial arts type of training did it without complaining. Nobody said, "I'm not doing this shit." That wasn't the Japanese way. If the coaches had ordered them to practice twenty-four hours a day, I sincerely believe that they would have tried to do it. They were, if anything, more contrite than ever. Our prospects for a pennant on the fiftieth anniversary of the club were very dim, and our owner, Mr. Toru Shoriki, would not be happy paying for some other Japanese team to play the Baltimore Orioles in the much-heralded big U.S.–Japan baseball showdown. He'd be the laughingstock of Japanese baseball.

I'd only met Shoriki once. That was before the season started. He was the son of businessman Matsutaro Shoriki, the founder of the *Yomiuri Shimbun* and the Tokyo Giants. He was a short, brusque man with glasses who had looked at my major-league statistics and said, "Hmmmpf. OK. You hit thirty home runs for us. OK?" End of meeting. It was more of an order than it was a request.

Shoriki had no quarrel with me once I started blasting the ball, but word had it that he was going to take away some of the commercials the players were making—which were many and worth a lot of money—if they didn't start playing better. He had that kind of power.

Our pitching coach Horiuchi, a former Giant ace who had played with Oh, had vowed to resign if the pitching didn't get any better. And there was talk about dropping Hara out of the cleanup spot because he hadn't been producing. That would have been a really radical step, almost heretical, because Hara had *always* been our cleanup hitter.

A succession of former Giants' stars had been coming out to the park to analyze Hara's form, suggesting this and that correction, putting him through extra batting practice. It was like a national emergency. And Hara put up with it all like a good Japanese.

In my opinion, what Hara really needed was a rest. But in Japan, as I was finding out, you could never just rest, especially with the Giants. Not with the entire nation watching you all the time. They'd think you weren't serious if you did.

Photographers were everywhere. And you had to be extra conscious of your image at all times. A shot of Hara relaxing on the bench during pregame drills could do great damage to the good name of the team. It was hard even to go out and have a quiet beer after the game. You never knew what photographer would be waiting in the men's room to photograph you taking a leak for the nation's readers. There was a team rule that said we had to stay out of cabarets and certain types of hostess bars to avoid any hint of trouble. We had to dress a certain way. Reggie was the only one on the team who was allowed to have a mustache. That was in recognition of his long major league career. But people bitched about his mustache all the time; they thought it was a disgrace.

Being a Giant was like working for a Japanese company where, I was told, management control was absolute. Employees had no life of their own. There was the story of a Japanese auto maker which had a bad sales year and the workers all gave up their annual vacations to stay on the job. The Giants didn't get any time off either.

I'm sure the Giants would have had a better record if we hadn't had to practice so hard. That wasn't an option, however, and the result was that the manager and the coaches and the front office people abused the hell out of their resources. They used a pitcher until he burned his arm out, then they'd get somebody else. It was the throwaway pitcher philosophy. We had a young kid named Makihara. He was only 19 or 20 that year, a lean six-footer who wasn't even fully grown yet. But they let him throw 200 pitches in one game. In the States, that would be a criminal offense.

One hundred twenty pitches maximum was the rule on some major league teams for a starter, but on the Tokyo Giants, it was all this macho shit. A guy proved how tough he was by throwing his arm out.

All of our pitchers threw 100–150 pitches every day. Because they threw so many different kinds of pitches—curves, sliders, fork balls, *shooto* balls, and whatnot—management said that constant practice was necessary to perfect their form and have sharp control. The pitchers were good. You had to grant them that. They could snap off that breaking pitch on the outside corner on a 3–2 count every time. A lot of major leaguers couldn't do that.

But any American coach or sports physician would say that so much pitching is bad for the arm. The arm needs rest, they'd tell you. Every time you throw you tear muscles, and if you pitch a nine-inning game, three or four days are required for the muscles to heal and the tissue to regenerate. The Japanese either did not believe that, or if they did, they did not care. Everything was *samurai* guts and spirit. If you had enough of *that*, then you could throw all day.

Pitching coach Horiuchi once explained the Japanese philosophy to a BBC television interviewer: "You can overcome fatigue by willpower," he said. "If your mental attitude is right, you can make your body work. That's why we emphasize mental training. It's not exactly like there's no freedom here, but you have to sacrifice yourself for the fans and for the team. We aren't as strong as the Americans, and unless we practice a lot, we can't play ball."

It was a praiseworthy attitude, but it also explained why you seldom saw successful pitchers in Japan over the age of 30—and why so many pitchers on our team had arm trouble.

If the pitchers on the Giants were bothered by that unpleasant fact, it didn't show. No one dared to rebel against a coach. It just was not done. That was the quickest way to get a ride out of town.

Hard training wasn't all we had to put up with. There were also the meetings, which we had at every possible opportunity. We had meetings before the game where the coaches for hitting, pitching, and defense would go over the opposition's strengths and weaknesses. We had meetings between innings, where Oh would gather us around him in front of the dugout and dispense special advice like "Go for the curve ball," or "Hit to the opposite field."

Then we had postgame meetings where the coaches would go over all the mistakes that we made that evening, regardless of whether we won or lost; they were called *hansei-kai*, self-reflection conferences. We weren't in first place, but we led the league in meetings.

Every day, it was the same routine. Management had to tell you what to do. In the games, you were never allowed to show any initiative. The manager and the coaches controlled it all, from the first pitch on. Take an extra base without a coach's express order, and there'd be hell to pay.

In the U.S., in major league baseball, you are expected to figure certain things out for yourself. You're brought up to be an individualist. That's the American way. From grade school on, people tell you to stand up, to speak your mind, otherwise you're not a man. I gotta be me, tell it like it is, and so on.

In Japan, it's just the opposite. The Japanese motto is "We gotta be us." That's the main difference. Japanese kids are taught not to question authority and not to try to be different. They wear the same school uniform, cut their hair the same way. Their big lesson in life is to shut up and obey orders. And obey is just what my teammates did.

The most amazing thing about it all, though, was the harmony on the team. In the U.S., you always have some sort of conflict on a team. But these guys hardly ever wised off. They never complained out loud—even though they had good reason to—and I never saw one argument. It was incredible, but I had to admit it was kind of nice too.

If my teammates were restrained on some fronts, they weren't at all in others, like eating, which they did with great gusto. Their pregame food intake was impressive. They'd go out and do their practice, then come into the clubhouse and stuff themselves with noodles, sushi, rice, fish. To their thinking, you had to be nourished—full, in other words—to go out and play your best. To our way of thinking, there is no way in hell you can play well consuming the amount of food they eat before a game.

I would eat maybe some spaghetti around 3:00 before a night game, because it's carbohydrates. It was good energy and I could burn it off in the game. But my teammates gorged themselves. To say nothing about the cigarettes they smoked! That totally blew me away. You didn't see a lot of real heavy drinkers, but everybody on the team smoked. Everybody. And there were some very serious smokers.

I'd say on the average those guys smoked a pack a day each, from the time they reached the ballpark until the time they left the stadium after the game. I saw a player have somebody get him seven packs of cigarettes—as if he were in the navy and his ship was about to leave.

Much of the time we traveled by train—on the famous bullet train which zipped along, on schedule to the minute. To Nagoya to play the Chunichi Dragons, it was a two-hour ride; it was three-and-a-half hours to Osaka to play the Hanshin Tigers, and almost six to Hiroshima to play the Carp. And the entire time it took us to get where we were going, the guys smoked.

We'd board the train and everyone on the team, except me, would light up—some forty players and coaches and other assorted personnel. I had no choice but to sit there and suffer. Outside the rice paddies were whooshing by at 95 miles per hour, and inside I was choking in a haze of cigarette smoke. I felt like a fireman. I should have had a sweatband and a fireman's hat on.

Traveling on the team bus was no different. The windows were closed because that was a team rule. We'd sit there, dripping sweat, and everyone would be puffing away. It was torture. I decided I would endure it through sheer willpower—it would be a test of my fighting spirit—if I didn't die of smoke inhalation first.

THE BANZAI MAN

August nights at Korakuen were especially steamy. It was muggy, stifling beyond belief. The stands were packed as always, but people would sit there in T-shirts, wearing towels around their necks to sop up the sweat, waving paper fans in front of their faces. They all looked wilted. Even our normally lively cheering section, or *oendan* as it was called, seemed drained of energy.

But me, I loved it. The higher the temperature went, the hotter my batting seemed to get. I hit two homers against the visiting Carp early in the month, then the next night went two for four, including a homer and three RBIs, against the Swallows to lead us to a win. It was my twenty-eighth homer of the season, and I was now leading the league. My average was a decent .275 and climbing, and I'd been moved up to third in the batting order. I was getting the hang of things. The Cro was flying.

The pitcher who gave me the most trouble was a Whales' right-hander named Endo. Endo had one of the wickedest fork balls I'd ever seen, to go along with a 90-mile-per-hour fastball. He would have been a star on any major league team.

Most of the others I'd gotten used to, and now that they were all tired, I was feasting on them. Their *shooto* balls didn't have as much *shooto* as earlier in the year. By the fourth or fifth inning, their pitches were up high in the strike zone, the ball was looking bigger and bigger. It was paradise.

Other Americans had been telling me all year that would happen. "Man, we live for July and August in Japan," Leron

Lee had said. "That's when we make our money." Now I understood what he meant.

My 28 home runs were not bad for someone whose best season in the major leagues had been 14. Still, Reggie advised me to stop thinking about hitting home runs. I wasn't really long-ball hitter, he said. I was just benefiting from the smaller parks. But Reggie was out of the lineup again with a bum knee. So what did he know anyway. I preferred to think that I had developed as a hitter.

With my increased home run production, I started a new thing: a *banzai* after every blow into the stands. *Banzai* is a Japanese-style cheer, something like Hip, Hip, Hooray! You raise your arms straight up in the air, and you yell, *Banzai! Banzai! Banzai! Banzai* meant happy times, they told me, ten thousand years' worth; so I thought, hey, wouldn't it be nice to share my home run delirium with the fans.

So after each mighty Cromartie clout, I would trot out to my position in center field to begin the next inning, and face the fans in our cheering section. I'd raise my hands, and they'd yell *Banzai!* I'd raise my hands again and another *Banzai!* would follow. I'd do it several times, and each time they'd respond—thousands of people wearing our cheering uniforms, screaming *Banzai!* at my command. It was great. I felt like a commander in the Imperial Japanese Army.

It became a regular thing—something the fans began urging me to do. In time, I developed my own technique. I would make them wait until they started calling my name. Then I'd raise my hand like the conductor of a symphony orchestra, signaling it was time to begin. Even the opposing players would stop to watch my performance. They'd never seen anything like it—or me—before.

I started doing other things too, like chewing bubble gum during the games, blowing bubbles between pitches, as I stood in center field. I'd also raise my fist while circling the bases after hitting a home run. I couldn't have gotten away with behavior like that in the States. They'd say I was hotdogging, and I'd have been dead meat. But in Japan, nobody seemed to mind very much. I livened up the games, which tended to be dull with their millimeter-by-millimeter emphasis on offense.

The Giants' management didn't object. They said it helped keep fan interest up. So, gradually, I became Warren Cromartie, entertainer and showman as well as would-be messiah.

REGGIE'S COMPLAINT, II

As the season wore on, Reggie became more and more irritable. Perhaps it was the heat, but more likely it was because he was going through such hard times. His shoulder was bothering him so much that he couldn't swing the bat properly. Every time he swung, he would recoil in pain. The end of his career was in sight, and it was not pretty.

Whatever the reason, he had begun to lose his tolerance for the razzing that opposing fans often subjected him to. They would single Reggie out, I think, because he was making so much money and not producing very much.

Hanshin Tigers fans were the worst because the Tigers were the traditional rivals of the Giants. They were the second pro team to be established in Japan, after the Yomiuri Giants, and they were based in Osaka which was the biggest city in Japan after Tokyo. Whenever the Giants and the Tigers got together, the mood in the stadium was volatile, and of late, Tiger fans had been zeroing in on Reggie. They would hurl batteries and other stuff at him and yell "nigger"—which was definitely the wrong thing to say to Reggie. He'd yell obscenities back at them. The more they saw that it bothered him, the more they did it.

One very hot day in August, when Reggie and I were coming out of the subway exit at Korakuen, Reggie spotted this one dude in a group of Tiger fans milling about in their yellow and black *happi* coats. It was the same guy that Reggie had seen the previous evening, while he was shagging fly balls in pregame practice, yelling "nigger! nigger!" at him. So Reggie walked over, looked the dude in the eye, and smoked him. He punched him right in the jaw and knocked him on his ass. Then Reggie picked the guy up by the lapels of his *happi* coat and spit in his face.

Me, I just kept walking.

The next day, as chance would have it, was August 15, the

anniversary of Japan's surrender in World World II. Reggie celebrated it by punching out yet another Tiger fan.

I'd taken a cab to the park that day. A Giants' official had advised us to take an alternate route until things cooled off. But Reggie refused to change his routine. He said he was going the same way he always did. It didn't matter to him. Hanshin be damned. This time, he took his 16-year-old son Reggie Jr. and another guy with him, for protection.

As he came out of the subway, there, waiting for him was a group of Tiger fans, holding yellow and black megaphones, ready for revenge. As the story went, there was some more shoving and jostling, Reggie Jr. got knocked down, and Reggie Sr. smoked another guy, knocked him out cold.

Two Tiger fans punched out in two days. It was a new Giants' record.

But victim no. 2 complained to the police, claiming that he wasn't the one who had shoved Reggie's son. Reggie was called down to the police station to undergo several hours of questioning.

After conducting their investigation, the police decided not to press charges. The commissioner of baseball ruled that the problem was with the fans, not with Reggie. But the fact that the police were involved at all was harmful to the team image, I was told; Reggie had not acted like a "gentleman." And I personally think that was the final nail in Reggie's coffin.

GAIJIN GO HOME

We won ten games in a row in the early part of September to come within one-and-a-half games of the first-place Carp. Then we turned around and went into a tailspin. By the latter part of the month, when the first cool breezes of fall finally arrived, we were eight games back, dead in the water, and our owner Shoriki, I am certain, was fit to be tied.

We played our last game of the season at Korakuen, against the Whales, before 48,000 fans. That gave us an attendance total of 2,970,000 for the season of sixty-five home games. Par for the course. The Tigers drew two million and so did the Dragons, while the pennant-winning Carp drew a million one.

Shinozuka, my first friend on the team, won the Central League batting title with a .334 average. Endo of the Whales, who was a thorn in my side, led the league in pitching wins with 17. And Dragons' shortstop Uno and Tigers' third baseman Kakefu tied for the home run crown at 37. Yours truly was runner-up.

I finished with 35 *banzai* blasts and a batting average of .280, which was enough to satisfy the Giants. But I also committed the serious error of going back to the U.S. before two makeup games had been played in mid-October. I had a pulled muscle and didn't feel like waiting around, so I left without getting the team's permission. For this I was fined two million yen, about $7,500, the highest fine in the history of the Yomiuri Giants. As a Giants' official later explained to me, I still had a lot to learn about team harmony.

Reggie finished with .255 and 17 homers and, as expected, was released. I didn't see him after he got the news. I got the feeling he was avoiding me. Before I left, I called him at his apartment to thank him and to say goodbye. He told me that he really didn't want to come back anyway. Maybe that was true. But I know that he did try to promote himself in the Pacific League, without any luck.

Reggie had put in his years—some very spectacular years. But he was 39. It was time to hang it up.

In the Pacific League, Boomer Wells, who'd once belonged to the Minnesota Twins, won the triple crown. No foreigner had ever won a triple crown in Japan, and only three Japanese had ever done it, including Oh, who'd won it twice. But hardly anybody paid attention. People said, "It's the Pacific League. It's not the league of the Giants."

Nor, I understand, did anyone pay attention as the Carp beat the Braves in the Japan Series, in seven games, to earn the right to take on the Baltimore Orioles in the "Showdown Series" sponsored by a very unwilling and embarrassed *Yomiuri Shimbun*. The Carp lost four out of five to the jet-lagged O's, who had almost backed out on the deal. Yomiuri had had to increase the amount of money it paid each player, which I'm sure did not help Mr. Shoriki's sense of humor.

All in all, it was a good year for the *gaijin*. Randy Bass of the Tigers finished with .326 and 27 homers, Leon Lee of the Whales hit .321 and 21 homers, Ken Macha of the Dragons .316 with 31 homers, Leon's brother Leron .309 with 31 homers, and Tommy Cruz hit .348 with 29 homers.

Yet, at the end of the year, the executive committee of Japanese professional baseball, made up of the twelve team owners, recommended the exclusion of foreigners from Japanese baseball within five years. The position was that the *gaijin* cost too much money and caused too much trouble; Japanese talent was "competent enough" to fill team rosters.

Even Oh agreed. He had given a speech at the Foreign Correspondents' Club in Tokyo, while I was back home in Miami, in which he said that a true world series between Americans and Japanese would be impossible with foreign players still in the game.

I read about his speech in a Miami newspaper.

I put the paper down and, muttering to myself, thought hard again about packing it in and returning to the major leagues.

1953-83

I've always been a *gaijin*, you might say. I grew up in Liberty City, the poor black section of Miami, where most people were lifetime outsiders and it was a struggle to get from one day to the next. The things I remember most about my childhood are not knowing where my next meal was coming from and having to move all the time because my mother couldn't afford to pay the rent.

My father split when I was a couple of years old. So it was my mother, Marjorie Keaton Welbon, who raised me and a stepbrother, working at a lot of different jobs—assistant nurse, secretary, and what have you—which she never seemed to hold for very long. She was a fox, and she liked to party more than anything else. Working nine hours a day was something she couldn't handle.

There was never any money, and we lived in some dumpy places—mostly cold water tenements. I remember waking up in the middle of the night to find rats chewing on my toes and cockroaches crawling across my lips. I usually had to share a bed with my stepbrother Wendell. Two meals a day was a luxury. I would go for a week on a diet of mayonnaise and spam sandwiches or pot pies.

We were always one step ahead of the landlord. We'd change apartments whenever we'd get an eviction notice —which was about every six months. On one block alone, we moved into three different houses. We also slept on people's couches and in seedy hotel rooms.

But we never had to sleep on the street. Somehow or other, my mother always came up with the money to prevent that. She'd get it from a boyfriend, or from one of the in-and-out jobs she had, or from my grandmother and her sister, my Auntie Loo. I remember my mother once took us to a shopping mall and stuffed some clothes in her bag when she thought the clerks weren't watching. She got caught. But when the store manager saw she had two kids, he let her go. It was very hard for her, but she did what she had to do for us to survive. And for that she has my respect.

I really didn't know much about my father when I was growing up. I did know that his name was LeRoy Cromartie, and he was this big, strong guy who had been a star athlete at Florida A&M, where he made All-America in three sports and was inducted into the school's hall of fame. In football, his main sport, he was a quarterback; in fact, he was the first quarterback to throw a jump pass in the Orange Bowl. In basketball, he was a guard, and in baseball, he played shortstop and third base.

My father married my mother when they were both quite young, and they divorced in a very short time. My mother soon married a man who was a backup singer for James Brown, but then had an affair with another member of the band, which produced in turn a baby stepbrother, a second divorce for my mother, and the rapid disappearance from the scene of my stepbrother's father.

As a child, I was a terror. Sometimes, my stepbrother and I would go to my aunt's house after school to wait for my mother to come home from work, where I would regularly beat up my cousin, Auntie Loo's son.

We also played ball a lot with a two-by-four and some beer cans because nobody had any equipment. My father was a recreational instructor for the Miami City Parks and coached a little league team. When I became old enough, he came around and recruited me. He introduced me to the basics of the game, and from then on, my life would be going to the parks to play baseball.

The city park is where I originally met Mickey Rivers, the first big name ballplayer from Miami. It was Mickey who gave me my first glove. I also met Muhammed Ali. I remember watching him run down 17th Avenue in training, when he still had the name Cassius Clay. That was when he was starting from scratch, and we didn't have any idea who he was. He was just this tall, well-built guy running down a street in the heart of Liberty City, with army boots on. Everybody thought he was a fucking fool. The next thing we knew, he'd knocked out Sonny Liston and bought a chicken restaurant across from the park where we played our games.

In little league, I started to realize I had special talent. I could play with the thirteen- and fourteen-year-olds when I was only ten. Then I joined the Boys' Club, where I played ball until I was 18. I made some good friends there. It was like a second family, and it also helped keep me out of trouble.

My father taught me correct baseball techniques, but he was a loner, and he kept his distance from me emotionally. We never talked father-and-son. We never went fishing. We never had a real relationship. To this day, I don't know how many brothers and sisters he has. I don't even know when he was born.

I did learn that he was adopted, that his mother had been blind from birth, and that he took care of her until she died. I also found out that he had a brother who'd been paralyzed on one side and that my father had to take care of him too.

Maybe all that taking care of people wore him out, and he didn't have anything left for me. Whatever the reason, he remained aloof. No matter how hard I tried, I couldn't seem to impress him. In one little league game, the bases were loaded, with two out in the bottom of the last inning, and our team down by three runs. It was my turn to bat. My father was standing in the third base coaching box staring down at me. I was so nervous I was shaking.

Somehow, I managed to hit a home run. I was overjoyed. As I rounded the bases and approached third, I looked up at him. No way he wouldn't be proud of his son now, I thought. But when I crossed home plate, I was tagged out. I was so busy looking at my father that I had forgotten to touch third base. The game was over. I had blown it, and I could have died from embarrassment. My father didn't say a word, but the hard look he'd flashed me for a second was enough. It was devastating. I cried all the way home.

Still, he was around, if on the periphery, which was something a lot of other kids I knew didn't have. If I was having trouble at school—getting bad grades, getting into fights—or giving my mother a real bad time, she would sometimes call my father over. In front of him, I didn't dare wise off.

Usually, however, my mother would take matters into her own hands. She had a temper that was hard for her to control, and she would whip me with an extension cord when I misbehaved. Once she hit me in the face with a shoe and put a scar over my eye that is still there. I was twelve at the time. Today, maybe that would be considered child abuse, but then, it was pretty common in a black family. It was typical of the environment we lived in. I saw my mother getting beaten up by her boyfriends plenty of times. I didn't like it, but I figured it was normal. That was just the way life went.

My mother wasn't an evil woman, by any means. In her own way, she always looked after me and tried to see that I went on living my life as straight as possible. And she was loyal. She'd come to all the games. Even later when I was in the major leagues, she'd show up from time to time and scream her lungs out. At one game in Atlanta, she was yelling so loud that Chris Chambliss, the Braves' first baseman, turned to me and said, "That your ma, Cro?"

Even under these circumstances, I felt blessed. I could have taken a much different road from the one I wound up taking. Once when I was around ten years old, I was aching to go fishing. I was given a couple bucks for fishing equipment, but when I got to the department store and saw how much the stuff cost, I knew the money wouldn't go very far. So I got the bright idea that if I slipped some small things—you know, hooks and sinkers, things like that—into my pocket without anyone knowing, then I'd still have money for a cheap pole. After all, the pole wasn't going to fit into my pocket. Only thing was, I got caught and pulled down to security. I wasn't any better at crime than my mother was.

The person in charge was a woman. She looked over the stolen goods and stared down at me.

"What's your name, kid?" she asked.

Terrified and crying, I told the truth: "Warren Cromartie."

"Cromartie?" the woman asked, her eyes lighting up, almost unbelieving.

"Yeah, Cromartie."

"Your father's not LeRoy Cromartie?"

"Yeah, that's my father," I mumbled.

"I know your father," she said, now smiling. "I've known him for a long time." Then she cheerfully called him up with the bad news.

My father came down and got me, but he wasn't happy to learn about his kid, the thief. Later, he let me know just how unhappy he was, and you can be sure it wasn't pretty. But the good thing about the whole incident was, I didn't get dragged down to some juvenile delinquent hall and my career as a criminal ended right then and there.

It was harder for Wendell, my stepbrother. At least my father was at the park, and at least he dropped in on us, from time to time. But Wendell's father was never, ever there. He eventually got shot in a liquor store. Some people were fighting, and Wendell's father just happened to be there buying a bottle, minding his own business. He wound up dead by the cash register after paying his bill.

The only one Wendell had was me. I was his friend and his protector. We slept in the same bed, without any pajamas because we couldn't afford any. My mother yelled at him all the time, and I would try to keep her from getting too violent. Once he got shot in the eye with a slingshot by my cousin, and he had to go into the hospital for an operation. He couldn't play sports very well after that, so I think he felt left out. All of that had a lot to do with him later getting involved in crack.

The word drugs wasn't in our vocabulary then. Probably the drugs were around, but the neighborhood wasn't as dirty or bad off as it is now. People were poor, but they weren't running around loose and wild, shooting up or shooting folks like they are these days. Some people even had jobs.

Still, Liberty City wasn't what you could call easy. The big crimes at that time were breaking and entering, and a lot of people I grew up with landed in jail. Mickey Rivers would have been one of them if my father hadn't made Mickey one of his pet projects. Mickey'd had a rough childhood, and he used to hang out with a bad group of people. He was always in trouble, stealing cars, and he'd accumulated a record as long as your arm. My father helped get Mickey out of hot water more than once. He would go over to Mickey's house and literally drag him to the park, because Mickey had ungodly ability.

Mickey went on to have a great career with the Yankees, but now he's out of ball and probably out of money. He liked to throw it around when he had it, especially at the racetrack.

My father arranged for me to go to Miami Jackson High, a big sports power and, then, a predominantly white school; today it's mostly black and Spanish. He made me put on a coat and a tie and took me down to meet the Jackson High coach, a man named Lenny Booth. We went into the locker room, a muggy, grungy place. You could smell its toughness right away. On the wall were pictures of all the stars who had played for Jackson: Freddy Norman, Jim McDuffy, Oscar Del Busto, and others.

Coach Booth showed me the uniforms, sleeveless green and gold jerseys with names on the back, just like the Oakland Athletics. It felt good right away.

The school itself was a turning point in my life. I got along pretty easily with the blacks, the whites, and the Latinos; color didn't make any difference. My world had suddenly grown bigger. There were big pep rallies and plenty of good-looking girls, and I quickly fell in with the jocks. We used to hang out in the halls at lunchtime and rank the other students walking by. We'd jump on the socks someone was wearing, or his pants, or the size of his head. "Hey, you got Frankenstein shoes, man. Look how big they are." "Hey, check out that vinyl belt. Why don't you just tie a rope around your pants. Then you'd really be a Beverly Hillbilly." We weren't real mature, but what the hell, we were kids, and we thought we were hot stuff because we wore jocks.

We'd cut people to shreds. We'd all be standing there, snapping our fingers and having the time of our lives. But, of course, I was never on the receiving end. That would come later—much, much later.

As a student, I was a disaster. I put all of my energy into baseball, and Lenny Booth became like a second father to me. He was the one who molded me, who purified my play, and who helped me develop a good, quick left-handed swing. (In everything else, I'm right-handed.) Come to think of it, he was almost like a Japanese trainer, teaching me to hit tires to gain strength.

I had such good stats in high school that I was drafted by the Chicago White Sox in the ninth round. I was thrilled, but they only offered me $15,000 to sign. When you have nothing, $15,000 seems like a lot, but my father said it was too low, and I was in no position to argue. So I went to Miami Dade North, a local junior college, instead.

Dade North was one of the most famous junior colleges in America for baseball. It had produced a number of big league ballplayers: Mickey Rivers had gone there; so had Glen Borgman, Bucky Dent, Curt Bevaqua, Harry Chappis, Pat Putnam, and even Steve Carlton, for one semester.

I worked hard at the game, and in my first year I was named to the All-America team, along with Freddy Lynn, Al Bannister, Roy Smalley, and Dick Ruthven. We were sent to Japan, of all places, to play the Japanese collegiate all-stars. Never in my wildest dreams did I imagine I'd wind up there as a pro. This was 1972, and I just thought of the trip as a great adventure. I was 18 years old, going abroad for the first time, and very impressed with myself.

It turned out to be an unforgettable experience, not for any good reason you can think of, but for the terrible thing that happened. Years later, standing in the outfield at Jingu where we played those games, I could shut my eyes and still see *it* clearly. *It* was a routine play. The shortstop Al Bannister fielded a ground ball and threw hard to second base to get the Japanese runner out. The second baseman was late in covering, the Japanese runner *didn't slide*, and *whock*! the ball hit him square in the head. The sound was horrible. The guy dropped like he'd been poleaxed. He just lay there on the field, unconscious, and had to be carried off.

Everyone was in shock. Play continued, but I don't remember if we won the game or what. We were all too tense. I do remember that sometime later in the game, the ball was hit to Bannister in almost an exact replay of the earlier incident. Bannister fielded the ball again, and this time he hesitated. When the Japanese runner didn't slide, Bannister didn't throw the ball. He was too shook up.

The guy who got hit in the head died later in the hospital. I don't know if he ever regained consciousness. All of us attended the funeral, still numb over what happened, but also more than a little nervous. We were worried that someone would come after us. Nothing like that happened, but we really didn't feel safe until we boarded that plane for home.

The following year, I hit .340 for Dade North, leading the nation in stolen bases with 55. Then, in the summer, I played for the Anchorage Glacier Pilots in a very good Alaskan semi-pro league. Bump Wills was a teammate. Dave Winfield and Roy Smalley played for the Fairbanks team. So did Suguru Egawa, one of my Giant teammates, three years later.

In Anchorage, I lived with a local family, worked at McDonald's—unloading buns from their big delivery trucks and stacking them in back of the freezer—and went salmon fishing when I had the time.

When our team went to a nationwide semi-pro tournament in Wichita, Kansas, a Montreal Expos' scout saw me. He offered me a contract calling for a bonus of $38,000, which I accepted—at lightning speed. The next summer, 1974, I was playing for the Expos' minor league affiliate in Quebec City in the Eastern League, making $500 a month.

By September, I had been called up to Montreal.

I was only 20 years old, and already I was playing in the

major leagues. I was on top of the world.

MINOR LEAGUE

I'd hit .336 in Quebec City, playing first base and the outfield, with 13 home runs, 61 RBIs, and 30 stolen bases—which was why I'd been called up. So there I was, bright-eyed and eager, putting on my major league Expos' uniform alongside all these guys I'd seen on television. Reality would set in later.

The Montreal franchise had only just been founded in 1969, and the Expos were playing in an old broken down Triple A minor league stadium called Jerry Park, where you had to wait until twilight to start the game. That was because the sun set right in the first baseman's eyes and you couldn't play baseball under those conditions. The Expos had a mix of young, up-and-coming players—like Tim Foli, Mike Jorgensen, Kenny Singleton, and veterans playing out their string—like Ron Hunt and Willie Davis. Steve Rogers was just beginning to make his mark as a pitcher.

Willie Davis, the former Dodger star, took me under his wing and introduced me to the various night spots in Montreal. Willie was having his problems with the front office and with his life as well, and Expo executives John McHale and Jim Fanning ordered me not to associate with him. They said Willie screwed around too much off the field and that he would be a bad influence on me.

I didn't know what to think. When you're a young rookie and a great veteran like Willie Davis, a man with 2,000 career hits, wants to hang around with you, Jesus Christ, it was an honor of the highest degree. But after the lecture by McHale and Fanning, I obediently ended my relationship with Willie. There were things more important.

After that I became friends with Hal Breeden, a guy who would later play for the Hanshin Tigers. He was a real redneck, but nice even if he did have a weird sense of humor. Breeden was from Georgia, and at season's end I followed him home, driving from Montreal to Miami. When we got to the Georgia border, he pulled over, got out, came back to my car, and said, "OK, boy, you're on your own now. This is Georgia territory, and if some of my guys happen to stop ya up the road there, well, I don't know ya. So just keep on going, straight ahead until ya get back to Florida. And don't look back."

I took him seriously. I gunned it the rest of the way home. But that had been Breeden's idea of a joke. He called me later from Atlanta to have his little laugh.

I had only gotten 3 hits in 17 at-bats that September, but the following year, I had a very good spring camp. I knew I could play in the major leagues. I felt absolutely certain of it. But Jim Fanning, then the Expos' general manager, sent me back to the minors. He wanted me to have another year of experience down there so he assigned me to Memphis in the International League.

I wasn't eager to go. I had gotten used to major league treatment in the short time I was there. You'd take a chartered bus to the airport. They'd open a gate and take you straight to the plane. They'd handle your bags for you, carry your shoes, and give you decent meals after a game. But it wasn't just losing these perks. I felt cheated. I was good, and I firmly believed it was part of my destiny to be in the major leagues.

Then there was the matter of Carole, my new wife, a French-Canadian woman I'd met and married in Quebec. I was not overly excited about living in a place like Tennessee with her. I didn't think the combination of a white woman and a black man would go over too well there.

Myself, I had never really made a big deal about race. My high school coach, whom I thought the world of, was white. And I'd played ball with all kinds—Cubans, Puerto Ricans, the whole spectrum. If people were decent, *that* was what counted. I wasn't blind to racism, because it certainly existed. I knew a stone redneck when I saw one, and I could spot a black guy who didn't like white guys in a minute. But my attitude was to ignore it. I just tried to do my own thing and I was lucky in that I was accepted wherever I played—even when I was the only black on the team.

Being married to a white woman, however, was a different matter.

Carole was a slim, very pretty 21-year-old Montreal native

with fine brown hair and a quiet manner. She was working in the front office of the Quebec City Carnival when I first met her. Larry Parrish, a teammate, and I went on a double date with Carole and her girlfriend one night, and I liked her right away. We saw a lot of each other that summer of '74, and in the winter, I took her home with me to Miami. We got married the following year.

I gave more than a little thought to getting involved in an interracial marriage. Not only was she white, but when I first met her, she couldn't speak much English either, her native language being French. But none of that seemed to faze Carole in the least. She was very independent-minded.

She had quit high school at age 17 to go to work and had been on her own since then. Her parents were separated, and she never had much family closeness—which was something we had in common.

Carole's only weak moment came when she first visited Miami. It was her first time out of Quebec, her first visit to a black family, and the first time she'd ever met my mother, who tended to overwhelm people. In the beginning, she was shaking like a leaf. But somehow, it all worked out. My mother and my grandmother took to Carole right away, and our wedding plans proceeded. Then we found ourselves in Tennessee.

If you're a black man and you've never married a white woman and lived in Tennessee, I recommend it just for its educational aspects. It will certainly broaden your outlook on human behavior. People would literally stop and stare at us. Carole would come out to the park every day. She'd sit there looking gorgeous and suntanned. Then, after the game, I'd walk out, she'd grab my arm, the fans would see she was my wife, and mouths would drop open. Their jaws would be dragging on the ground.

We never had any serious confrontations, but there were many unpleasant moments. Once, we were sitting on the balcony of our apartment, and two girls drove by in a car. They looked, their eyes popped out, and they yelled "nigger" and "nigger lover," among other imaginative curses, at us. Carole tensed up. I just smiled and waved. But it wasn't easy to maintain a sense of humor about that sort of thing.

Larry Doby, a roving hitting instructor with the Expos, told me that the reason I was kept in the minor leagues so long was because I was married to a white woman. One of my junior college teachers even sent me an article about mixed marriages which described how most of them didn't work. The thoughtfulness of my fellow man was amazing.

But the thing that bothered me most about being in Tennessee was not racism. It was having to play for a manager named Karl Kuehl. I hated his guts.

Kuehl was my first professional coach. He'd worked with me in the Expos' instructional league and also at the Expos' camp. He was a hard-assed guy who did things only by the book, and he was always on my case. I hated how he tried to teach me to do things his way instead of letting me develop my own style.

Kuehl's big success had been Gary Carter. He had molded Carter in the minor leagues and had a lot to do with Carter becoming a successful catcher. He was also Carter's best friend.

At Memphis, Kuehl continued his efforts to mold me too. He wanted to change everything about the way I played. He didn't like my swing, my running, my throwing, or my fielding. He also thought—wrongly in my opinion—that I didn't work hard enough. He was on my back all year.

"No, Cromartie, no, no, no, no, Cromartie," he'd yell. "That's *not* the way to do it."

His attitude toward me was totally negative. He wouldn't start me. Or he'd start me and then pinch-hit for me in my second at-bat. When he did that one day, I got into such a violent argument with him that I stormed off the field and out of the ballpark.

I had a bad year at Memphis—not surprisingly. But I got hot the last three weeks, raising my average from around .240 to .268 with 3 home runs. I was hoping the Expos would call me up that September, but Kuehl stopped them. He told Fanning that I wasn't good enough yet. And Fanning, who did not appear to be a big Cromartie fan either, agreed.

The next year, I found myself in Denver, with another Triple A team, where I played under Vern Rapp. Rapp was hard-assed too. He was from the old school, but he respected me and let me play every day.

I hit .337 in Denver, on a team that might have been the best in minor league history. We were 86–15 at one point. Ten guys were called up to the majors that September: Rodney Scott, Jerry Manuel, and Wallace Johnson among them. I was the tenth and last guy because the Montreal manager that year was none other than Kuehl.

When I finally did go up, I played part-time, hitting .210 in 81 at-bats and helped the Expos lose their hundredth ball game. Then the fates finally grinned at me: Kuehl got fired, Dick Williams got hired, and things started to go my way.

YOSEMITE SAM

I had heard about Dick Williams, about how tough he was, about how if Dick Williams liked you, then you were in like Flynn and if he didn't like you, then you were like screwed. But there was something I did during spring training in 1977 that turned him on toward me. We were playing an exhibition game. I was on third, and I'd made the pitcher balk by acting as if I was going to steal home. I broke the guy's concentration, and Dick went crazy over that in the dugout. "That's it!" he cried "That's it!" Dick loved that sort of aggressiveness. And I loved that sort of praise.

Dick was a very intense man and very ornery. He reminded me of Yosemite Sam. But he never really showed his horseshit side to me. I think he took a liking to me right from the beginning. He called me by my first name, and he put me in the lineup every day and left me there, whether I was hitting well or not, which was quite a compliment considering the players he had had in his last job with the Oakland Athletics: Reggie Jackson, Catfish Hunter, Sal Bando, and Joe Rudi.

I had only one run-in with him. It was in my second year. He had taken me out for a pinch hitter in a game, and I started telling Chris Spier how stupid Dick was for doing it. Dick was right behind me. He moved by, stopped, looked at me with that flinty-eyed stare he had, and said, "Real stupid, eh? Real fucking stupid, eh?" Then he turned and walked off. I didn't know what to say, but Spier thought it was extremely funny. He doubled over laughing, which caused everyone else on the bench to start in too.

Playing outfield and first base in my first full big league year, I hit .282 with 5 homers and 50 RBIs. I was off and running. My second year I hit .297 with 10 homers and 56 RBIs. In 1979, the figures were .275, 8, and 46; in 1980, they were .288, 14, and 70; and 1981, my best year, I hit .304 with 6 homers and 42 RBIs in the strike-shortened season to help the Expos win the eastern division title.

Montreal was a town with a European feel, lots of night spots, and horrible weather. People said there were two seasons in Montreal—winter and July. By 1977, we had moved into Olympic Stadium, a huge monster of a park with no roof. And it was cold. The wind was always whipping in off the St. Lawrence River, and we often played baseball in 40-degree weather. In the early and latter part of the season, the temperature would sometimes dip below freezing.

In Olympic Stadium, there was a track around the baseball field. About 150 feet of open space separated the stands from home plate, and there was a 100-foot-long area between the outfield fence and the bleachers where construction materials were stored in anticipation of a roof going up one day.

The people of Montreal were mostly French-speaking and didn't know anything about baseball. Most of the reporters had covered hockey all of their lives. They would ask funny questions like, "Warren, if you hit .280, will the Expos win the pennant?"

But the Expos were popular because we were new and because we had a really good team of young stars: Andre Dawson, Tim Raines, Gary Carter, and Steve Rogers. We also had Tony Perez, Dave Cash, Chris Spier, and Larry Parrish. We looked so good that we were picked to win the pennant every year. We always came in second instead. It wasn't until 1981, the year of the strike, that we finally won, beating the Phillies in a special five-game division playoff.

I like to think I was the one of the big spark plugs of the team that season. My on-base percentage was over .500. I got a lot of key hits and also scored a lot of runs. Some writers said I carried the team on my back. And I was not about to argue with them, even though Dawson had hit .302 with 24 homers. You took whatever you could get.

It really was an emotional time. Montreal usually went apeshit over its hockey team, the Canadiens. But this time, it was the Expos who were in the limelight. The entire nation of Canada, it seemed, had gone crazy over us.

Our series with the Phillies went the entire five games, and in the last contest, in Philadelphia, we had to face Steve Carlton, who was at his peak. He had been 24–9 the year before and was 13–4 in the short 99-game season. He had a slider you couldn't even see.

I remember the feeling in the hotel coffee shop the morning of that game. The guys were sitting there not saying very much at all, dreading Carlton. It was depressing. Finally, Jerry Manuel spoke up. "What's the matter with you guys?" he said. "Why is everyone so quiet here? We can go out and beat Lefty. You know we can."

It wasn't exactly Gene Hackman in *Hoosiers*. But it seemed to work, because we won 3–0, behind Steve Rogers. In the bottom of the ninth inning, as we took the field, 50,000 Philly fans in Philadelphia were screaming bloody murder at what we were about to do to their heroes. When I assumed my position at first base, my stomach was churning from a serious case of nerves.

A ground ball to third took care of one out. A fly ball to the out field took care of another. Dawson caught it with one hand, just to rub it in perhaps. "Shit," I thought, "how icy can a person be?"

Dawson's cool must have infected me, because I suddenly found myself yelling, "Hit it to me! Hit it to me!" Rogers wound and fired, and Manny Trillo hit a line drive right above my head. I leaped and caught it and the game was over. We went fucking nuts.

There were a lot of Canadian fans in the stands, and some of them came down onto the field. One of them had a Canadian flag, which I took and started waving. Suddenly, the whole place started booing, and people were throwing things at me. A cop came running over to me and said, "What're you trying to do? Start a fucking riot in here?"

According to a newspaper article, a Canadian high school teacher started her class the next day by asking her students, "What shall we talk about today?" One kid said, "How about Warren Cromartie holding up the Canadian flag?"

When we arrived home at the airport in Montreal, the fans were everywhere—in the parking lot, on the roof, up in the trees. We stood up on a dais that city officials had built for us so we could wave at the fans. When we got on the bus, the fans surrounded it and started shaking it so much that we had to get back out again and up on the stage a second time. You would have thought the Pope had come to town.

Then, we played the Dodgers for the National League title. Two games in sunny Los Angeles, then three at night in frigid Montreal, with snow flurries thrown in for good measure. Rick Monday hit a ninth-inning home run off Steve Rogers in the fifth game, and it was all over. My picture was on the front page of one paper the next morning, crying like a baby. It reminded me of the time I forgot to touch third base in little league.

HAWK AND THE KID

There were some bona fide superstars on our team, and Andre Dawson was one of them. People only talked about his hitting, but I saw him make plays in center field I couldn't believe. He could run like a fucking cheetah.

Andre came from Miami, too. He'd been born in poverty, like me, and because of that, perhaps, we became close friends. We called each other "Homey."

Andre's nickname was the "Hawk," because his facial features resembled a hawk's. He had a body like one, too. We also called him "Cobra" because when he got mad, his shoulders would rise up and spread out, just like a cobra, and he'd look even bigger than his 6'2", 190 pounds.

Andre was a very strong-minded person who could be very intimidating. Once, I saw him run Tony Perez out of the batting cage during spring training. It totally blew me way. It blew Tony Perez away too, because Tony Perez was one of the all-time greats and Dawson was only a rookie at the time.

At this particular juncture, however, Dawson was feeling his oats. He had destroyed the Pioneer and Eastern leagues and had made it up to the majors in just one year. He knew he was special. On this spring day in 1977, when we were at Expo camp in Daytona Beach awaiting our turn to hit, Perez suddenly stepped into the cage, out of turn. Andre decided he wasn't going to stand by and take it.

"It's my turn," he growled.

Perez turned around and said, "I won't be hitting long."

Dawson took that very, very personally. His back proceeded to swell, and he took a couple of steps toward Perez and said, "You wait just like everybody else. It's my fucking turn."

I'm saying to myself, Jesus Christ, Hawk, this is Tony Perez, future Hall of Famer, you're talking to. At that time, Tony was 35 years old. He'd just come to the Expos from the Reds where he, Pete Rose, Johnny Bench, Joe Morgan, and others had formed the Big Red Machine—the great Cincinnati dynasty of the seventies. At 6'2", 210 pounds, Perez wasn't exactly a pipsqueak either. But to his credit, and my great surprise, he walked out of the cage.

Later, I told Andre that I thought what he'd done was wrong. "It might not have been Perez's turn," I said, "but you shouldn't have made such a big deal out of it. It really didn't matter that much." It was still early in spring camp, the hitting order hadn't been set in stone yet, and everybody was going to get his swings regardless. I mean, the batting cage wasn't going anywhere. If anything, a little respect was called for.

Andre scowled. "Perez is like anybody else," he said. "He waits his turn." Being loose was not one of Andre's big traits.

"Hawk," I said gingerly, "don't you think you ought to lighten up? You're way too uptight."

"Fuck you too," he replied.

I decided not to pursue the conversation. Andre had very quick hands. One move and I wouldn't be talking to anyone for a while.

Andre was a very dedicated person, though, and very loyal. He had worked hard all his life to get where he was. And I admired him because he always played in pain and never complained about it. He had bad knees, and sometimes the pain was so bad he could hardly walk.

I remember sitting with him on the bench one time. He was rubbing one knee and grimacing. I asked him if he was all right, and he said, "Homey, this fucking knee is killing me."

Andre had bad knees from playing on the Astroturf. He also had a congenital growth in one of them. A piece of bone was sticking out. The doctors wanted to go in and fix it, but Andre wouldn't let them because he was afraid he would lose his speed. Despite the pain, he always played, he always gave 100 percent, and he never said a word about it to the manager or the front office or the press. That was Andre.

Because of his knees, he never had the super year in Montreal that everyone expected, but he was always in the .300, 30 home-run range. Later, when Andre went to the Cubs and had a chance to play on natural grass, he really showed what he could do. In 1987, he hit 49 home runs with 137 RBIs and was voted National League MVP.

In Montreal, the media always paid more attention to Gary Carter than to Andre—perhaps because of Carter's blond hair and blue eyes. This bothered Dawson because he was every bit as good as Carter—better, in my opinion. In fact, I thought that Carter was even a little jealous of Dawson's ability. A rivalry between the two developed, which the press eventually caught on to and magnified—especially when Carter started getting endorsements and Andre got none.

Dawson may have respected Carter's talent, but he wasn't crazy about him personally. Neither were any of the other guys, because of the kind of guy Carter was. Instead of just letting his ability—which was considerable—speak for him, Carter was always trying to promote himself, gleaming in front of the photographers, showing his teeth to the camera. I used to call him Teeth because of that. The press would ask him one question, and he would linger on it for about twenty goddamn minutes.

There is nothing wrong with self-promotion, but Carter put himself before the team. He used to whine a lot, like a spoiled kid. If we won a game and Carter didn't get any hits, he would come into the locker room mad. He was always moaning about passed balls too. If he got charged with one, he would call up the official scorer and try to get him to change his ruling to a wild pitch.

Carter didn't want to catch on Sundays. That was another thing. He wanted to play first base instead so he could rest his legs. The guy was making two million dollars a year, and he didn't want to catch. Give me a break. None of us wanted to hear that shit. I remember when Carter got his 1,000th career hit. He ran to first base tipping his cap to the stands. Then he got bent out of shape because the team didn't put a notice about it on the scoreboard.

All he had to do was be a team player, like he later was with the Mets. When he went over there in 1984, those guys straightened his ass out. Some of them like Keith Hernandez and Dwight Gooden were just as big as Carter, and they played in New York. They knew how to play on a championship ball club. So he became more of a team man there, and I think that had a lot to do with the Mets' success.

But on the Expos, he was too much in love with himself. He would take more than his allotted swings in batting practice before a game. You were supposed to take eight cuts and then get out, but Carter would take twelve. You'd have to tell him his turn was up; then he'd say, "Oh," and leave. What Carter wanted was to stay in until he hit a home run so he could impress the fans.

Carter was also cheap. One time he bought these chairs and had each player's nickname put on the back. That was his way of making friends. But when his dog, a golden retriever, had pups, he turned around and tried to sell them to the guys at $350 each. He wasn't breeding them or anything. He was just trying to make an extra buck. There he was, baseball's highest paid player, hustling spare change. Another time, Carter invited the team over to his house for a party. The only food served was potato chips.

Carter's nickname was The Kid. Don Carrithers gave him that name when Carter first came up in 1974. Carter had had this big reputation, and everybody knew about him even before he arrived. Barry Foote, who was then the regular Expo catcher, got sick of hearing the name Gary Carter and about what a big star Carter was destined to become. When Carter actually showed up, we saw he had this kind of wide-eyed, squeaky-clean, Disneyland type of attitude. He was like a little kid. So Carrithers nicknamed him The Kid. And it stuck. Kid Carter: that's his nickname to this day.

Carter could not take needling. The guys used to love to rip him because he couldn't handle it. He had the weakest comebacks you ever wanted to hear. We used to tease him all the time. He would wear bellbottoms that would drag on the floor and pick up dirt wherever he walked. We'd get on him about that. Or maybe we'd all be out having a beer and Carter would be talking to some girl. He'd whip out pictures of his family—his wife and daughters—and show them to her.

We ranked everybody really—just like back in high school. We were a very loose ballclub, with Spier, Bill Gullickson, Doug Flynn, Bill Lee, and yours truly. We all loved practical jokes. Once in a while we'd find some brown stains in a guy's underwear, which he'd thrown in the laundry basket. The guy's number would be on his clothes, so we knew whose it was. We'd pull it out of the basket and hang it right on his locker for everyone to see. When the guy came in, the first thing he'd see was his dirty shorts. Someone would say, "You're a pro. Can't you even keep your ass clean?"

We did that to Carter and to Larry Parrish and to a lot of others. It wasn't terribly mature, but Carter was the only one who couldn't handle it. We'd throw a few jabs in there to see how he'd react and he usually got mad. After a while, I think he adopted the attitude that everyone was against him.

Mind you, Gary Carter was a great ballplayer, and he is going into the Hall of Fame. It was just that he had all these negative points. I know that everybody has his negative points, including me; I've got an ego as big as anyone else's. But with Carter, it eventually got to the point where he couldn't stop talking about himself. He was like that character Al Franken on "Saturday Night Live." It was always, "I, I, Me, Me, I, Gary Carter." We all hated that. We used to call him "I, I, I, Gary Carter," or "I, I, I, Kid Carter," because that's all we heard.

Carter in his autobiography wrote that I was the one who turned Dawson against him. Well, let me set the record straight. Dawson learned to dislike Carter all by himself. It wasn't so much the jealousy over endorsements, because Andre, in the end, got his. Dawson just wanted Carter to put all his self-promoting aside and try to be more of a team player, because he knew we needed him to win. But it wasn't in Carter to do that. Not then, anyway.

Tony Perez taught me more about playing the game than anyone on the Expos. "Doggie," as everybody called him, taught me the importance of a winning attitude, which he had picked up from playing in Cincinnati. He taught me about game strategy, how to use my head while at bat, how to think ahead, how to anticipate all the way up to the triple play.

If I was in a slump, I'd turn to Tony, and he'd always help me out. On the road, I'd go up to his room, and we'd talk for hours about batting. He stressed hitting the ball up the middle, and sticking to my natural stroke. "Go back to the basics," he used to say. "Do what got you here in the first place."

Steve Rogers was our ace pitcher, and I liked him a lot. We called him Cy because we expected him to win the Cy Young award one day. But he never did. He never won 20 games either. Steve was a very intelligent guy—he'd majored in engineering in college—and on the mound he was very technical, very precise. He thought about every detail of his motion.

But Cy had the unfortunate reputation of not being able to win the big games. The home run he gave up to Rick Monday, which cost us the National League pennant, didn't help his reputation at all.

Cy lost it in a hurry. I think that having to pitch in a cold climate hurt him, because he had a chronically sore elbow. Being player representative didn't help either. He had too much to do. Cy started to lose it during the time of the strike and the rise of the player's union. And when he started to slip, the front office did not demonstrate much patience. They released him after one bad year.

Rogers had several run-ins with Carter, too. They wouldn't agree on certain signs, and after the game Carter would try to cover his tracks with the press. A reporter would ask Steve, "Why didn't you throw a fastball on that home run you gave up instead of a curve?" And Carter would say, "I called for a fastball." Rogers didn't like that at all.

Another guy I'll never forget is Bill Lee. Everything they said about him was true. He really was very strange. He was a nice guy, who meant well, and was a very good competitor, but he was different from you and me. One night, Bill, Ross Grimsley, and I were walking down 42nd Street in New York City, near Times Square. It was pouring rain, and there was this old mushy hat lying on the sidewalk. Lee said, "Hey, look at the hat, man," and he picked it up and put it on his head. It was soaking wet. There was no telling where that hat had been in New York City or what had been done to it, but Bill Lee put it on and wore it for the rest of the evening.

Lee used to have the reporters going in circles. We all looked forward to some of the quotes he would give them. Once we played a doubleheader in Wrigley Field in Chicago, and it was about 95 degrees in the shade. Lee pitched the first game, went the whole nine innings, and banged out three hits. After the game, he was sitting in front of his locker, drenched in sweat, and eating a banana.

A reporter asked him, "Where did you get the energy to pitch a complete game and knock out all those hits as well?"

"Bananas," Lee said. "Before the game I eat a lot of them. Bananas have a lot of potassium. And that's what does it."

"Are you serious?" the reporter said.

"Of course, I'm serious," Lee replied. "Why do you think monkeys eat bananas? All the swinging they do through the trees and around the bars at the zoo. You ever see a monkey get tired or have a cramp? It's the potassium, I tell you."

They called him "Spaceman," because of the outrageous things he would do. Once he was fined by Bowie Kuhn for saying he had marijuana with his breakfast. He said he put it on his pancakes. He was fined two or three thousand dollars for that. And he paid up. He sent it to Kuhn's office all in pennies.

Larry Parrish was another guy I felt close to. Larry played third base, and he had some good seasons, but they ran him out of town because he made so many errors. Larry was always the whipping boy. His number was 15, and as soon as the fans saw it emerging from the dugout, they would start to boo. Parrish eventually found a home in Texas.

And after he left, I became the whipping boy.

The Drugs of Summer

Ellis Valentine was one of our starting outfielders. He liked to smoke pot. He smoked it all the time, even on the team bus. He'd sit in the back and light up a joint like it was nothing. I'd even seen Ellis smoke it in the back of a chartered plane.

A lot of guys used marijuana. When I was in the minor leagues, it seemed everybody was into grass, including me. We'd get together in the evening after the game was over and toke up.

We used it in moderation. Or at least I did. I never had a joint before a game or during one. After I got married and had kids, I started putting things into perspective and realized what could happen to my career if I got caught or if things got out of hand. So I cooled it.

But Ellis continued to smoke dope even after he made the Expos in 1976–77. He was even known to be puffed up before a game. Ellis was an arrogant guy, a hulking 6'4", 200-pound black dude, and when he lit up, it was as if he was daring people to say something to him. But nobody ever did. He was supposed to be this big phenomenon, and the team wanted to protect him.

Ellis wasn't the only guy on the team to smoke grass. Rodney Scott did too. It eventually caught up with both of them. Rodney was released by the Expos in April 1982. Ellis was traded in the middle of the 1981 season and was on his way out by 1984.

With Ellis, it was a real pity. As a player, he had all the tools in the world—power, speed, a sense of the game, and a cannon of an arm. But I think his head got screwed up using some of the drugs that he did. A lot of people think marijuana doesn't have any effect on you, but it does. It did in Ellis's case, especially, because he abused it. Ellis used to party until the wee hours of the morning, all the time. He didn't take care of himself. He only wanted to pounce around in his fancy cars and his jewelry. He'd come late to the ballpark. He never wanted to do his pregame workouts or make the effort necessary to excel. As a result, he kept getting hurt, but even so he'd want more money every year. In the end, Ellis gradually got slower, his reflexes started to go, and before you knew it, he was gone.

Ellis and I never did get along. Part of it, I think, was jealousy because I'd come up at the same time he did, and there had been as much talk and hoopla about me in the press as there was about him. But also, there was a personality conflict. I used to laugh at him when he fucked up, and he hated it.

One night he kept me up until 3:00 in the morning, blasting away on his big portable stereo. This was the night before a doubleheader, and I was trying to get some sleep. The team was staying at a hotel in Atlanta, and his room was next to mine. Some lady was with him, and they were making a racket. I called the front desk to complain, and the guy called Ellis to tell him to tone it down. But Ellis didn't pay him any mind. His attitude was, "You know, I'm Ellis Valentine. I can do what I want."

The next day Ellis confronted me in the locker room. I was standing there in front of my locker in my Expo undershirt, when he walked up and stuck his jaw in my face. "What the fuck you doing calling the front desk?" he snorted.

"Fuck you," I said. "You were making too much goddamn noise."

He took a swing at me, and we started going at it right there. Ellis was about four inches taller and twenty pounds heavier than me, but I didn't care. I wanted to kill him. We exchanged a couple of punches to the head, scattering chairs, knocking over a trash can, and smashing a mirror in the process. A couple of guys stepped in and threw me to the ground while a couple more grabbed Ellis and held on. Wayne Twitchell was the one who first got between us. At 6'6", 220 pounds, he was a little braver than the rest. When they finally let me up, I threw a chair at Ellis and that started things all over again.

Although almost everybody on the team did marijuana at

one time or another, I never actually saw anyone snort cocaine. There were a couple of guys who I thought were doing more than marijuana. Those guys weren't married, they had their share of women, and they'd party after every game. They'd always come into the clubhouse looking tired. At first I thought they were just hung over. It was 1982; coke was a new thing, and nobody knew anything about it. But then the stories about it being used in the big leagues started, and I began to put two and two together.

Tim Raines had joined the team in 1981, at age 21. Andre had moved to right field, and Raines took over in center. There was a lot of talk about Raines using coke, which later turned out to be true. In his first season, he'd been an athlete to behold. He'd hit .304 with 71 stolen bases in only 88 games. But the next year, he began to deteriorate. He dropped to .277 with 78 stolen bases in 156 games, and at the end of the season the coke scandal came out.

Raines was close to Dawson, whom I considered my best friend on the team. The three of us gravitated toward each other at the park. But when the coke story broke, Andre and I were totally blown away. It was hard for us to believe that Raines was actually doing cocaine—because it was such a taboo thing, and also because Raines was so young. Booze or dope, we could believe, but coke? Whatever it was, we knew there was something wrong because of the way he was playing.

He would show up at the ballpark late, his eyes bloodshot, looking extremely fatigued. His locker was like a junkyard. He had clothes in there that hadn't been washed for days. In games, sometimes he would miss fly balls or he wouldn't be as quick on a play as he normally would have been. His reactions were so slow that even the average fan could tell something was wrong.

Raines looked up to Dawson. He even named his kid after Andre. But not even Dawson knew what was going on for sure, because Raines kept his private life private.

The reporter who wrote the story about Raines's use of cocaine was a man named Bob Dunne. Dunne got the story from the guy who sold Raines his coke, a lowlife named Bob White. White had supplied other Expo players with drugs, too, before he turned around and let the word out about Raines.

White was a black guy who hung around the nightclubs in Montreal. Nobody knew what his occupation was, but he was the type of dude who seemed to know everybody. He tried to make friends with the Expo stars, particularly the big-name black players. I saw him outside the stadium once or twice, and I was introduced to him once at a nightclub. But thank god, the only thing I ever did was meet him.

There were guys like White in every city—New York, Pittsburgh, Chicago—sleazeballs who knew they could make a quick buck selling cocaine to professional ballplayers. They would tell the guys that they needed a stimulant like coke to keep them going over the long, hard season, that it would make them feel more powerful, enable them to do more than they ordinarily could. It was expensive but young stars like Raines—and Dwight Gooden later on—had money to burn and before you knew it, they were into the white powder. They got caught up in the fast lane. And it caught up with them.

The Raines story appeared in the winter of 1982–83. And it began to look like cocaine was a problem on nearly all the twenty-six major league teams. Expos' president John McHale told the *New York Times* that he suspected eight or nine of our players had used cocaine the previous season. He didn't name names, but he seemed to think that I was one of them—perhaps because I had only hit .254, or perhaps because I was close to Raines. Whatever the reason, he called me in for a little chat about the subject the following February at his executive suite in the Fort Lauderdale Holiday Inn, just before the 1983 spring camp began.

We sat down facing each other across a table in his office, McHale, a silver-haired middle-aged man in an expensive suit, me a 29-year-old ballplayer in a polo shirt and jeans. Florida winter sunlight filled the room.

"Warren," he said, fixing me with a firm look, "if you're on drugs, let us know, and we'll get some help for you."

It struck me how much McHale looked like Charlton Heston. I returned his gaze as best I could and replied, "John, I'm not on drugs. I just want a chance to play and redeem myself for the bad year I had."

"You're sure?" he said, his eyes piercing me in the best Heston tradition.

"I'm sure," I said, trying not to blink.

It was demeaning, but that's the way it was then. Everyone was paranoid as hell about coke. And if you were black, they were even more paranoid. If a black guy went into a slump, right away people began to think he was on something. Carter had slumps too, but nobody ever accused him of snorting coke. The color of the ball, as the black players always used to say, was white.

Bill Virdon took over that year, and I didn't play regularly. I always wondered about the reason. I thought that McHale, and by extension, Virdon, still believed I used drugs—although there were other reasons too, which we shall get to shortly.

In camp, the Raines story was all the press talked about, and there was a lot of pressure on Tim. But he handled it the best way he could. He closed the subject. There were no speeches in front of the team. No tearful apologies. He just came back and had a good year: He hit .298, with 11 homers, 71 RBIs, and 90 stolen bases—batting leadoff.

I never asked Raines about his drug problem. And he never volunteered any information to me or anyone else. So I felt, why bring it up? What he did, he did, and the whole world knew about it and that was that. It was over and done with. The only thing for him to do was to turn his life around.

Raines's recovery was strictly on his own. But, believe me, the front office was watching his every step and probably had people following him, too. I wouldn't be surprised to find that they had private eyes following all of us that year. A lot of guys on the team were still smoking grass. I don't know if any were snorting coke, but they certainly didn't give up grass. They were just more discreet.

That summer the FBI started coming into the clubhouses around the league. They were men in suits and ties and button-down shirts. Real clean-cut and tough. They showed us what marijuana looked like and told us what marijuana did to you. Then they went through the same routine with pills, and with cocaine. They held a real seminar.

The FBI visited the Expos in San Francisco. They filed into

the visitors' locker room and told us that they knew which Expo players were on drugs, who was doing what, and where we were getting the stuff from. They were watching us, they said, and if they caught us, they were going to take away our cars.

"You see, if you get caught," said one earnest-looking young guy with very short hair who was doing most of the talking, "your car is evidence. And the FBI has to keep it." He was trying his best to sound sincere. To drive the point home, he added that some of the investigators didn't mind driving the Porsches they impounded. Therefore, if we had any information, be sure to let them know immediately.

That had been Baseball Commissioner Peter Ueberroth's brainstorm. The owners wanted the FBI to scare us because they were worried they wouldn't be able to stop the spread of drugs. That day after the Feds lectured us, they paid a visit to the San Francisco Giants. They eventually went to every major league team.

The players didn't care for that at all. Some of the guys were scared, I suppose, but others, the ones who hadn't had anything to do with drugs, were resentful. They were just trying to make their mark playing major league baseball, which was stressful enough without having to deal with FBI agents in the clubhouse and undercover investigators following them around.

So when the media asked us about our meeting with the FBI, we were sure to tell them that the government was invading our privacy and that the fine institution of major league baseball was now the subject of federal surveillance.

THE COLOR OF THE BALL

If Dick Williams had stayed in Montreal, my major league career might have turned out differently, and I might never have wound up in Japan.

Trouble was, Dick hated Montreal. He hated everything about it. He hated the weather. He hated flying into the airport there with the two-hour wait going through customs. He hated all the people he had to deal with who didn't know baseball, including the French reporters and the Expo front office, because they didn't know anything about the game either.

By his last year in Montreal, he was fed up. The things that Dick Williams normally did as manager he wasn't doing anymore. He wasn't taking the initiative on the hit and run, he wasn't planning strategy, he wasn't geared up at all. He wasn't the same man we had come to know and fear. We thought he was trying to get himself fired, and that's just what happened, right before the strike in 1981.

When Dick left, he really gave it to them. He blasted McHale. He criticized the owner. He told everyone how disorganized the whole Montreal franchise was. And he was right. But it did absolutely no good. Jim Fanning, moving down from the front office, took over as field manager and we went on to to win the division title. It made Dick look incompetent and Fanning look like a genius.

Of course, the reality was that Fanning didn't know shit. Hiring a guy from the front office to manage the Expos is like putting me in charge of Texaco for six months. Fanning leading us to the pennant was one of the great accidents in the history of organized baseball. And the next year, it began to show. We slipped to third in our division. A year after that, under Bill Virdon, we barely finished over .500.

In retrospect, it was a crying shame. The FBI should have focused its investigation on the Montreal front office instead of drugs, because as far as I was concerned the higher-ups in the organization took a winning team and completely destroyed it.

People said the Expos were spoiled. They were puzzled that the Expos had all that talent and yet continually failed to win. Well, it wasn't puzzling to me. The turnover rate in Montreal was tremendous for a team that was predicted to win the pennant every year. Faces changed all the time. In 1980, the Expos got rid of Jerry White, which they never should have done. They brought him back later in the year which just goes to show you but, nevertheless, they dumped him in 1978 and they kept a player named Kenny Macha, whom I didn't particularly think we needed at that time.

Jerry White had been our fourth outfielder. He was a good pinch hitter who batted from both sides, had good speed, and played good defense. Macha was a backup catcher and pinch hitter. Although Macha swung a good bat, defense wasn't his trademark. He had bad hands, and he couldn't run. I had played against him in the minor leagues, and I knew about him. We were born on the same day, September 29, and Macha had beaten me out for a minor-league batting title in 1974. I considered him a friend. But regardless, I couldn't see any use for him on the Expos in that particular year.

I was inclined to believe that cutting White and keeping Macha was a racial thing. Macha was white. White was black. (Any fool could have seen that.) I wasn't the only one who was upset about White. All the black guys were too. But I was the one who spoke out. When a reporter asked me why those two had gotten the ax and Macha hadn't, I replied, "Look at the color of his skin. That'll tell you why."

The reporter's story appeared in the paper, and when McHale asked me about it, I told him yes, that was what I had said: Jerry White should have never been sent down and the color of his skin had something to do with it. McHale didn't like that at all, but I sincerely believed it was true. Unfortunately, I just couldn't prove it.

People who maintained that racism did not exist in professional baseball were, in my opinion, blind and deaf and mentally handicapped, to boot. How many black field managers and black executives have there have been in baseball? People said Canadians were supposed to be more liberal than Americans, but it was no better or worse in Canada than anywhere else. There wasn't one black person in the Montreal front office.

All the blacks on the team in 1978 thought that Ken Macha had been kept because he was in tight with the front office, that he had a pipeline upstairs. We thought the same about Woody Fryman too, another white guy, that he had a latch-on relationship with McHale. Fryman was losing it. He had 7 saves in 1981, 12 in 1982. Jeff Reardon had 26 in 1982 and was coming on strong. Yet Fryman managed to stick around another season, during which he racked up zero saves, and get half a million dollars in the bargain. Some of those guys—the pipeliners and the asskissers—stayed around longer than the guys who actually played.

I did have a lot of respect for Woody Fryman, personally. He was another guy from the old school, and he helped me a great deal. He taught me about mental readiness and what to do to become a complete ballplayer. But I thought he got preferential treatment.

In 1981, when we won the division, we had a lot of blacks on the team: Jerry White, Andre Dawson, Jerry Manuel, Rowland Office, John Milner, Ellis Valentine, Rodney Scott, Ray Burris, Tim Raines, and me. The next year that number was cut in half.

The Expos screwed another black, Roy Johnson. He was an outfielder with pretty good potential. But they never gave him a shot. They kept sending him down. I learned throughout my professional career that being a black athlete means always having to do it better than the white guy. If all things are equal, the white guy will get the break.

Al Campanis, the former Dodger executive, said later that blacks didn't have the necessities to be managers in baseball. Bullshit. Do you know how many blacks there are who have what it takes? The San Diego Padres had Willy Stargell, Don Robinson, Joe Morgan, and Tony Perez to choose from. But who did they give the managerial post to? Larry Bowa. The least qualified of all, in my humble opinion. Give me a break.

That business Campanis said about blacks not wanting to go to the minors to manage is more bullshit. Anybody would go. Give them a chance and you'd see.

THE POSTGAME BUFFET

When Jim Fanning took over, my position in Montreal began to deteriorate. Fanning had this reputation of being a mild-mannered guy, but he and I didn't get along at all. I resented him because he had kept me down in 1975, on Karl Kuehl's advice. And over the years, he and I had had our problems.

One time after I'd first been called up, I was talking to

Charlie Hough, then with the Dodgers, in the outfield. I knew Hough from Hialeah. So I said hello to him and then when I went in to take batting practice, Fanning called me over.

"Cromartie," he said, "you're not supposed to talk to the opposing team before the game."

"Well, everybody else does it," I replied. "Why pick on me?"

"It's against the rules."

There should have been a rule against front office executives like Fanning trying to be big league managers. Because he was always trying to play the role—especially with me.

One day in a game against St. Louis, I was on first and Dawson hit a line drive to second base which doubled me up. It was a bullet shot, and I didn't see how I could possibly have gotten back in. I was a third of the way down the base path when they got me. But when I came back to the dugout, Fanning complained that I hadn't slid.

"How can I slide when I'm thirty feet away and the ball is hit like a rocket?" I asked.

"If you can't do it, I'll get somebody who will," he said.

I blew up. I lost my cool completely.

"Goddamn it man, you do that," I yelled. "And another thing you can do, you can quit fucking with me. You been trying to fuck me ever since 1974."

I was steaming. I felt like strangling him.

He backed off some. "I know you don't like me," he said. "I don't know what it is."

"What do you mean you don't know what it is?" I roared. "You been trying to fuck with me ever since I signed on."

"You truly believe that?" he said. "That's not true."

"You're full of shit," I said. And I stormed off into the clubhouse.

It was not my finest hour.

Until Fanning took over, I had played in 96 percent of the games. I was in there almost every day. But in Fanning's first full year, I played mostly versus right-handers. I had 100 fewer at-bats than in seasons past. Although I did hit 14 homers and have 62 RBIs, my average dropped 48 points—from .302 to .254.

Then the drug scandal broke. And rumors began to appear

that I was the odd man out in the Expos' plans for the future.

The rap against me was that I was too controversial, because I spoke out—which I did. People in the front office remembered my comments about Jerry White. And about racism. And other remarks I'd made about us needing more left-handed pitching and so forth. I had a hard time keeping my mouth shut.

The next season, Bill Virdon took over, and when I showed up in camp, I found out how radically things had changed for me.

Virdon, who'd won a division title with Pittsburgh, was highly regarded. He was supposed to be the man who would bring more discipline to the team after the supposedly easygoing Fanning. Al Oliver, who was with the Expos that year, had played with Virdon on the Pirates, and he told me how much he respected him. But I had difficulties with Virdon right from the start.

In camp, he told me that I would have to bust my ass to win a starting job, which was predictable, but didn't bother me a great deal because I always busted ass in camp. I was in the lineup on opening day, but when I got off to a bad start, Virdon benched me. That, I suppose, was the main reason why I wasn't overly fond of him. And the nagging suspicion that he, and McHale, assumed I had been on drugs.

To be fair, Virdon benched everybody that year at one time or another, even Dawson, and even his big fan, Al Oliver. He was so concerned about discipline, it seemed, that he wouldn't always use his best players. He would play guys that couldn't do the job, like Jim Wohlford.

He was strictly military. He acted as if he was running a boot camp at times. When he was with Houston, he'd had mounds of dirt built so that his players could run up and down them. He was the type of guy who wanted to look mean and tough, like an army general. He kept his hair short, GI-style, and during a game he'd sit on the bench, flexing his muscles. He'd flex his forearms and admire his biceps and try his damnedest to look intimidating.

A lot of players didn't care for Virdon. Cesar Cedeno almost tore his head off in Houston one year. Cedeno hadn't been playing, so he went into Virdon's office and asked why and the next thing anybody knew, he had his hands around Virdon's neck. It took several guys to pull him off. By the middle of the season, I was beginning to understand how Cesar felt.

There is nothing wrong with a manager not being well liked. Dick Williams was a prime example of that. Most of the players were terrified of him. But Williams could make things happen. His teams were usually in contention. He had won his share of pennants and World Series. But in Virdon's case, you couldn't exactly say that.

I had one big run-in with Virdon on a hot day in Atlanta, after a bad loss. We were falling out of the pennant race, and we'd looked pretty sloppy in this one particular game. The guys didn't seem to give a shit. I was already pissed off because of the bad year I was having, and their attitude pissed me off that much more. It was a good excuse to lose my temper. So after the game, I walked into the clubhouse to where our usual postgame buffet was laid out and turned it over.

I remember walking over to Al Oliver at first base from my position in right field during a pitching change and saying "Scoop," which is what we called Oliver, "you better get in the locker room real fast and grab something to eat because we stink, and I'm turning the goddamn spread over. It's time somebody did something about the way we've been playing."

"I'm glad you told me that," Scoop said. The very second the last out was made, he hauled ass into the clubhouse to get some food. I was running right after him, up the stairs, into the locker room, as fast as my legs could carry me. I got there and some of the guys had already started eating, acting as if we'd actually won the game. Guys were digging in like they hadn't had anything to eat for a week. Oliver was doing his best to load up too.

Bill Gullickson was at the buffet, and there were cold cuts and watermelon and all kinds of good stuff that he was helping himself to. I said to Bill, "You know what? We don't deserve to eat. We're lousy. We suck."

I said it again. Gullickson looked at me quizzically, his plate full of food, a slice of watermelon in his mouth. Then I turned the fucking thing over. I flipped it as hard as I possibly could. Food flew from one end of the locker room to the other.

Virdon came running over. "You got a problem?" he asked, jaw jutting out.

And I answered, "Yeah, I got a problem. My problem is we stink."

And he said, "Well, if we stink it's my job to do something about it."

And I said, "Well, I'm just saying what I have to say. We stink and I'm putting the emphasis on 'we.'"

And he said, "Well, that's my responsibility and if you can't handle that then *we*'ve got a problem."

And I said, "We don't have no problem."

It wasn't a real intelligent conversation.

We stood there and stared at each other for a moment, bologna and potato salad all over the floor. Then he turned and headed back to his office. I could see him flexing his forearm muscles, clenching and unclenching his fists as he walked away.

I guess Virdon was upset because he hadn't thought of doing it—which he should have, but much, much sooner.

I stood there in the middle of all the scattered food, starting to feel a little foolish. Then Dawson came into the locker room with an angry look in his eye.

"Hey, man," he said, "Where's my watermelon?"

I decided it was time to go take a shower.

THE DEFECTION

I finished the season at .278 with 3 homers and 43 RBIs in 120 games. It was the last year of my contract, and I was going to be a free agent. McHale, shaking my hand at the end of the year and wishing me good luck, said that he wanted to get a hold of my agent and start talking. But perhaps he couldn't find the number because my agent never heard from him. Then Virdon announced to reporters that I did not figure in the Expos' plans for the future, and that was that.

I didn't mind so much. I was actually looking forward to testing my worth in the free-agent market and playing with some other team besides Montreal. I preferred to be out of that situation.

Unfortunately, Virdon had made such a big deal about my being persona non grata as far as the Montreal Expos went, that my standing in the free-agent draft was not exactly enhanced. I was drafted by San Francisco in the first round, and in the second round by Boston and Seattle. Then the Yomiuri Giants came along and the rest is, as they say, modern Japanese history.

How I came to sign with the Yomiuri Giants and give up my major league career in what might loosely be called my prime is a complicated story. You might say that the practice of the owners ganging up on the players to suppress free agency started with me. And if you did, you might even be right. Because I was the first one to feel the bite.

The San Francisco Giants seemed the most interested in me, and my agent flew up to San Francisco immediately after the draft to negotiate with their general manager, Tom Haller. Haller offered a three-year contract for $450,000 a year—about 50 percent more than I'd gotten from Montreal, with an option for a fourth year—and we agreed to it.

However, when neither Boston nor Seattle matched his offer, he put the squeeze on. He lowered his terms to two years at $400,000 a year, with an option for a third at $450,000. That was pretty rotten and underhanded of him, we thought, so we put him on hold.

Andre Dawson and Tim Raines went through similar experiences in 1987 when they declared free agency and couldn't get decent offers. Andre was forced to take a cut over his previous salary in order to sign with the Cubs and later an independent arbiter ruled that this all constituted collusion to keep players' salaries down.

To be brutally honest, I really didn't want to go to San Francisco in the first place. Haller wanted me to play first base, a position I didn't particularly like. Besides that, I hated the ballpark. It was cold, windy, and depressing, and most of the guys who had played there felt the same. I didn't care much for the idea of living in the City by the Bay, either. I liked the Wharf, but San Francisco was too far from home—not that Montreal was around the corner.

As fate would have it, the Yomiuri Giants made me an offer a few days after Haller revised his terms. Originally, Yomiuri had had its sights set on Dave Parker or Amos Otis, who were also becoming free agents. But those two guys were not interested in going to Japan. Parker, in fact, said flat out, "You couldn't pay me a bucket of money to play over there." So Yomiuri came at me full blast.

It turned out, ironically, that Reggie Smith had recommended me to the Yomiuri organization. He knew me and my style of play from the majors. I could hit, he told them, play the outfield, and would work hard. Since Reggie could switch-hit and I swung from the left side, the Yomiuri management thought that both of us together would do great things.

Through their representative, Hiroaki Hirano, they offered me a three-year contract at $600,000 per year. At first I was reluctant to go. Why do I have to leave the major leagues and travel all the way over to Japan just to play baseball? I asked myself. If San Francisco was too far away for me, Tokyo was out of this world. Why couldn't I just get the money I deserved in the States? It wasn't like I was asking for the moon. I just wanted what I deserved for my accomplishments and for the time I put in.

But it also occurred to me that I really didn't have anywhere else to go. We had put Haller on hold, but I was still furious at the way he'd lowered his terms. So I said, "The hell with it, I'll go to Japan. And damn the distance."

When the news came out that I was going to join the Tokyo Giants, Haller was very upset. Apparently he had been getting ready for a press conference to announce my signing with San Francisco, even though I hadn't agreed to their last offer, only to their first.

There were some accusations later by San Francisco that the Yomiuri people had played dirty, that they had neglected to get permission from the commissioner's office to talk to me, that they had interfered with an American team's negotiations. But not so. The Japanese were free to do what they wanted. I was a free agent. That meant exactly what the words said. I was entitled to talk to whomever I wished. If I wanted to go to China, or Mars, to play ball, I could.

Relations between San Francisco and Yomiuri were chilled for a while because of my signing on to go to Japan. But I didn't care. Yomiuri had just given me a ton of money, plus all sorts of benefits like housing, first-class airfare for my family, an assortment of bonuses if I did well, and full dental.

I'd defected in style.

1985

HELLO AGAIN FROM MIYAZAKI

I came to the conclusion that I'd had it with Japan. I was back with the Tokyo Giants for another year, but that would be it. Enough was enough. I was going home.

The realization came to me late one afternoon midway through my second camp in Miyazaki, after another exhausting day of workouts. It was twilight, and I was sitting alone in my miniature room, staring out the window at the mountains in the distance, thinking how unpleasant my life had become.

I'd come to Japan to play baseball and discovered that I'd joined the marines instead. I had to wash my own clothes, carry my bags, and endure constant harping by coaches who were worse than drill sergeants.

They made us do everything together and dictated our every move. Even when we did our jogging, we had to run in a cadre-type formation, counting out cadence, the coaches off to the sides shouting at us not to slough off.

They wouldn't stop messing with me, either. The year before, it was my batting stance that disturbed them. Now a Giants' defensive coach, Shibata, was trying to tell me how to play the outfield. He'd taken me aside for special fielding practice—an entire afternoon of catching fly balls. He made minute adjustments in my stance and lectured me about the proper way to come in on a hard-hit ball and to go back after one hit over my head. It was stuff I'd learned in high school and the minor leagues. At one point he turned to me and said sternly, "*Kuromatei*, always catch the ball with two hands."

Gee.

They'd had us on the field for eight fucking hours that day, and evening workouts were coming up. Oh's new byword was *kyosei*. It meant compulsion and, according to press reports, he'd instructed his coaches to act like "demons" in camp. I could understand everyone's disappointment at not winning in 1985, but this was like preparing for war.

It was not the way to approach baseball. It was why Don Money and others had left, and it was why I had decided to hang it up too.

I got up, opened the window, and yelled as loud as I could.

"Fuck this shit and fuck all of you too."

Then I closed the window and lay down on the bed, bumping my hip on the table and my head on the bedlamp in the process.

"Goddamn," I thought, "this is no way to live."

I lay there and I thought about my family back home and tears came rolling down my cheeks.

I'd finish out the year and do my best, but fuck them for a third. I'd return to the major leagues. That's what I'd do. I'd sharpen my tools this season and go back where they played real baseball.

Fuck this shit, indeed.

Frankly, I didn't see how the Japanese players could stand it. Take Makihara, our young pitching star, a kid with a 155 kilometer-per-hour fastball—that is, a 96 mile-per-hour fastball. He was a big, simple, country boy who kept tripping over things and was a magnet for the coaches' fury. He had developed a sore arm during camp, and that made them furious. They sent him down to the farm, where they devised a program to whip him back into shape—to teach him spirit. And it was brutal.

Every day the coaches would hit grounders to Makihara until he couldn't stand up, yelling insults at him all the while—"*Me wo samase!*" (Open your eyes!) and "*Shikkari shiroo!*" (Show some spirit!) Then they'd make him run four or five miles. Once, when a coach thought Makihara wasn't trying hard enough, he grabbed him by the neck and hit him over the head with the end of a bat.

They treated him like dogshit. He couldn't even scowl. The head coach ordered him to report to his special workouts every morning with a smile on his face. If Makihara wasn't smiling when he showed up, that meant even more punishment. It was all part of his "training." Makihara hated it, I'm sure, but there was nothing he could do, short of quitting.

If might have been one thing if Makihara and the others had at least gotten paid a decent salary for their trouble, but that wasn't the case. About 75 percent of the pro baseball players in Japan earned less than $50,000 a year, compared with the average of $450,000 in the U.S. (The average Japanese household income was about $25,000.) The players' minimum salary was a joke, while the top money earner among all Japanese, Carp veteran star Koji Yamamoto, only earned about $300,000 a year. I made twice that; Boomer and Bass nearly as much.

The Japanese always complained that we *gaijin* were overpaid. The commissioner of Japanese baseball in fact was always urging a complete ban on foreigners, saying it was degrading to Japanese baseball to have to pay big money to Americans who were washed up in the U.S.

The reality, however, was that the Japanese were getting screwed.

Most of the teams had money. The twelve clubs drew about twenty million in attendance a year—but they were all advertising tools for larger companies. The Hanshin Tigers promoted the Hanshin railways, the Hiroshima Carp helped sell cars made by the Hiroshima Toyo Corporation, and so forth. They weren't profit-oriented entities in themselves, and that left the players with no leverage. Not that they'd use it if they had any.

When the Japanese players finally formed a union, the guy who was elected chief told me they'd never strike because it wouldn't be fair to the fans. So much for the union. As a Japanese writer once explained to me, pro ballplayers were supposed to be "clean, simple, and obedient."

The members of the Giants were not only underpaid, they were also kept under lock and key. In the huge crowds that always surrounded us in camp and on the road, there were lots of attractive females who were ready and willing to sneak into the players' rooms. But there was a big fine if you were caught with a girl in your bed. Sex was bad for the team's image.

A third of our fans were teenage girls. They were out there every day at the park and at practice too—sweet young things, lovesick and squealing wildly at the sight of Hara and the others. But I didn't see how these younger guys could have had any kind of social life at all. Makihara and the other unestablished players were required to live in the team dormitory outside Tokyo. The curfew there was 10:00 P.M. What kind of date could you possibly have?

I assumed they found discreet ways to sow their wild oats. It was hard to tell in any case, because everyone on the Giants was so secretive about his private life. One of the dormitory residents, a 19-year-old pitcher named Mizuno, got caught breaking curfew and drinking beer with a girl who was also a minor (the legal age in Japan is 20). For that he was fined $10,000—about a third of his annual pay! He was also suspended and confined to his dormitory quarters for a month.

So all that was left for them was work, which I guess was the idea. They paid a high price for the privilege of being a Tokyo Giant.

Because the Giants were the most popular team in the country, we played everywhere, and some of the places we appeared in were almost indescribable. We played in parks where the dugout benches were only half the length they are in the majors, and with no bull pen. We'd have thirty-five guys on the team, all trying to sit on the bench, crammed up and squeezed in like subway commuters. I'd usually wind up sitting on the ice cooler at one end of the dugout. There wasn't even enough room to hold your bat in some of those places.

It was like going back in time, like playing baseball in Bedrock with the Flintstones. I'd look at it all, and I'd say to myself, "Just hang on, Cro. Hang on until October. Then it will all be over."

PLATOON

By my second year, I had seen enough of my teammates to have formed some opinions. Our best pitcher and coolest dude was the round-faced, plumpish Suguru Egawa, a solid 15-or16-game winner every year. He was a nice guy and his attitude was more like that of an American major leaguer than any other Japanese player I'd met. He thought that all the training and all the strict rules of the Giants—no beards, no long hair, suits and ties on the road—were basically bullshit. He thought that words like "fighting spirit" and "guts" were nonsense. He was a real professional.

Egawa had played semi-pro ball in the States for a year after graduating from college. He had seen the American way, and he thought it made sense. In practice, I noticed, he would slough off a little more than the other guys, trying to conserve himself. The other pitchers would throw two or three pitches in the time it took Egawa to throw one. He would clean his spikes between each delivery, adjust his belt, remove his cap, and check the ball. The coaches never seemed to notice.

The players liked Egawa, and he had a huge following among young Giants' fans. When I walked with him in airports and train stations, people were always calling out his name and wishing him luck. Egawa was a very smart cat. He could speak English fairly well from his time in the States. On a scale of 100, I'd say Egawa's English was about 70. That was a lot more than most guys on the team, or most Japanese in the country, period. The average I'd say was about 10, but everyone had some idea of the basic form of written English because it was required in school. What's more, most of the baseball terms they used were the same as ours—*banto*, *tsubesu hit*, *homu ran*, while others were close enough—*ranningu homu ran* (inside-the-park home run) and *dedo boru* (hit by a pitch). So on the team there was at least some form of communication going on.

I enjoyed playing behind Egawa. He had a 93-mile-per-hour fastball, a big sweeping curve, and lots of poise. His best year had been 1981, when he was 20–6, with a 2.29 ERA, 221 strikeouts, and led the league in just about every pitching category. He was 6'1", 200 pounds, and, at his peak, some people had compared him to Nolan Ryan; in one all-star game, for example, he'd struck out eight men in a row. But at age 30, he was losing his speed. He was giving up too many home runs.

Takashi Nishimoto was our number two pitcher, and another solid 15-game winner. He had a wicked *shooto*, a mean look to go along with it, and was perhaps the most superstitious guy on the team. The Japanese, I discovered, were just as superstitious as Americans; they just did things a little differently. They'd carry salt in their pockets to ward off evil spirits. They'd take a drink of green tea, then pour some into their crotch to purify their balls—like the old *samurai* who'd spit *sake* on their swords before going into battle. They would even change their names to change their luck. I'd also heard about a former manager of the Nippon Ham Fighters, who refused to change his underwear after a win. If the team went on a winning streak, it was said that all the players sat as far away from him as possible. After a loss he would change his underwear but take a different route to the game the next day. If the team went on a losing streak, he would run out of ways to get to the park. His uniform number was 86. One way to read "86" in Japanese was "*ha-mu,*" which was also the Japanese word for "ham."

Every time Nishimoto was scheduled to start, he would bring out a brand new pair of batting gloves, and he wouldn't put them on until one of our interpreters, Ichi Tanuma, had tried them on for luck. When the game was over, he would throw them away. Nishimoto threw salt in various places, and after the last out of every inning he would come back to the dugout, pick up the pot of cold tea the club kept on the bench, and pour some on the back of his neck, also for luck.

Nishimoto had very few friends on the team. Egawa seemed to think he was all right, but most of the others disliked him.

They thought he was too uppity. Nishimoto was making about $200,000 a year, which was a lot for a Tokyo Giant, and he liked to show it off. He drove a flashy sports car, wore gold accessories, and dressed in the finest threads. Japan was becoming a super-rich, materialistic country, but poverty was still a virtue. Nishimoto, therefore, was regarded as unvirtuous.

Nishimoto was also a Korean, I was told, or part Korean, which was perhaps the real reason for his lack of popularity. The Japanese don't like Koreans, and they'll come out and tell you that. People on the Giants would turn to me and say, in a hushed voice, "Nishimoto's Korean," as if he had leprosy or something. Nishimoto was born and educated in Japan, which meant that he wasn't technically a *gaijin*—even though Koreans, no matter how many generations they'd lived in Japan, aren't allowed natural Japanese citizenship. His status on the social ladder was even lower than mine...much, much lower.

We had a battery coach named Yoshida, who actually smacked Nishimoto one day in practice at Tamagawa. Yoshida was mad because Nishi had ignored his orders to practice bunting. So he grabbed him around the neck and let him have it in the forehead with the buff of his palm. Yoshida was fined for that, but so was Nishimoto, who was also ordered to apologize for insubordination.

Our big batting star was Tatsunori Hara, 6', 175 pounds of handsome, red-blooded Japanese hero. He'd hit about 30 homers every year with an average around .300 since joining the team out of college in 1980. The huge communications conglomerate of the *Yomiuri Shimbun* (magazines and newspapers) and Nippon Television, to which the Giants belong, were constantly building him up. It seemed that every time you turned the TV on, there was Hara smiling out at you, plugging eardrops, chocolate bars, and what have you.

Hara was our glamour boy. More than once I caught him looking in the mirror, gazing at himself, admiring his image. Sometimes, after our workouts, he would stay outside, standing in front of our bench, so he could get his picture taken. It could be hot as blazes, and everyone who'd finished his drills was inside where it was cool. But not Hara. He'd be out there posing for the photographers.

Kiyoshi Nakahata was our first baseman and our team captain. At age 31, he was coming off his best season, a .294 average with 31 homers. He was lean, tough, energetic, and cheerful, and he would do anything for a laugh. He would turn to the stands and mug for the fans or run in place at his first base position. The crowd would eat it up.

Nakahata was the team leader, and everyone looked up to him. When he walked into the clubhouse, the players really snapped to and showed him respect. He pretty much demanded it. He'd walk by their lockers, and if he didn't hear that "*oosss*"—a greeting like "hey, bro"—from each one, he'd stop and grumble about it.

"*Nani?*" he'd say. What?

Nakahata would make younger Giants apologize for not greeting him properly. Once I saw him pop one of the kids across the head for insubordination. Even with his good cheer, he could intimidate the hell out of people. So when he reported for duty each day, it was like an army muster.

"*Oosss...*"

"*Oosss!*"

"*Oosss...*"

"*Oosss!*"

"*Oosss...*"

"*Oosss!*"

"*Oosss...*"

"*Hmm...*"

"*Nani?!*"

"*Oosss!*"

The clubhouse was much more formal than in the U.S., and you didn't see many practical jokes. Screwing around like we did on the Expos was not appreciated—or tolerated—in Japan. I'd also yet to see my first fight. Those guys were 100 percent baseball, and despite their differences, they showed outward respect for each other, which, again, was very different from life with the Expos. Old Shoriki's dying command, it was said, was that the Giants must always be gentlemen—as well as always be number one. And they tried to live up to it.

Nakahata had a great voice. He was always singing in the

clubhouse or on the team bus. He would sing old Japanese ballads—*enka*, they were called. And he was very good, good enough to be a professional singer. Many a time he told me that if he hadn't become a baseball player, he would have tried to become a recording artist. In fact, he'd once cut a record in the off-season, and it was mildly successful.

Another star was our 28-year-old second baseman Toshio Shinozuka, a soft-spoken dude and my first friend on the team. Shino was a singles hitter, always over .300, with an inside-out swing that was perfect for Japan. A lot of players on the Giants got on his case. They said he didn't like to get his uniform dirty, that he was a pretty boy. But Shino just had his own smooth style. He was also one hell of an infielder, with a good arm, terrific range, and fast hands.

Shinozuka had fast hands in other ways too. In the course of his career, he compiled an impressive set of statistics with members of the opposite sex. He got engaged to one of the girls who always hung around the Tamagawa practice field, then broke the engagement when he became involved with a nightclub hostess. Later on, he had an affair with a well-known actress, which supposedly continued even on his way to two subsequent marriages and one divorce.

It was the quiet guys you had to watch

Then there was our catcher Kazuhiro Yamakura—our all-star catcher who had a hard time batting over .250. Yamakura was an OK guy. I got along with him just fine. On the road, we would often have drinks together in the bar of the hotel where we were staying. But as a catcher, Yamakura was lazy. He was complacent. That was his problem. He was 30. He'd been the Giants' first string catcher since 1980, and he knew he had the catching job locked up for years, because the Giants didn't have anyone else on the farm to take his place.

That was another thing about Japanese baseball. Because the teams were owned by big corporations purely for PR purposes, each franchise had one farm team and that was it. There was no Triple A, Double A, Single A, as we had in the States. The Giants had about two catchers in their entire farm system, which was why Yamakura felt he could relax.

Yamakura was tired most of the time, because he caught

almost all of the games. Even on off-days he'd be down in the bull pen catching pitching practice. So he had good reason to cool it on occasion, I guess.

None of the guys on the Giants were big fans of Oh though. Egawa, Nishimoto, Nakahata, Hara, Shinozuka—none of them liked Oh very much.

But that was another story.

DEATHBALL

I had started out the season just fine, hitting over .350 in the first two months, with 10 homers. Other teams had put defensive shifts on me, but I learned how to hit right through them.

The Carp, for example, would move the shortstop behind second base, and I would poke the ball through the hole at short. Then I'd stand on first base and tap my head with my finger, as if to say, "See, I'm using my brains to beat you."

A lot of people resented my doing that. They thought it was bad manners, that I was making fun of the opposition—which I wasn't, exactly. I was just trying to psyche them out.

Hara, batting cleanup, with me fifth, had a horrendous start and we went through one stretch, in early June, of thirty-one innings without scoring a run. As you might imagine, the coaches had Hara out for special practice nearly every day. They made him do extra running and extra batting and they analyzed his form up the wazoo. Hara smilingly put up with it all. He'd have stayed at the ballpark all night if the coaches ordered him to.

"You sleep in the batting cage tonight, Hara."

"Yes sir! With or without a *futon*?"

We were in a three-way pennant race with the Carp and the Tigers, but by mid-June, the season had already become a drag. The daily routine wore you down, the practices, the constant meetings, banging the same things into your head.

The rainy season was unbelievable that year. There'd been a total of eighty-five games rained out all the previous year, but this year the number would nearly double, which was bad because rainouts just meant more practice. You could never just go home.

It rained for twenty-one days straight at one point, the air thick and sluggish, morning and night. The fields were wet and soggy, the dressing rooms clammy and moldy. In parks with natural grass, the stadium attendants used towels to sop up the water so we could play.

By the all-star break, I was hitting .316 with 16 homers and 63 RBIs. I was voted into the starting lineup for the three all-star games by the fans, along with Randy Bass of the Tigers, and was even chosen MVP in one of the contests when I got the winning hit.

Despite the kudos, however, there was always a rap on me—bad defense or something. I had a tendency to make high arching throws from deep center and that was a frequent kvetch: Why couldn't I fire bullets all the time?

As if saying it would make it come true, I had told the press about my decision to leave Japan at the end of the year, and some people held that against me too. Masaichi Kaneda, a former 400-game-winning pitcher, said on television, "A man who is planning to quit is no good. That's why Cromartie has spiritless play."

I didn't think I had "spiritless play." But I wasn't doing as well as Randy Bass—*that* was a big reason for my bad press. Bass, a big, powerful blond guy from Oklahoma, had 29 homers, 73 RBIs, and a batting average of .357 in his first 68 games. Not only was he threatening to win the triple crown, he also had a good shot at breaking Oh's single season home-run record of 55.

Fat chance. Bass told me one night in Tokyo that he was sure the pitchers would never let him do it. He'd get close, he said, and then they would start walking him. No way they'd let an American take a record like that.

It always seemed to come down to Us vs. Them. In one game in Yokohama in July, Jerry White of the Taiyo Whales hit a long drive to center field. I ran back and jumped, but I missed the ball. When I came back to the bench, two coaches on our team asked me, *"Presento desu ka?"* Was that a present? It was the same thing they had asked me in a previous Whales game when Leon Lee's single took a bounce over my head.

The Giants stayed in the race despite the loss of Keith Comstock, our new American pitcher who had gone out with arm trouble, and Makihara, who had slipped on the Astroturf at Korakuen and broken his leg.

But you could really see a big difference between the Giants of April and the Giants of August. Our players just wilted. Egawa would lose his fastball after three innings. Nishimoto's slider started to resemble a change-up. Yamakura looked like he needed a blood transfusion.

Oh had to switch his relievers nearly every inning because they were so exhausted from the heat and all the training. Our games would last four hours in July and August primarily because of all the pitching changes.

The other teams were just as tired. Endo of the Whales was usually good for seven or eight innings in April and May. He could challenge me with his fastball and win. But in August, he was dead tired. His control was off, and his fork ball wouldn't break. His arm was hanging.

If they hadn't practiced so much, I thought, they might have been stronger, but you couldn't tell that to anyone. Oh himself believed that what players didn't have naturally in speed and power they had to try to make up for it with fighting spirit. "We have to emphasize mental training," he once told me, "because if a man's mental attitude is right, he can make his body work."

It was the legacy of the martial arts—the idea that an athlete had no limits. If you were tired, the coaches would say that what you needed was not more rest, but more training to develop your fighting spirit. You used your spirit to conquer the weakness of your body.

Most of these guys had been practicing the same way since Little League. In high school the system was to practice 365 days a year. Seriously. Perhaps there were four or five days off over the New Year holidays, so make that 360 days. I watched some of the national high school tournament games on television in August. The forty-nine regional champions played off for the title. It was a huge thing in Japan, like the Olympics, and it was televised live, nationwide, morning to night, for two solid weeks. Those kids, some of them as thin as bean poles, were out there playing in the heat like there was no tomorrow, as if it was the last game they were going to play in their lives.

Because of all the conditioning and training they had to endure throughout their young careers—high school pitchers, I discovered, threw 200 pitches a day every day of the year—many of them burned out early. Just like the Latin ball players who played baseball all year around. That was one big reason you didn't see even more big name Latin players in the major leagues. They wore themselves out in winter ball.

Japanese high school kids (and their coaches) felt strong pressure to make it to the big tournament. That's why they trained so hard. Then if they became pros, they felt strong pressure to practice all the time to make the starting lineup. And if they did that, they felt strong pressure to keep up the hard work to show how serious they were. It was endless.

As a result, by August, these guys were so tired they were bobbling routine balls or letting them go through their legs. They'd lost that extra hustle. Maybe in September, if their team was involved in a pennant race, you'd see them reach back and find something extra to give, but in July and August, they were barely ambulatory.

OH-SAN

August should have been a happy month for Oh. Our attendance passed the two million mark for the twenty-third straight year on August 20, and four days later, we moved into first place.

But on the night we took over the league lead, beating the Carp in a sweat-soaked match, 8–4, Oh's father died. He had passed away during the game, and Oh's wife called our traveling secretary Yamazaki, in the third base dugout, with the news and instructions not to notify her husband until the game was over.

As soon as the last out was made and Oh finished congratulating his players, Yamazaki approached him. "*O ki no doku. O naku ni narimashita,*" he said. I'm sorry, but he is gone. Oh's eyes misted slightly, and he hung his head. His father was 84, and the two of them had been very close. On the one occasion that I'd visited Oh's home, a plain six-room house in a suburb of Tokyo, I met his father. The respect and affection they had for each other was enviable.

Everyone in Japan knew the story of how Oh, as a youth, had badly blistered his fingers while pitching in the national high school tournament and how his father had taken the all-night train to Osaka to help Oh out. He applied a special herbal pack which enabled his son to pitch the next day—and lead his team to the national title—before hurrying back to his job as a cook in Tokyo. It was one of the great tales of Japanese sport.

On the night Oh broke Hank Aaron's career home run record, Oh brought his mother and father out onto the field in front of 50,000 fans to thank them personally for all they had done for him.

The unfortunate death of Oh's father provided me with a rare glimpse into Japanese attitudes toward family and work. When we got back to our hotel, the Hiroshima Grand, Yamazaki assembled all of the players, still in our grungy uniforms, in the tenth-floor lobby to stand and observe a minute of silence. Then Oh stepped in front of us and began to speak, in a voice cracking with emotion, "Thank you for your concern. My father's health wasn't very good, so his passing was not unexpected. I said my goodbyes to him before we began this road trip. This is a private matter, and it has nothing to do with baseball. I plan to go on as before. We will still take each game one at a time, and there will be no more days off until the end of the season."

It was certainly not the way an American would have acted, but it *was* Japanese. The next morning Oh took the first plane back to Tokyo, 560 miles away, to make a brief noontime appearance at his father's wake. Then he grabbed the bullet train for Nagoya. By 5:00 P.M., he was on the field for the opener of our three-game series with the Chunichi Dragons.

"A man's work is more important than anything else," the Japanese were constantly telling me. And now I had seen just how important it was.

The more I saw of Oh, the more I liked him, personally. He had helped me in many, many ways, most of all as a hitter. He taught me to be more patient, not to get upset if the pitchers wouldn't challenge me, and to intensify my concentration at the plate. He gave me a lot of interesting insights into Japanese pitchers, such as the fact that they hardly ever throw the same pitch twice in the same at-bat.

I had started doing a little downswing routine that Oh had taught me, one which he'd used in the on-deck circle when he was playing. It countered any tendency to swing up. Now, there was a tremendous amount of disagreement on the best way to hit. Some guys preferred the upswing, like Ted Williams. Others liked the downswing. Me, most of the time, I liked the level swing. But I had a tendency to lift my shoulder, which the downswing drill helped cure. I couldn't very well go out on the field with a book under my arm, so I tried Oh's drill: swinging down and trying to hit the fat part of the ball. Oh was big on it. Whenever I did it in batting practice, he'd really get off. He'd stand there and watch the entire time I was up.

Oh was becoming a friend, I felt, and when my second son was born in April that year, back in the U.S., I named him Cody Oh Cromartie, in Oh's honor. Oh had three daughters but no sons, and when I told him what I'd done, I think he was genuinely moved.

Now, he had a godson.

Despite my affection for him, Oh was not really a popular manager. In fact, a lot of my teammates were against him. Many were supporters of previous manager Shigeo Nagashima, the man who had played third base and batted cleanup behind Oh on the old "V-9" Giants, as the team that won nine Japan titles in a row was called. Nagashima had managed the team from 1975 to 1980, when he was forced to resign by the Yomiuri board of directors because of his failure to win a Japan Series. He was, hands down, the most popular player of all time in Japan. He didn't have Oh's hitting power—his lifetime home run total was 444—but he won more batting titles than Oh (six to Oh's five), had a higher lifetime average (.305 to Oh's .301), and had a reputation as a clutch hitter. He was named Japan Series MVP four times and had hit a game-ending *sayonara* home run in the only professional baseball game the Emperor Hirohito had ever attended. Doi, our infield coach and the second baseman on the V-9 teams, once said, "Nagashima was a great batter because he could see the heart of the ball as it came speeding toward him from the pitcher's mound."

Nagashima was charismatic, people said, colorful and fun to watch. I'd seen films where he would hit a home run and do a little dance coming around third base. Other players of his era were too restrained to do something like that. I met him once at Miyazaki airport. He was a good-looking, exuberant man, with a high-pitched, excited style of talking. You could see why the fans took to him.

In contrast to Nagashima, Oh suffered image-wise. He was quiet and shy and, it was said, somewhat mechanical as a player. Whereas Nagashima would swing at bad balls, Oh would refuse to swing at anything outside the strike zone. He was too well disciplined. He'd bat third, ahead of Nagashima in the order, and with the game on the line in the ninth inning, Oh would draw a walk if he could, which was what he usually did because the pitchers were afraid to pitch to him. Nagashima would be set up to drive in the winning run. The pitchers had no choice but to challenge him.

I didn't understand how people could say Nagashima was the greater player when Oh was walked 150 times a year and still won two triple crowns. He'd done it back to back in 1974–75; in those two seasons, he'd had 128 and 166 bases on balls. Oh had hit 49 and 51 home runs when he won his triple crowns, and he'd done it in 130-game seasons. (His single-season mark of 55 homers came in a year when the Central League played 140 games.) He had also won fifteen home run titles, thirteen of them in a row. Nagashima couldn't compare. No way.

But at age 50, Nagashima's popularity was still sky-high, and he was making a million dollars a year in endorsements—far more than Oh. He just had that aura—a pure-blooded Japanese aura. That was the big difference.

Davey Johnson, who'd played for the Giants in 1975–76, told a story about the time he was out running with Nagashima. They were jogging near a temple in Ashiya, and several people were following them, including Nagashima's attendants and several members of the press. Nagashima took off his jacket and threw it down, without looking back. One of the attendants dutifully picked it up. Johnson was flabbergasted, but that was the treatment that Nagashima expected.

Oh was not like that. He never acted like he was above anyone. Fans, little kids, other ballplayers would constantly come up to him for his autograph. He'd always comply. His locker and his office would be full of things for him to sign. Very few players in Japan—or the U.S. for that matter—would have the patience. But Oh would sit there after each day, going through stacks of Japanese "sign cards" and buckets of baseballs, autographing them all. He never said no.

I think it bothered Oh that the Japanese treated Nagashima as the greatest ballplayer in the land. Once I saw him in his cramped, little manager's office signing a boxful of balls in English.

"What are you doing," I asked, "Are those for Americans?"

He gave a little laugh and said, "Yeah. I'm more famous in the United States than I am in Japan."

He was joking, but I think he was quite proud of the ton of mail he'd get from the States. He had a great name in major league circles, because he had always done well against visiting big-league teams. You could ask any American major leaguer about Oh, and they'd say, "Yeah, Oh, what a hitter!" Ask them about Nagashima, and they'd say, "Who?"

For Americans at least, Sadaharu Oh was, and is, Japanese baseball. Not Nagashima. People in the Giants' organization didn't seem to realize what they had in him.

I doubt Oh would have hit as many home runs as he did if he had played in the U.S., but he would have been able to do just fine. He'd hit Tom Seaver in his prime when he visited Japan with the Mets. He'd also hit the other big boys too, while Nagashima wasn't that successful. Ernie Banks told me about a spring camp in the States long ago when Yomiuri had trained with the Dodgers; Oh had taken Sandy Koufax deep. Banks didn't know who Nagashima was, but he certainly remembered Oh and respected the hell out of him.

As manager of the Giants, however, Oh didn't get nearly the respect he deserved. Many of the players blocked Oh out.

They just couldn't get into his wisdom or his knowledge. They all talked about Nagashima instead. Nakahata, our team captain, was a Nagashima man and did not particularly care for Oh. Nakahata had been raised under Nagashima, and he remained loyal to him years after Nagashima had departed.

Oh's name in Japanese meant "king." It was pronounced "wan" in Chinese which also sounded like Oh's jersey number, "1." Nakahata, however, occasionally referred to Oh as *wan-ko* behind his back; it meant dog.

The main reason people didn't like Oh, I'm sure, was that he was half-Chinese. Nobody ever said anything to me about it, but it was there, believe me. I saw the looks that people would give him. One time, Yamazaki, our traveling secretary, was trying to tell Oh something when Oh was talking to somebody else. Oh turned and said, "*Chotto matte,*" Just a minute, and continued with his conversation. Yamazaki looked around and said to nobody in particular, "*Chotto matte?!*" as if he had just been insulted. There was an expression of total disclain on his face.

As manager, Nagashima did win two pennants. But the general consensus was that he wasn't in Kawakami's class—Kawakami being the V-9 manager. People said that Nagashima would do silly things. He'd forget the rules. He'd go out to the mound twice in an inning without realizing what he was doing and then be forced to take the pitcher out. He also had a revolving door policy toward his pitchers. The *gaijin* called him "Captain Hook."

Oh was generally regarded as smarter than Nagashima. And Oh was, in fact, a very smart man. Reggie Smith certainly respected Oh's brains. But he also thought that Oh was too wishy-washy, that he didn't ride his players hard enough, and that he made too many player changes too early in the game—leaving the wrong people in the game in the ninth inning with no one left on the bench. Once Oh put Reggie in a game as a pinch hitter in the fourth inning. Reggie complained that it was too early to do something like that.

"Why don't you save me for the late innings?" Reggie protested.

"It's never too early to hit a home run," replied Oh.

Many managers in the States, like Dick Williams, would leave their starting lineups alone until the seventh inning or so. But Oh was constantly tampering. He'd bunt in the first inning. He'd change his strategy on every pitch. He'd move people around. He couldn't seem to leave his players alone. The guys never knew how long they were going to play, and it got on their nerves.

Oh prided himself on concentration and dedication on an everyday basis, but his lack of managing experience hurt him because basically the people around him—the press as well as his coaches—were always second-guessing him. Oh would follow a coach's suggestion, and then when it didn't work out, the coach would turn around and criticize him to a reporter. The coaches were not going to take the blame for his mistakes even though they didn't mind taking some of the credit when things worked out. We weren't as good a team as the Carp or the Tigers that year, but I thought Oh could have gotten better results if our coaches had been more supportive and if so many of our players hadn't been so pro-Nagashima.

Frankly, I didn't think Oh enjoyed his job. Once he said to me, "Cro, today I star, you manager." And he laughed, but I think he was half serious. Oh didn't have any illusions about his managerial skills. "A good player," he would say, "doesn't mean a good manager. Ted Williams, .400 hitter, but no good manager."

I'd joke with him, "You're a great hitter. That's why you're a bad manager."

Reggie was right when he said that Oh was too wishy-washy. Oh's main problem was that he was way too nice. Instead of ordering a player—"Do this!"—he'd say, "How about doing this?" It was his character.

The word was that when Nagashima lost a game as a manager, he would smash the trees in his garden with a baseball bat. But when Oh lost, he would go home and play his piano—which he was rather good at, incidentally. He left the screaming and yelling and the nasty work to his coaches. And because he didn't have that tough guy image, he didn't have the firm grasp on the team that he should have had.

Oh once said that as a player he always tried to avoid causing any disputes among his teammates and tried to get along with everyone. It was partly because that was the way he was, he said, partly because that was what his father had taught him.

If Oh had a gentle demeanor on the surface, however, he also had his other side which you could see on rare occasions. Once, in a spring training game, Yamakura had looked just terrible. He'd played as if he didn't care at all. After the game, Oh came in and chewed him out, right there in the locker room in front of everyone. He really got on his ass for a couple of minutes. Then he calmed down and turned to leave. As he was walking away, Yamakura gave him a little snarl behind his back.

Oh spun around. He was absolutely furious. The veins in his neck stood out. His eyes were like fire. I'd never seen him like that. I thought he was going to hit Yamakura, but then he caught himself and went into his office.

Not that Oh's anger wasn't called for. While Yamakura and the others were driven extremely hard and their lives controlled and restricted, they were also aware of the prestige they enjoyed as starters—starters on the Tokyo Giants. And they tended to take advantage of it, by not giving 100 percent all the time. It was an arrogance that was unhealthy.

Oh could also be narrow-minded and a stickler for form. Once, when a reserve outfielder named Nakai walked into the hotel dining room in Hiroshima wearing designer jeans and a Kansai Yamamoto sweater, Oh burst out, "What a shameless way to dress!" Shibata, who was also there, voiced his agreement.

"What's wrong with these clothes?" Nakai asked. "What should I be wearing?"

"A white polo shirt and golf pants," Oh replied, referring to the costume that pro ball players in Japan had been wearing off the field for thirty years.

Zzzzzzzz

The longer I stayed in Japan, the longer the games seemed to get. In August, we played a nine-inning marathon in Hiroshima which took us four hours and fourteen minutes to win, 9–8. I almost fell asleep in the outfield. The games just dragged on. The pitchers screwed around with the batters so much that every count, it seemed, went to 3–2. They'd get two strikes, then inevitably throw three straight balls—junk on the outside corner. They never tried to blow the guy away.

What's more, the batters and the pitchers had to psyche themselves up for each pitch. That took time too. They'd step out of the batter's box, or off the pitcher's mound, take a deep breath, stare at the sky, maybe touch the good-luck charm in their pocket. And then they'd be ready.

There were also the endless meetings on the field. If the catcher wasn't always going out to the mound, the coaches were always interrupting the game to give advice. They seemed incapable of just getting on with the game. They had to analyze the hell out of every situation before proceeding. It was like paying chess.

After a while, the routine got to me—the sameness, the predictability of it all. We'd take the train to Nagoya to play the Dragons, to Osaka to play the Tigers, then to Hiroshima to play the Carp. Then we'd fly back to Tokyo for a home stand—against the Dragons, the Tigers, and the Carp. After that we'd taxi across town to Jingu for a set with the Yakult Swallows, then hop a commuter train to Yokohama to play the Taiyo Whales. Then we'd go back home to host those two squads. I'd see the same teams and the same faces, and the games were always played the same way. Three hours into the game, we wouldn't have finished seven innings.

The Giants went into their second annual September swoon. We had played so badly in a loss to the Whales at Korakuen that the fans in the bleachers stormed the field, halting the game for a time. I was counting the days until I left Japan for good, on my way back to the big leagues. At night, I'd actually have dreams about playing for Pete Rose and the Cincinnati Reds.

The Tigers took control of the pennant race, infecting the country with Tiger fever. The team hadn't won a pennant in twenty-one years, and their fans were going nuts. Bass was nearly unstoppable, despite suffering from a broken bone in his ankle. He merely put on a foot protector and kept playing. By September 9, he had 45 home runs and people were beginning to think Oh's record was in serious jeopardy. Oh had hit his 45th homers in game 109; Bass hit his 45th in game 102.

The question everyone had begun asking was "Can a *gaijin* do it?" Actually that was the question the *gaijin* were asking. The Japanese were trying to ignore the situation.

By September 26, Bass had hit 46 homers, with twenty-three games left. He was also leading the league with a .354 average and 116 RBIs. I was hitting .323, with 32 homers and 110 RBIs second to Bass. I was the only one who could block his triple crown.

Despite this, the Japanese press was singling me out as the reason the Giants were eight games back and fading. The knock on me now was that I didn't hit in the clutch, because I hadn't gotten any hits in a big September series with the Tigers in Osaka. The writers said that I wasn't serious enough about baseball, that I suffered "lapses of concentration" on the field because my mind was on returning to the major leagues. Other critics said that because I was making so much money, I wasn't hungry enough.

A reporter for one evening daily, the *Yukan Fuji,* wrote that the Tigers' two Americans, Bass and Rich Gale, were far more serious about baseball than me, and so was my teammate, pitcher Keith Comstock, who was 8–8 since coming off the injury list. Those three guys happened to be white, so the reporter concluded that black players lacked dedication *and* were difficult to control. The paper quoted our infield coach Doi as saying that maybe the Tokyo Giants ought to stick to white *gaijin.*

On the same day the article appeared, Leron Lee, a black man who played for the Lotte Orions, logged his 4,000th career at bat in Japan; his lifetime average in Japan stood at .324, highest in Japanese baseball history. His brother Leon, who played for the Whales, had hit 200 home runs in Japan. But then again, perhaps they had white genes. You never knew.

If all this were not enough, the scandal magazines were having a field day, printing rumors about my private life. They built up a dinner date I'd had with a Japanese actress into a torrid love affair. Then there was a supposed "fight" I'd had in an Aoyama nightclub, which, in reality, had only been an argument.

I was having a drink at a disco that was your basic international scene—a mixed crowd of Japanese and *gaijin*. It was a place where all the visiting rock bands from the States would go, and lots of models and stewardesses were always in attendance. There were flashing lights and strobes, and huge Altech speakers you could get up and dance on.

I was sitting there with a friend named Charlie and a guy I'd invited along. Charlie was with a fox whom my other friend promptly tried to snag. Charlie got mad at me for having invited the guy along, and we ended up shouting at each other over the loud disco music. It was nothing really: Charlie went home in a huff, no blows exchanged. But a magazine reporter present at the scene built it up into the fight of the century.

The whole thing was silly, but because of my "poor" conduct, one sports editorial urged the Giants to seriously consider getting rid of me—even if I did drop my retirement plans.

Inflamed by all this criticism, I recklessly dove for a ball in a game at Yokohama in early October. I ended up busting a bone in my shoulder, which put me out for the remainder of the season. In this case, it amounted to two more weeks of makeup games. My stats stood at .309, 32 home runs, and 112 RBIs.

The Giants wouldn't give me permission to leave, even though I was in a cast. So I packed up and went home anyway. This time I was fined a million yen, but what did I care? I was sick of team harmony.

I missed seeing the final game of the season when the Giants played the Tigers at Korakuen and walked Bass, who had 54 homers, four times.

1986

SENDAI BONUHEDO

I sat in Miami and dreamed about playing once more in America. Pete Rose had expressed some interest in me for the Reds, and I sincerely believed I could get a good deal with Cincinnati or any number of clubs. Free-agent salaries had taken such a big jump since I'd come to Japan that I thought anything was possible. Although the Giants said they still wanted me, I was certain I could get them to release me from the last year of my contract.

At the same time, though, I'd grown attached to Oh. It bothered me that I hadn't been able to help him win a pennant. He was getting bad press, and I felt responsible somehow. What's more, the criticism that had been heaped on me at the end of the previous year left a bad taste in my mouth. I wanted to prove them wrong. I wanted to show them that I deserved as much respect as they were showering on Randy Bass for helping Hanshin win the pennant and the Japan Series. But how I was going to match Bass's triple crown statistics—.350, 54 home runs, 134 RBIs—remained a mystery to me.

So in the end I returned, with my big ego, to Miyazaki once

more for what I truly hoped would be the last time.

The revolving door of *gaijin* players was spinning. Ken Macha, Tommy Cruz, and Steve Ontiveros, who had each hit .300 for their respective teams, were no longer in Japanese baseball. Not enough power, their managers said. After what Bass had done the previous year, everybody wanted a player like him—including Giants' fans.

My new *gaijin* teammate was Luis Sanchez, a relief pitcher for the California Angels, who was from Venezuela. Keith Comstock returned as well, but got caught in the numbers game. Since the rules allowed only two *gaijin* per first team, Keith, a nice guy and a good pitcher, had to stay on the farm team as a backup.

Bobby Marcano, also from Venezuela and a man who had played second base for the Hankyu Braves for many years, was hired as the Spanish-Japanese interpreter for Sanchez, who didn't speak English. That meant we now led the league in interpreters. There was Ichi Tanuma, our veteran ace, who had been with the team since the days of Davey Johnson; Rocky Hirano, who had joined the team when Reggie Smith came along; and now Bobby M.

Originally the Giants had gone after Dave Stewart, the Dodger pitcher who went on to become a star for the Oakland Athletics. They had offered him two million dollars for two years, but that was before Stewart got in trouble with the law. In January 1987, he was arrested by the Los Angeles police for soliciting a prostitute, who turned out to be a man in drag. Team officials said that hiring Stewart would be bad for their image. One paper even wrote that there was the danger that Stewart would give the Giants AIDS. Jesus Christ.

Despite my great expectations, the season had barely begun before I found myself once again under indictment. The scene of my first offense was our practice field in Tamagawa on the outskirts of central Tokyo.

Oh had called a workout one morning in late April, which I thought was asking a bit much in view of the fact that we had a game scheduled that night back in town. It meant an hour-and-a-half ride to Tamagawa and back, not to mention the extra practice itself.

It was unjust, and to show everyone how I felt, while running laps I kicked a couple of team gloves that were lying on the ground, as hard as I possibly could. The gloves, I later discovered, belonged to Hara.

Oh was not amused. He yelled at me for the first time, ever.

"Don't kick the gloves," he screamed. "That's team property."

"They were in the way," I protested, trying to sound tough.

"You're fined, Cromartie," he said.

End of discussion.

After practice, we took a bus to the park where we played to a three-hour-and-forty-minute tie, thus concluding our twelve-hour day. But Oh was happy. A tie was better than a loss, and we'd had our practice.

My second crime took place a month later. I had gotten off to another slow start. By May 20, I had but 5 homers and 21 RBIs, with an average of .294. My batting form was off, and in the game that night, Oh ordered me to bunt. This was more than a little embarrassing. I executed my bunt, then stormed back to the dugout and angrily kicked a chair over. Reggie would have been proud, but my little outburst cost me another fine.

Then, in a subsequent game against the Dragons, I let a soft line drive to center field drop in front of me instead of diving for it. That was bad judgment on my part because the Dragons scored the winning run as a result. The next day I was lambasted in the papers for loafing, and when I arrived at the park I found myself benched—for the second time in my Nipponese career.

Oh called me into his office and shut the door. He told me I was playing like a minor leaguer. Maybe I was tired, he said. Maybe I needed a rest to clear my head. I urged him to reconsider. I told him that I was fine and that he shouldn't create a problem where one didn't exist. All I needed, perhaps, was a little extra practice.

Apparently, he didn't believe me (or see the humor in my statement) because my name was not on the lineup that night.

I bitched in private about being sat down. I told some people I felt like quitting. Somehow this got into the press. And when I wore Cincinnati Reds' socks in practice the next day as a subtle way of protesting my treatment, the reporters went nuts. The following morning, there were big red headlines splashed in all the dailies that I was planning to desert. CRO TO QUIT! CRO FLYING COOP! They were worse than the *New York Post.*

I had absolutely no intention of leaving during the season. And, in truth, I felt sorry for Oh. The Giants had fallen to third place, five games out, and the pressure on him was intensifying.

The media reports coming out just showed how crazy thing could get in Japan. The sports press scrutinized and magnified everything the Giants did. If you smiled while sitting on the bench, someone would criticize you for not being serious enough. If you scowled, some writer would a attack you for disrupting team harmony. God forbid clowning around.

They were like the Mafia, and whenever there was a *gaijin* involved in a controversy, it brought out their worst. We were easy targets. We were big money. We were supposed to be perfect. And, conveniently for the sportswriters, we couldn't read Japanese.

It wasn't long before I gave them more new material for their notebooks. On June 14, in a game in Sendai, one of the many faceless postwar cities we played in, I cost the Giants a victory with bad baserunning.

In the eighth inning, with the score tied, we had the bases loaded, with me on third. Nakahata hit a long fly ball to deep right field, which I lost track of in the lights. I thought it was a home run, or a double at least, so I trotted down the line halfway until I suddenly noticed that the right fielder had caught the ball at the base of the wall. I had to turn around and race back to third. I could have made it home easily if I had only waited to tag up. It was a stupid thing to do, and I should have known better.

Everyone was outraged at me, naturally. Doi, our third base coach, who had been screaming "Go! Go! Go!" at the time, angrily slapped my helmet several times, just so everyone watching on TV would know the blame was mine and that he hadn't given me improper instructions.

After the game, which ended in a tie, I was fined fifty thousand yen. The next day the Tokyo sports dailies reported they had been flooded with calls from Giants' fans demanding that Oh bench me. Our head coach Kunimatsu was quoted as saying, "What a bonehead play. Even a primary school player would know how to score on that." At the park the next evening, no one wanted to talk to me. Even my own teammates shied away from me. It was as if I had the bubonic plague.

The people of Japan never ever forgot my "Sendai Bonehead" —or *bonuhedo*, as they pronounced it. Believe me they never forgot. Years later Japanese would still ask me about that night. You saw bad base running all the time in Japan. Everyone fucked up at one time or another. Ask people about the time Hara screwed up or the time Nakahata screwed up, and it's water under the bridge—they've forgotten it. But ask about Warren Cromartie and the "Sendai Bonehead," and it's indelibly etched in the minds of every Japanese baseball fan.

When we returned to Tokyo, rumors began circulating that the Giants were going to dump me and sign up a new *gaijin*. Bill Cowens was the name being mentioned. A magazine writer summed up the general attitude toward me when he wrote:

> Cromartie doesn't hit, he doesn't hustle, and he doesn't field. He loafs on easy flies—letting them fall in for base hits. And he sloughs off in practice... Oh had dinner with Cromartie during the recent northern trip and that's something that is hard to understand. Why does Oh give that selfish *gaijin* such special treatment. Why does he even keep him on the team?

I felt like writing a letter to Pete Rose.

In time, my stock began to rise. On June 23, I hit two two-run homers in a 7–3 win over the Taiyo Whales in Yokohama. It was our fifth win in a row, and we were now only half a game out of first place and thirteen games over .500.

A few days later, I hit a grand-slam homer in the top of the ninth inning to beat the Swallows, 7–3. By the all-star break, I had gotten up to .327 with 17 homers and 51 RBIs. Although I didn't make the all-star team—the two *gaijin* slots in the Central League went to Sanchez, who had 18 saves, and Bass, who'd finished the first half hitting .399 with 25 homers and 69 RBIs—suddenly everyone was my friend again. Even Doi. This was getting to be an annual pattern.

QUALITY CONTROL: THE BIG COACH

Americans would find the power of the Giants' coaches and the deference the players showed them hard to understand. It was mind-blowing to me, but it reflected how the society as a whole was run. Harmony came first, the individual second; seniority ruled.

The coaches wanted perfection, which was difficult to achieve in a game like baseball because anything, even a strikeout, could be considered a mistake, and the best hitters in the game still failed seven times out of ten.

But the coaches tried. The Giants had what you might call a zero-defect policy. A sign in the clubhouse went: "The fewer mistakes you make, the more games you will win." They wanted us to be baseball machines, and the way they went about trying to achieve that goal could make life trying for even the most patient and agreeable of people—which I wasn't. We were constantly being watched. We had to submit ourselves to incessant badgering and nitpicking, which began in camp and continued all year long. That was Japanese-style quality control.

There were also the group discussions to make sure everyone was aware of the mistakes he was making or could potentially make, and understood how to avoid making said mistakes in the future. After the player had the theory drilled into his head, he would go out on the field to put it into endless practice.

The Japanese philosophy was that you had to teach the body and the mind together. Proper form and established procedure were more important than fast reflexes, quick thinking, or individual initiative. Repeated lectures and repeated practice were therefore essential. That was the way the Giants approached the game, and it was the way all the other teams in Japan approached the game.

It was also way of Japanese business and industry. If a factory employee screwed up, everyone in the company had to hear about it in a meeting. There had to be a discussion so that the same mistake wouldn't happen again. What all this meant was that if you were a company worker, or a ballplayer, you kept hearing the same shit over and over.

One of the distinguishing features of the Giants was the number of coaches that we had: eight. That was twice as many as the Expos had, and all eight took their jobs extremely seriously. They believed they had to be busy every minute of the day; they felt compelled to give constant instruction whether you needed it or not.

At Montreal, the coaches were more laid back. Players were allowed to develop their own individual routines, and the coaches were more like consultants. They were there if you needed them. If you wanted to know something, you asked. But they left you alone for the most part. If I had a problem with my hitting, I'd usually talk to a good batter like Andre Dawson. Or Tony Perez. But seldom a coach—because coaches didn't face the opposing pitchers; the players did. In Japan, however, behavior like that would not be tolerated.

Doi, a Giants' defensive coach, a little guy who had played second base in the V-9 years, was a fanatic about his job. Now I liked Doi, basically. He was a nice man, despite certain remarks he'd made to the press and the way he had whacked me on the head in Sendai. But the guy talked too much. He knew a little English, and he would just wear out my ears from the minute I set foot in the park—with advice.

For openers, I would get a daily weather report from him. If it had been raining, Doi would point that out and tell me the Astroturf was wet. If it was windy, he would mention that that too. The team flag in center field could be snapping like mad, pointing toward home, but still he'd have to tell me, "Cro, the wind is blowing in today, so you don't have to play so deep."

If the park we were playing in had a hard wall, he'd warn me that the wall was hard and that when the ball hit off the wall, it was going to rebound fast. It didn't matter that I'd been playing in the park for three years and that I had bounced off that wall myself, he had to tell me anyway.

He was unbelievable.

Our games would start at 6:00 P.M. In the twilight, between 6:30 and 7:00, a fly ball might be hard to pick up. So Doi invariably reminded me of that as well. "Cro, it's twilight," he'd say at the stroke of 6:30, "be careful.".

Finally, I asked him to back off. One day before a game, he came up to caution me about the wind and the twilight, and I stopped him in mid-sentence, holding up my palm like a traffic cop. "Hold it," I said. "You don't have to tell me. Not so often. I already know. I understand. *Wakarimashita*."

"But that's my job," he protested. "I'm supposed to tell you."

"I know that's your job," I said, "but I'm a professional. I've been playing for many years. You can tell the rookies about the twilight and the wind every day, but you don't have to tell me. I already know."

He couldn't understand that. It was beyond his comprehension. He'd keep telling me, and I'd keep asking him not to. But he refused to give up; he just changed his tactics and became more subtle. He would kind of sneak up on me. I'd be playing catch in the outfield and I'd turn and suddenly Doi would be standing there beside me.

"Cro," he'd say "How are you today? *Genki desu ka?* You OK?"

"Yeah, I'm OK," I'd reply.

Then it would come out.

"Windy day today, isn't it?"

We had a batting coach one year, a guy named Yamauchi, who wouldn't quit either. He was a real jabberer. In practice he'd stand behind the batting cage and talk to the batter while the guy was trying to concentrate on hitting. The batting practice pitcher would wind up and throw the ball, and as it was on its way, the coach would still be telling the guy how to hit it.

Now this was the guy's hitting time. How in the hell was he supposed to concentrate on hitting the ball and do what the coach was telling him at the same time. But the coach would be jamming the guy's head on every swing, and after too, constantly yammering.

"That swing is OK. Try to stay back. OK. Stop your swing. Do this. Do that. Put your hands out more. Keep your head down. Wait until the ball gets there." And so on.

It was a kind of compulsion, I guess, because he wouldn't let up. When the guy was finished hitting, Yamauchi would follow him into the locker room, still talking. He would make the guy sit down and watch videos of whoever the opposing pitcher was expected to be that night, his mouth still in high gear.

Even when the game was going on, he wouldn't quit. The batter would be in the on-deck circle, and the coach would be standing in the dugout yelling, "Don't forget what I told you about the elbows."

The player couldn't escape. He'd be in the batter's box. He'd foul off a pitch, and the coach would call him back. "Hey, Komada, come over here for a moment. What did I tell you about the elbows?"

You'd never see that in the States because it would disrupt the hitter's concentration. If an American coach ever tried it, the batter might tell him to fuck off. Just like in *Bull Durham*. But in Japan, it was standard operating procedure, and it never stopped.

Even after the game, it wasn't over. The coach would pull the guy aside to go over the mistakes he'd made in his at-bats. It was like school, or like parent and child. The amazing thing was, I never saw a player get mad and tell the coach to back off. No way. That would be a capital offense in Japan. You'd get hanged by the nuts for it.

The players might not have liked it, but they kept their feelings more or less private. They had to. If they didn't, they'd find themselves somewhere else. It was the same way in a Japanese company. If you went against the program, you'd find yourself in a branch office somewhere in the Japan Alps.

THE GROUP

In August, I was really stinging the ball. It was suffocatingly hot, but I felt great. My arms got longer, the ball got bigger, and my average started to zoom. By August 27, I was hitting .349 with 26 homers and 68 RBIs, trailing only Bass, who was having another incredible year with 36 homers and a batting average of .397.

We were also four-and-half games up on the second-place Carp, after demolishing them 12–2, with Egawa getting his thirteenth win and Yamakura, of all people, hitting three home runs. I'd given an impromptu pep talk to the guys earlier in the month, to try to get some energy flowing. Oh later told the reporters that I was the real leader of the team, and damned if some of them didn't begin to write that I should be chosen league MVP if the Giants won the flag.

Aahhh. How green was my valley. And how things had changed from the spring when they were all thirsting for my blood.

One reason I was doing so well, of course, was because I was in better shape than everyone else. Most of the guys were done in by the heat. They were running out of gas while I still had a full tank, because I paced myself and they didn't—or couldn't.

I had my own light routine, which Oh and the coaches allowed because I was a *gaijin* and a veteran big leaguer. My teammates, on the other hand, would be out there every afternoon in the god-awful heat, doing an hour of running laps, calisthenics, and whatnot before even beginning their hitting and fielding practice.

Even our big stars Hara and Nakahata did it. They had to do it. It was demanded of them. Perhaps they were jealous of the routine I was allowed. And if they were they had every right to be, in my opinion. Veterans like them should have been given the same leeway or freedom as me. But even if by some miracle the coaches chose to let them train their own way, they would have refused, because they were so hypersensitive to the feelings of others. Hara and Nakahata always said that they had to set an example. And that example was no special treatment for anyone—*gaijin* excluded. Star *gaijin*, that is.

You see, it was not considered enough just to show up for work and do your job—whether you were a ballplayer or a company employee. You also had to show your devotion to the group. Sacrifice was required. The greater the sacrifice, the better the product—that was what people who understood the Japanese culture said. You could see that philosophy everywhere in the country.

Once, when Nakahata was in a slump, he took two hours of batting practice, with all the press watching. Now maybe he didn't need two hours of BP, but he did it anyway—to please management, and to please the media, and to demonstrate to everyone that he was trying. Now maybe there's nothing wrong with that. But the Giants did that type of thing constantly, to excess. Consequently they ran out of gas mid-year.

There were very, very few Japanese who would do things on their own. Ochiai of the Lotte Orions was the only exception I know of. He was a real rebel. During the season, he'd do about five minutes of pregame. Sometimes he'd take BP with no bat. He'd just stand there in the cage "getting the feel" of the strike zone. Ochiai won three triple crowns in the 1980s. He was so big he could do what he wanted. Still a lot of Japanese resented him, and nobody tried to copy him.

BRIGHT LIGHTS, BIG MACHI

Carole and the kids left for Florida in the last week of August. It was time for school to start again. Here in June, gone in August.

I was all alone again, but much as I hated to admit it, I was getting used to this crazy life I was living. And I had Tokyo nightlife to keep me company. That meant more bars, nightclubs, coffee shops, discos, you name it, than you could possibly imagine. If you tried to have a drink in each place, you couldn't do it. You couldn't live that long.

In Tokyo, one place the American players liked to go was Nicola's Pizza House in Roppongi. Red tablecloths, good pizza, and huge mugs of draft beer. The owner was a gruff, stocky guy from East Harlem, New York. He had come to Japan with the marines when the war ended and stayed on to make a fortune for himself in the Italian restaurant business and other more clandestine activities.

Nick had put up a huge TV screen for his customers to watch baseball. After the games, the ballplayers would file in to watch the Fuji-TV Pro Yakyu News, an hour-long review of the evening's pro baseball action which started at 11:00. We would cheer our hits, boo our called strikeouts, and count how many derogatory remarks the commentators would make about the *gaijin*. Usually, we needed a calculator.

Other places we would visit in the area were Tony Roma's, the Hard Rock Cafe, and the Lexington Queen—a disco that attracted the best looking women, both American and Japanese, in town. Then there was Chaps, a country-and-western bar, with bluegrass singers imported from Nashville.

Roppongi was like Disneyland for adults; there were all sorts of amusements to partake of. The energy level was amazing. Neon signs were everywhere—a hodgepodge of English, Chinese characters, Japanese *hiragana* and *katakana*—and the area was always bursting with people. The most popular meeting spot was in front of the Almond Coffee Shop at the Roppongi intersection. It was there that you could see the new ultra-modern, ultra-rich Japan that was emerging.

Just about everyone, it seemed, was dressed to the teeth in the latest Japanese and European fashions—the girls in their designer dresses, hair and make-up perfect, the guys in Giorgio Armani suits and ties looking like they'd stepped out of *GQ*. Every other car was a BMW or Mercedes. It made you realize just how wealthy the Japanese were becoming. I'd never been to Paris but I couldn't imagine the Champs-Elysées having any more flair than the heart of Roppongi.

It wasn't easy for us to go out. Fans recognized us on the street and stopped to stare. But it was much harder for my teammates. The crowd around them would magnify ten times. They'd be mobbed, which was one big reason why they didn't like to go out without careful preparation.

If they wanted to go to the movies, for example, they would

have to call the theater and arrange for the manager to let them in a side door once the lights had dimmed. They also had to leave before the film ended, while the theater was still dark, to avoid being recognized.

My teammates, I was beginning to discover, liked to go to hostess bars—both in Roppongi and the Ginza—even though the Giants did not approve. I joined in the fun a few times, and, let me tell you, it was like nothing I'd ever seen in the States or Montreal. Where we'd go was usually some soft-lit salon with deep-cushioned sofas. You'd sit down and immediately be surrounded by several beautiful girls in long gowns with long, flowing hair. Many of them were shy, virginal, innocent-looking—the way Japanese men liked them.

You would buy them all drinks and make conversation. Half an hour would pass, and they'd get up and leave. Then a new group of girls would arrive, all as beautiful as the first batch. You'd buy them drinks too, talk for thirty minutes and it was time for the next shift. You'd go on like that for two or three hours, and then you'd get your bill—about two or three thousand dollars. It wasn't my idea of a great way to spend the evening.

The girls were not prostitutes, exactly. You just couldn't walk out with one and spend the night the first time you met her. You had to develop a "relationship"—which could cost you a lot of money in the process. After you had romanced a certain fox for an appropriate time, then perhaps you could meet her after closing hours and take her to a love hotel, one of those glitzy places in the back streets of the city, where you could rent a room for about a hundred dollars a night and enjoy yourself with overhead mirrors, a revolving bed, complimentary condoms, and, if you were into that sort of thing, video equipment to record your performance.

Visiting hostess bars was my teammates' way of relaxing. They said they really couldn't open up to their wives, like they could talk to these girls. Japanese men were supposed to be reserved and stoic at home. Traditionally, wives greeted them at the door, slipped a *yukata* robe on them, served them dinner, prepared their bath, and followed their orders. Conversation was almost nonexistent. But in hostess bars the guys could let fly. They could sing, dance, tell dirty jokes, and generally make fools of themselves. And no reporters would be watching because nobody in the press could afford such places. Well, each to his own. I preferred the Lexington Queen.

If I didn't feel like a night on the town, I'd just go home and play my drums, fool around with some other percussion instruments, and maybe write some song lyrics. Music had been a hobby of mine for a long time, and I was toying with the idea of organizing a rock band at some point in the future when I was liberated from Japanese baseball.

The Migrant Worker

I hit .439 in the month of August with 8 homers and 23 RBIs. I had several game winning hits, too. But the league MVP for August went to Makihara, our young right-handed ace, who was 4–0 for the month with an ERA of 0.63. A Giant executive mentioned to a sportswriter that I had to produce even more, that I made too many stupid errors, and that I had to get my act together overall. Was this some sort of contract-negotiating ploy?

At the end of the month, we went into a tailspin. We lost four in a row to the Tigers and the Carp. Our lead dropped to three games. Hara and Nakahata were in a slump.

The one who'd been carrying us was our little reliever Katori. Katori was only about 5'6". In the shower, he looked so slight you'd think a gust of wind could blow him over. But he'd come in every night and get them out with his *shooto*. I didn't know where in the hell he got his stamina. And I wondered how long he could keep it.

We had a brutal road trip in late August. Six games in a row in the stifling heat of Osaka and Hiroshima. I'd sit in the dugout at the Carp stadium, and the sweat would flow off my brow, cascade down my nose, and splash on the floor. I felt like Niagara Falls. Then there was the ride back on the bullet train with the air-conditioning on full blast. It was 95 degrees outside, and here I was shivering. It struck me how hard it was to stay healthy in Japan.

From Tokyo Station, I went straight home to an empty apartment. I looked in each of the five rooms on the off chance that somebody might actually be there. No such luck. I fooled around with my drums, then switched on CNN. It was time for Larry King, my main man. After the show, I took a shower and headed out into the Roppongi night—for a cold draft beer at Nick's and other amusements.

I think the heat was starting to wear on everybody's nerves, especially the Whales' catcher Wakana, a big, sturdy dude who had spent some time in the States playing ball. I bowled him over on a hard slide at the plate in Yokohama, and he didn't like it at all. Some Japanese still considered hard sliding bad manners.

"*Nani surun da!*" he yelled at me, then pressed his limited English skills into service. "What the hell you doing!"

"Just sliding home."

"You do that again," he snarled, "I trip you and break your leg."

Then he pushed me. I pushed him back. He pushed me back harder. I grabbed his uniform. The umpire stepped between us. Wakana's teammates came to his rescue. Mine rushed out to pull me away.

What the hell. It was a close play. We were in a pennant race. You were supposed to slide hard. Wakana was a big boy, He could take it.

For my money, Wakana was a jerk. He had no manners and he had a big mouth. I'd be up there at bat and the pitcher would go into his motion, and Wakana would start with his broken fucked-up English, trying to disrupt my concentration.

"*Nekusuto wa kabu!*" Next is a curve!

Wakana had the wrong profession. He should have traded in his uniform for an announcer's mike.

We beat the Whales that game, 7–1. Egawa pitched a complete game to move his record to 14–4, but our lead over the Carp now stood at two games, six over Hanshin.

I went home but I couldn't sleep. I couldn't stop thinking about Wakana and his big mouth. I got up and went out to my balcony. In the distance the lights of Roppongi beckoned.

Maybe a trip to the Lexington Queen was what I needed. I got dressed and headed out into the Tokyo night heat. This was getting to be a habit.

If the pennant race was tight, the batting races weren't. Primarily they were between Bass and me. On September 9, Bass was hitting .390; I was second with .362. I had 32 homers to Bass's 38, 84 RBIs to his 95, and 14 big game-winning hits to his 8.

Hey, I was doing just fine, but did I want to hang around any longer? My three years were almost up, and despite all the pain and frustration, I had to admit I wasn't sorry I'd come here. But I yearned for the big leagues too. That was where I really belonged—or so I thought.

A widely read article appearing in the *Weekly Asahi* magazine attempted to answer that question by predicting my return in 1987! It carried a full analysis of my baseball playing ability, by a former catcher named Katsuya Nomura, a man who had hit 657 home runs in his career. A friend translated it for me. I had never read anything quite like it.

LEARN FROM THE MAJOR LEAGUERS
WHO HAVE CHANGED JAPANESE BASEBALL
—Cromartie's Big Contribution—

Cromartie hit .254 in April, was at .278 by the end of May, and didn't reach the .300 mark until June 7. But since then Cromartie's average has been climbing steadily.

During the recent Tiger series, Cromartie shone with six hits in eleven at-bats, lifting his average to the .360 mark. He has been hitting the ball so well that it is hard to believe that this was the same Cromartie we saw back in the spring. Still, Cromartie has given us many moments of anxiety.

He gives up easily on defense. He has a tendency to make high arching throws back to the infield, which allows the baserunners to advance a base. And there have been times when he doesn't run hard to first base.

It seems that I am not the only one who thinks this way. The sports dailies often write articles about this. But even so, Manager Oh always defends Cromartie.

Said Oh, "If we tried to force Cromartie into the Japanese way of playing baseball, he would lose that special something that makes him good. It's my job to see that he plays well. Both of us want to win. It's only natural that I would stick up for him in the face of all this criticism."

By the data alone, Cromartie is certainly the leader in team batting. Fifteen times thus far, he has had three hits or more in a game. In August alone, he did it eight times. In those fifteen games, the team has a record of 11 wins and 4 losses.

On the days when Cromartie has two hits in one game, the Giants' win-loss record is 19–6. Therefore, Cromartie's hits lead to wins. In the category of game-winning hits, Cromartie has 14, three ahead of Chunichi's Gary Rajisch and Hiroshima's Koji Yamamoto.

By contrast, if you look at the games in which Hara, the Giants' cleanup hitter, has three hits or more—six games thus far—the Giants won-loss record is only 3–3.

Let's look at the other side of the statistics. On the days when Cromartie had no hits, the Giants record is 11–14. In Hara's case, it is 23–12. Whether Hara hits or not doesn't seem to have any effect on whether the Giants win or not. But in Cro's case, it does.

These statistics remind one of the case of Bass and Kakefu on the Hanshin Tigers last year. On the days when Bass had three hits or more, the Tigers were 15–5. In Kakefu's case, it was 5–3. On the days when Bass did not get hits, the Tigers were 10–17. With Kakefu, they were 23–25.

Since the all-star break this year, the Giants have led the league in wins on the road. Their driving force at bat has been Cromartie.

Oh had this comment to make: "Cromartie, like Bass, is one of the few *gaijin* to learn to understand Japanese baseball. He realized that Japanese pitchers would not come at him full speed, and he has adjusted his batting style accordingly, so that this year he is right on the mark."

Cromartie uses his head.

On August 29, in a game against the Tigers, Cromartie struck out twice and grounded out against Nakada's breaking ball pitching. In his fourth at-bat, he swung hard on a slow curve and lined it into the outfield for a clean hit. If you looked at his swing, you could tell that he had given up all thought of a fastball and was guessing curve. The mathematical probability that a curve would be coming is about 20% to 30%. That Cromartie had the guts to wait on a curve ball is a sign of his excellence at bat.

During this last three-game series with the Tigers, Hara did not hit with men in scoring position. He had one hit in twelve at-bats with men on second and third. He did not have the courage to guess.

Both Cromartie and Bass are clever hitters. They are both good at reading pitches. In America, Cromartie was a big leaguer and Bass only Triple A level, but both of them have improved and realized their potential in the same way in Japan. How did this happen?

If you look at their home run zones, you can understand easily. The strike zone is divided into nine smaller zones: three up and down on the outside, three up and down on the inside, and three in the middle.

Cromartie's home runs have come in the outer three zones. Most of them have been off-speed pitches in the middle zone of the outside corner. If the pitch is a little high, Cromartie usually strikes out. If it's a low pitch, he usually grounds to second or short.

Of his thirty home runs so far, only thirteen have been to right field. Four have been to right center. And thirteen have gone to left or left center.

The left-handed Bass has a bigger home run zone. He can hit an inside pitch to the opposite field. He hits a pitch in any corner of the strike zone.

The triple crown–winning Bass was the MVP last year.

This year, if the Giants win the pennant, a lot of voices will be calling for Cromartie to get the MVP. At the very least, one should think, he will battle it out with Egawa.

Bass and Cromartie are the best players on their teams and at the top of Japanese baseball. Yet, what will be their legacy when they leave? I wonder.

Most big leaguers who come to Japan to play have helped raise the level of Japanese baseball before they go back home. Daryl Spencer was blacklisted in the major leagues for his hard sliding, but when he showed it to the Japanese, he changed the quiet color of his team, the Hankyu Braves.

He was a man who showed his teammates how to read the opposing pitchers by their habits. He taught them that by studying a pitcher's form and his delivery, they could learn things to improve their batting. Their famous base stealer Fukumoto learned about studying a pitcher's set position. Without Spencer, he might not have been able to steal all those bases. *(Editor's note: Fukumoto stole 1,065 career bases.)*

Spencer made the Japanese players notice that there are a lot of different ways to play baseball.

Don Blasingame taught the Japanese a lot about thinking ahead to the next play. He taught the Japanese that the game is never over until the last man is out. Even if his team was behind by many runs, Blazer would lead off the bottom of the ninth inning trying his best to get on base. He taught Japanese how to use the drag bunt to upset an opposing pitcher's rhythm, or to somehow make the pitcher throw a ball outside the strike zone.

He taught that there are three strikes in every at bat, but the most important one is the last one.

Don Buford, who played for the Taiheiyo Club Lions, taught us about base running, how to rile the catcher into making a bad throw by taking a big lead off third base. He would position himself between the catcher and the third baseman's glove so that the ball thrown by the catcher would hit him in the back when he ran back to third base.

The gentlemanly George Altman realized that major league pitchers and Japanese pitchers did not throw at the same speed. He dropped his batting hitch when he came to Japan, started using a heavy bat and changed to a "half-batting" style in order to adjust to slower breaking-ball Japanese pitching. He showed us brains and technique in hitting .300 every year.

If you compare these big leaguers of the past to Cromartie, you will notice that they did not make fun of Japanese baseball. They did not take it lightly. They showed their major league pride. Cromartie, however, is quick to grasp the realities of the situation he is in. He gives up quickly; when the score is lopsided, he sloughs off on defense. When I see Cromartie's arching, looping throws, I think of the spirit of the migrant worker.

However, Manager Oh says, "Cromartie has passed the stage of being just a *suketto*—a "helper." He serves the team in a spiritual way, too. When the team is down and depressed, he creates a mood of "never give up."

In the early part of August, in a team meeting held after the Giants reached first place, Cromartie became the first Giants *gaijin* to ask to be allowed to speak before the team.

He was quoted as saying, "I'm in top form right now. Let's see if we can all pull together and win the championship."

Near the end of Cromartie's first season, with two games left on the schedule, Cromartie reportedly said, "This season is over." That remark and his early return to the United States the next season following an injury are the things that people remember.

This season, too, he has made controversial statements for which he was criticized. Has that Cromartie changed?

Cromartie had spoken of his respect for Pete Rose and of his wish to play for Rose and the Cincinnati Reds. But teams in the major leagues these days are undergoing youth movements. It's not that easy to just go back to the big leagues and play. Rod Carew and George Foster and other famous veterans have been released. Moreover, the team rosters in the U.S. have been reduced from twenty-five to twenty-four.

Cromartie is already 32, and his arm is not that strong. At the end of this year, his three-year contract for two million dollars will expire. One can imagine that he will want to continue to play in Japan.

Cromartie named his son after Oh—Cody Oh Cromartie. In that sense, he is different from Bass, who has criticized his manager Yoshida. He is very close to Oh.

In April, in one close game, Cromartie was ordered to sacrifice bunt and did so with a clearly visible lack of enthusiasm. Then he was fined for his behavior. Some coaches on the team wanted to send him to the farm team.

Perhaps it's unreasonable to expect that Cromartie will leave an important legacy in Japanese baseball.

But still he has shown me, at least, about major league style energy conservation. He insists that hard pregame training and practice on travel days are not necessary.

To me, Cromartie is not simply saying, "Japanese style practice is crazy." There is a rationale for his theory. To me, major leaguers hate laziness more than Japanese do.

What could I say? I laughed. I cried. And I asked myself. Well, was there really no place for me in the big leagues? Was I, as Nomura said, too old? Or would I fool them all?

I thought about those things on my subway ride to Yokohama for another Whales game. These days, I drove to work when we played at Korakuen or Jingu—in a Mercedes Benz the Giants had rented for me. I did it for the privacy. But for Yokohama, I would take the train. It was an hour's drive or more, so the train was faster, more convenient, less hassle. You bought a ¥200 subway ticket (about a dollar and a half) in Hiroo, and you were at Yokohama Stadium in thirty minutes. What's more the trains were spotless, gleaming. It was great, as long as the fans left me alone.

I sat with my head down, hoping that nobody would notice who I was and try to talk to me. It was still early afternoon, on a weekday, and the car was fairly empty. But I could hear a couple of young college-age girls, standing nearby, squealing excitedly as they looked my way.

They were hanging onto train straps. Long black hair blowing gently under the overhead fans, lithe, slender bodies in thin summer dresses. Nice, I said to myself. I lifted my head a little to get a better view and tuned into their conversation.

"*Ne, are Kuromatei ja nai?*" Isn't that Cromartie?

"*So, kashira.*" I wonder.

"*Kuromatei da yo. Kyojin no Kuromatei.*" That's Cromartie, all right. Cromartie of the Giants.

I looked their way, and they began to giggle. One of the almond-eyed lovelies looked like Mariko Ishihara, a popular actress I was particularly smitten with. She covered her mouth with one hand, dabbed the perspiration off her brow with a white handkerchief, and slowly turned red as I smiled at her.

Very nice, I said to myself.

I wondered what they were thinking of me. What was I to them? Was I Warren Cromartie, the spiritual leader of the Giants, or was I Warren Cromartie, the listless migrant worker?

Or were they just admiring my muscles? Did they want my body? I thought of going over to ask them, but they got off at the next stop. Still giggling. Still looking. And Mariko still blushing.

After the game, which was routine migrant work, Yamakura gave me a ride part way back to Tokyo. He dropped me off at Denen-chofu station, and I hopped on the subway for Hiroo. I looked around for the two girls, Mariko and her friend. Maybe they'd like to have a drink with me at the Lexington Queen and discuss my legacy.

But no luck. I got off at Roppongi instead of going home. I was restless.

THE BLACK CANNON

The question of what legacy I'd leave dogged me over the next several days. I sat in a hotel room in Nagoya, alone, and thought about it, as I waited for the *sushi* I'd ordered—a big tray of shrimp and eel and tuna and other goodies.

I had asked the hotel clerk not to say it was for me. One could never be too careful in Japan. After all, maybe the guy who ran the *sushi* shop was an avid Dragons fan. If he knew it was me that had placed the order, perhaps he'd put an extra dose of *wasabi* inside each piece of *sushi*. *Wasabi* was a green Japanese horseradish that was absolutely deadly. Great stuff, but it would clear your nasal passages out from here to next week if you got too much at one time.

We lost that night. A guy named Sugimoto, whom we should have beaten easily, shut us out 5–0. The Dragons knocked Nishimoto out in the third inning. I didn't think we were trying as hard as we should have been. We'd get it up for the Carp and let it down against a second-division club like the Dragons who didn't have diddly squat. It irritated the hell out of this migrant worker.

Autumn finally made its appearance, but the pennant race was getting hotter. we'd blown our lead, and going into a final three-game series with the Carp in late September at Korakuen, the standings looked like this:

Hiroshima Carp	62–42–11	.596	—
Yomiuri Giants	66–47–7	.584	0.5
Hanshin Tigers	55–54–10	.505	9.5

Hiroshima beat us in the first game, on a cool breezy evening before the usual packed house. They got to Egawa, who hadn't won a game in four weeks. The big hit was a home run by their third baseman, Sachio Kinugasa, who had played nearly 2,000 games in a row. It was Kinugasa's twentieth home run, which gave him thirteen straight years of twenty homers or more.

We played like shit. But after the game, the guys acted as if they didn't even care. They were laughing and giggling, about what I don't know. I couldn't understand what was so funny about losing a big game like that. But I was just a hired hand. What did I know?

I had two big bottles of beer that night. It took me a long time to go to sleep.

We lost the following night again as the Carp knocked out Makihara. Koji Yamamoto, their other big star with 536 career homers and on the verge of retirement, got a key ninth-inning single. We managed to win the third and final game, 6–2, mainly because I played like a wild motherfucker. I was getting hits and sliding into bases all over the place. One headfirst job into third base was on the front pages of the sports dailies the next morning. It was measured at five meters.

We lost Hara, batting .283 with 36 homers and 80 RBIs, when he broke his finger swinging on a pitch. Several nights later, in the midst of a surprising five-game win streak that had put us back in first place, we almost lost me, setting up what was perhaps my finest hour in Japan.

In a chilly night game at Jingu on October 3, a Swallows' left-hander hit me smack in the damn head. It was a fastball that hit my helmet at exactly the wrong angle. I dropped to the ground and immediately started seeing stars. I lay there thinking, "This hurts." I had to be carried out of the stadium.

I spent the night in nearby Keio Hospital. As chance would have it, there was an American doctor—a surgeon visiting on some kind of exchange program. He gave me a CAT scan and went over my X rays. The staff put me in a tiny room, in a bed that was much too hard and much too small for me to get any sleep. It reminded me of the Miyazaki Grand Hotel.

In the morning, the doctor gave me another CAT scan and judged me fit.

"You've got a hard head," he told me.

"My wife has been telling me that for years," I said.

There was a mob of press photographers waiting in the lobby. They called out my name, jostled each other for position, took a hundred pictures. Naturally, they were oblivious to the fact they were in a hospital.

I waded through the crowd repeating, "*Daijobu, daijobu,*" I'm OK, I'm OK, and grabbed a cab for the twenty-minute ride home. Then I took a nap.

At 5:00 P.M., I got into my Benz, which someone had thoughtfully driven home for me, and drove to Jingu. The press animals, who had camped outside my building, followed in hot pursuit.

Everyone was surprised that I showed up for the game. But our winning streak stood at six games, our lead over the Carp at two, and it was show time, folks. I didn't want to miss the fun.

I sat in what is laughingly called the visitors' clubhouse at Jingu—a tiny dressing room with no cubicles, only hooks on the wall for clothes, and a massage table in the middle that was in danger of collapsing—and talked to a Japanese reporter about my speedy recovery. Then the subject switched to Prime Minister Yasuhiro Nakasone. Nakasone had made a remark about the intelligence level of Americans being lowered by all the blacks and the Puerto Ricans in the country.

It was an out-and-out insult. It was worse than being called a migrant worker. I told the reporter that if Nakasone himself had walked into the clubhouse right then and there, I'd refuse to shake his hand.

But soon I forgot about Nakasone. Because it was my night for drama. Oh didn't start me. But I did pinch-hit.

In the sixth inning.

With the score tied, 3–3.

And the bases loaded.

And I walloped a home run.

A grand slam.

I remember every detail. Things had the extra clarity that comes when you've just had a brush with danger. I came to the batter's box, a little shaky, but sure. The pitcher was a hard throwing right-hander named Obana. The count was *tsu-wan* (2–1, as the Japanese called a ball and two strikes). Somehow, in my bones, I knew he was going to throw me a fastball and when it appeared, I was ready. I slugged it over the center field wall. Hot dog! And God damn!

O, to see the faces of my teammates as I crossed home plate! Some of them had tears in their eyes. They jumped on me and grabbed me and pummeled my back and whacked me on the head, forgetting that I had just been beaned and CAT-scanned.

I'd never seen Oh so happy. He threw his arms around me and hugged me as tight as he could. I hung on too, as tight as I could, because, frankly, I was getting a little dizzy from being hit on top of the head.

It was a pretty emotional scene. Some of our coaches were

even crying, including Doi of all people.

We won the game, 8–3. I was on the postgame TV "hero interview." The press was all over me in the clubhouse and hundreds of fans were lined up outside the park, waiting to shake my hand. I thought maybe I *had* died and gone to heaven.

The next day my picture filled the front pages of the sports dailies. One paper called me "The Phoenix." Another described me as the "Black Cannon." One columnist flatly termed me the best *gaijin* ever to play for the Giants. The *Nikkan Sports*, which did a three-page spread on our game, quoted a doctor as saying that he'd never ever seen anything like me in his twenty-four years of treating sports athletes. I wondered if Nakasone read the *Nikkan Sports*.

Ah! What a fabulous moment. How I loved it! I loved seeing the reaction of my teammates. Giant fans, were euphoric. We were two-and-a-half games up on the Carp. We had three games left to their eight and the standings looked as follows:

Giants	127	73-47-7	.608	—
Carp	122	66-45-11	.595	2.5

And still we managed to lose the pennant.

We won two of our final three games. Then, in one of those oddball finishes that only the Japanese leagues are capable of, we waited for the Carp to finish their schedule. They won seven of their last eight. Their retiring star Koji Yamamoto wielded a hot bat down the stretch. And they—not the Giants—took the flag.

I watched that last Carp contest on TV, on October 13, stupefied. The Carp defeated the Swallows at Jingu, and as they hugged each other for joy, the final standings flashed across the screen.

広島	Hiroshima	73-46-11	.613
巨人	Yomiuri	75-48-7	.610

The team that won the most games finished second.

The Carp had out-tied us for the title.

My final stats were .363, 37 homers, 93 RBIs, and 14 league-leading game-winning hits. It was the best season I had ever had anywhere, including little league. But it wasn't good enough to match Bass, who won his second straight triple crown, with .389—a new Japan record—47 home runs, and 109 RBIs. Bass should have gotten the MVP, hands down. But instead they gave it to the Carp pitcher Manabu Kitabeppu instead, who was 18–4 with an ERA of 2.43.

Still, it had been quite a year for me. I had gone from Public Enemy No. 1 in the spring to being a hero in the fall. What a transformation! During the last few weeks of the season, I couldn't even walk down the street without people stopping me and wanting to shake my hand.

I think that if you had asked my teammates then and they had answered honestly, they would have said that they really liked me, which was not always the case in Japan when a *gaijin* was involved. I think I had gained their full respect. And that of the fans and the press too—if only temporarily.

Of course, I had to get hit in the head and spend a night in the hospital for this to come about. But, at least, it had happened.

My three-year contract had expired, and it was time for the Giants to put up or shut up. It was also time for me to put up or shut up. I'd announced my retirement from Japanese ball two years in a row, and I didn't want to extend my streak to three.

But I wasn't stupid either, you know. After the year I'd had, my value to the team had doubled. Maybe tripled. There were reports in the papers that Cincinnati was ready to offer me half a million dollars to play for them. But as much as I'd have liked to play for Pete Rose, half a million was chicken feed compared to what I figured the Giants would pay me if they were to reward me properly for my contributions. My idea of a proper reward was at least a million dollars a year. More, maybe. Would you believe a million and a half?

I went into the Giants' front office in the Yomiuri Shimbun

building in downtown Tokyo to open preliminary negotiations. The real bargaining would come later when my lawyer back in Miami got involved. But I thought I ought to tell them what kind of figures were dancing around in my head.

Now the Giants may have been the biggest thing in Japanese baseball, but the front office was nothing like you might expect. Certainly not like the plush accommodations the Expos had. It was just a huge, dreary, depressing room on the ninth floor of a twelve-story building, with desks jammed together, no partitions or separate offices, and full of nondescript salarymen and uniformed young women whose main function seemed to be to serve tea. All Japanese offices were like that. It helped foster that feeling of togetherness the Japanese liked so much and at the same time allowed management to keep a close watch over the employees.

I ran into Oh, coming out of a conference room, looking dapper in a blue serge suit. He was in fine spirits. It had just been announced he would be returning as manager, despite losing the pennant. After all, his team had led the league in wins. I told him how glad I was, that without him in charge I really wouldn't want to return to play for the Giants.

He said, "Thank you," in English, and smiled at me in a strange way. I think deep down he suspected that for a million and a half dollars a year, I'd play for anyone.

Perhaps he'd be right, but then again, perhaps I wouldn't like it as much.

I shook his hand, then headed for the general manager's office.

1987

CRACK

THREE million dollars. Three MILLION dollars. Three million DOLLARS. *San byaku man doru.* No matter how I said it, it sounded great. That was how much the Giants had agreed to pay me for the next two years, plus housing, plus travel, plus bonuses, plus et cetera, et cetera, and et cetera. They even allowed me to stay home until March first. I didn't have to go to camp with the others. Now *that's* what I called compensation.

But being in Miami was no vacation. I spent most of my time trying to get my stepbrother Wendell out of jail. He had been arrested in the summer of 1986 for dealing crack. His best friend tried to escape and was shot and killed by the cops—a scene my brother had the unpleasant experience of witnessing firsthand, close up.

It happened at a crack house in Miami where people came to buy drugs. Wendell had been sleeping in one of the rooms when the police burst in. His friend tried to run out the back door, and the cops blew his fucking head off. My brother saw that. The next thing he knew, the police had him down on the floor with a gun to his head. One move and you're dead, that sort of thing.

Wendell was not the criminal type. I think that more than anything the problem was a deprived childhood. We had an aunt who was on crack, but it was his growing up without a father that screwed him up more, in my opinion. I know how Wendell felt because my father was hardly ever around, except on the edges. And not enough to matter to Wendell.

My mother was constantly on Wendell's back—she'd bust his chops every day, even more than she'd do mine. I became the only person Wendell could turn to.

Sports was my salvation, but Wendell wasn't so lucky. He was never able to put it together. He started using crack around the time I came to Japan. He wasn't happy doing what he was doing—construction work here and there. He didn't like the fact that the white man was always the boss. As a result, he didn't stay in any one job very long.

His social life was a mess, too. He wanted to be in with the in-crowd and have what all the other young kids had—what all the young white kids had, that is. But he never had any money. He wanted nice clothes and a car, but he couldn't afford them. He got more and more frustrated, and things sort of snowballed. He would go out, get a job, and go to the credit union for a loan to make a down payment on an expensive new car. Then, before you knew it, he would lose it to the repo man. He wasn't using his head.

My mother was constantly nagging him about the way he acted. She would call me in Japan and tell me what my brother was doing and order me to talk to him. Then I'd call him and he'd bitch that she wouldn't leave him alone.

I got him a job doing delivery work for a big liquor company. It was a good job, but it was then that he started doing coke. He wasn't making enough money to pay for his habit, so he started stealing—first from my mother—and before you knew it, he was robbing stores.

After the crack raid, he was put in a lineup where people from a 7-Eleven store that he had robbed spotted him. The cops said they were going to put his ass away forever. They stuck him in the Dade Country jail, where he was packed in in a little cell with five other people. He would get out of his cell once a day and call me collect.

I'd be in Tokyo getting ready to go to Korakuen and there would be this call from the Dade County Correctional Facility. If Shoriki and Mutai, the honorary chairman of the simon-pure Yomiuri Giants, only knew that their center fielder was trying to get his criminal brother out of the jailhouse...

When the season ended, I went to see my brother back in Miami. I'd sit there and talk to him through a plastic window, almost not believing it was happening. It was like a scene from "Miami Vice." Except that this wasn't television.

I hired a good lawyer and spent weeks trying to get my brother out. It cost me $30,000 in all, including bail. Then there were the rehab payments. Rehab is where my brother had to go for therapy.

My brother could have gotten five-to-ten years for drug possession on top of armed robbery. But the judge decided to give him a break because I was there to stand up for him and look after him. Half of the court cases in Miami were drug-related, and when a guy came up for sentencing, there was usually nobody in the courtroom with him. Most of them were teenagers with no parents. Nobody gave a flat fuck.

My brother was lucky. He could have stayed in prison. He could have wound up dead in there. Instead he went free. Except that wasn't quite the end of the story.

Two years after he was released, he was arrested again for armed robbery, and twelve months after that he was sitting in solitary confinement in the state penitentiary, doing sixty days in the hole for fighting. With time off for good behavior, he'd be out by in 1991.

PARANOIA

On Opening Day, our opponents were the Chunichi Dragons, who had been making news with their new manager and their new cleanup hitter. The new manager was a former Dragons' pitching star named Sennichi Hoshino, a cocky little ass who talked and acted like Billy Martin and had made "fighting baseball" his motto for the year.

The new cleanup hitter was Hiromitsu Ochiai, the 32-year-old third baseman who'd just won two straight triple crowns in the Pacific League. In 1986, he hit .360, with 50 homers and 116 RBIs, and the season before that, .367, with 52 home runs and 146 RBIs. Even so—and where else could this happen?—he'd been traded by the Lotte Orions in the off-season. A new manager had decided he didn't like Ochiai's independent ways and his unwillingness to practice hard.

The press was trying to a create rivalry between Ochiai and Bass, making Ochiai out to be the Great Japanese Hope. I didn't want to feel left out, and I thought the least I could do was to introduce myself to Ochiai when I had the chance.

The chance came in the first inning. With two out, I hit a drive into right center to knock in a run. I rounded second, chugging for third, but the throw beat me. I was two-thirds of the way down the line as the ball came in to Ochiai, who was standing there waiting for me. No way I was going to be safe, so I stopped dead in my tracks and signaled for time.

Ochiai didn't know what to think. When he came to tag me out, I threw my arms around him, giving him a big bear hug. He didn't like that at all. He scowled and pushed me away. But our fans got a kick out of it. I trotted off the field to a big round of applause.

The real stars of Japanese baseball, however, were not Ochiai or Bass or Koji Yamamoto with his 536 home runs or Sachio Kinugasa with his 2,000-game playing streak. The real stars were the Giants' players. Just this opening series made that clear all over again—SRO crowds at Korakuen for all three games, which were also among the top ten most watched TV programs for the week.

When I say Giants' players, of course, I mean the Japanese Giants' players: Hara, Nakahata, Egawa, Shinozuka, and so on. We're talking racial purity here. The list did not include me. I was liked, I was famous, but even after the year I had just had, my face was noticeably missing from the "Gallery of Stars," a big permanent display of photos of big-name Giants that had been installed outside Korakuen stadium.

Then too, there was the fact that Yoshimura, a young outfielder who had done very well in his first full year with the Giants, now had three commercials on prime-time TV; whereas I, Warren Cromartie, the messiah if you recall, had exactly none. I didn't even have any bat or glove endorsements. And I suspected that's the way the Giants preferred it.

That old paranoia again....

If I had been Japanese, if my name had been Kuroyama, or if my skin color were different, my picture would have been all over the place. I didn't like it. I felt left out and cheated. But what the hell. Yoshimura only made three hundred thousand dollars a year. I made three million dollars for two. THREE MILLION DOLLARS.

ROBOBALL

The beginning of May brought Golden Week—a string of national holidays—and baseball fever was running high. Spring had warmed the city, and at the Korakuen amusement park outside the stadium, people were lined up around the block for the parachute drop. Gondolas were winched up about 100 feet in the air behind our left-field wall and parachuted down. The riders would have a thirty-second glimpse of the game going on. Some die-hard fans who didn't have tickets would go up and down all day on that parachute ride, like crazed yo-yos.

But we were playing so badly, we really didn't deserve their attention. We weren't hitting. Our fielding stank. And our pitching was embarrassing.

We had a new ace—a pint-sized, 5'7", 160-pound, 19-year-old named Masumi Kuwata—who had a great split-fingered fastball which he called his *sundaboru*, his thunderball. He looked like a mini-Tom Seaver. But the rest of our staff was a joke.

Our *gaijin* hurler Sanchez was so fat, his gut got in the way of his follow through. Our young reliever Mizuno was in purgatory on the farm, having been caught with two girls in his hotel room, and our other reliever Katori was criminally overworked.

To add to our problems, Makihara was hurt, and Egawa

wasn't doing his job anymore. He'd pitch five or six innings, then he'd get in trouble.

Personally, I liked Egawa. He had a good sense of humor, for one thing. He liked to imitate the way I talked. He'd go around saying, "Say, man... Hey, baby," with a Japanese accent. It cracked me up. But he was getting fat and lazy.

Egawa said he had a sore arm. He'd been saying he had a sore arm for the past four years, but I didn't entirely believe him. There were times when he could have pitched; he just didn't want to. He didn't like to pitch in the rain; he didn't like to pitch in Osaka. It's true that his old speed was deserting him and that he had to rely on his curve all the time. But the facts were, he was tired and his heart wasn't in his game any more. At age 32, he was ready to hang it up.

Egawa was fed up with the Japanese style of play and the Giants' style of running your life. He once told me, "Cro, I hate baseball. I'm only playing to pay off the loan on my home." Now that his loan was almost paid off, he was ready to move on. He wasn't about to throw himself onto the pyre for the sake of the team. Instead, his plan was to play this last year then retire, become a TV commentator. So what did he fucking care whether we won or lost.

Egawa had always complained that he was underpaid. The other players did too. And with good reason. I didn't blame them for being resentful of my pay, as most of them were. If a Japanese had come over to the big leagues and made more money than me just because he was a foreigner, I'd be pissed too.

And what did they get even if they did make it into the Japan Series? The player's share in 1986 had been about $5,000, which was little more than taxi fare, basically, in expensive Japan. Ideally, you played not for the money but for the game, to win. But for $5,000, you were really straining your ideals.

I'd talked with those guys enough to know how they felt. They were tired of being used. They wanted to make the kind of money that *gaijin* were making. And they should have been making that kind of money. There was no doubt the owners could afford it. But they were too cheap. And of course, the players were too docile to do anything about it except grumble in private.

Money wasn't all the Giants' players complained about. They griped about all the restrictions, about how they never had any free time, and about how the coaches pushed them around. And the coaches did *literally* push them around. During one game, I saw Kunimatsu, our head coach, slap Junki Kono, a young infielder, in the face—twice—all because Junki was smoking a cigarette down in the runway behind the dugout.

Numerous times I saw scenes like that—coaches yelling and screaming, especially at the younger boys—shoving them around, treating them like shit. It burned me up. In the States, a coach who did that wouldn't last ten minutes. The players would kick the crap out of him. But although the Japanese guys bitched among themselves, again they just took it. Obedience to higher authority was drilled into them from an early age, at home and at school. That's why their union never did anything.

Nishimoto was the only one on the team who showed his temper. He'd slam his glove and kick the bench and speak his mind. That's because of the Korean blood in him, I was told; he didn't know any better. In March, he was fined two million yen for criticizing Minagawa, our pitching coach, and his days were numbered. By the end of the year, he'd be gone.

Not being allowed to think for themselves, most of those guys really didn't know how. Their lives were one constant pattern. You showed up. You got dressed. You did the same running, the same batting, and the same fielding as everyone else had always done.... It was all rote. Then you played the game. Even that was rote.

Our 8–2 loss to the Swallows during Golden Week was a good example. A young shortstop named Okazaki made one hell of a mental error. There was one out, a runner on second, and Okazaki caught a bullet at shortstop. All he had to do was run two steps and step on second to double up the guy trying to get back to the base. But instead, he flipped the ball to the second baseman, who wasn't there.

If he'd only thought for an instant, he would have known

immediately to step on the bag to get the double play. But he was so used to doing his pregame fielding drills—fielding the 100 ground balls the coaches hit to him every day, picking up each one and shoveling it to second—that it became automatic, mechanical. He played the infield like he was taking practice fungoes, because of that same routine, day in and day out.

And Oh was letting it happen.

In America, players learn by emulating their better peers. But that's not exactly true in Japan. Tim Ireland, an American who played for the Carp, did a lot of one-handed and backhanded tosses to the shortstop covering second, but you didn't see the Carp players try to follow him. They were too used to having the coaches tell them what to do. And the Japanese coaches' way of teaching was A,B,C orthodoxy, right down the line.

I would look at young players fielding ground balls to their right side, for example. They were crossing their bodies with an open-handed glove and winding up out of position to make the throw. That was because some coach, once upon a time, had determined that the "proper way" to field all ground balls was with an open glove in front of the body, that a player had to get in front of the ball. But for fielding a ball that, say, is coming down the third base line, the most effective way is backhand.

Hara always had trouble on balls coming down the third base line because he had systematically been taught to get in front of the ball. As a result, he would sometimes be off balance when he caught the ball and wind up in an awkward position or he'd bobble the ball and find himself unable to make a good throw.

Sometimes by reacting naturally—by relying on reflex rather than form—you can extend your range much farther and play with more precision and quickness. If you stay crouched down and glide over to backhand the ball, you can take it out of your glove quicker, and throw with the full power of your body. The person who fields the ball the orthodox way has to stand up before he can make the proper throw. It's unnatural and uneconomical.

The Japanese players were not allowed to work on these

techniques because the coaches always said, "Do things the traditional way." The Japanese were good at fundamentals, but, as Reggie Smith liked to say, in terms of managing and coaching techniques, the game in Japan was no different from little league to the pros.

THE DEVILS

All anyone talked about in May was Bob Horner, the ex–Atlanta Brave who'd just signed a one-year contract with the Yakult Swallows for two million dollars. He'd hit .273 with 27 home runs in 1986 for the Braves, but he couldn't get the free agent deal he wanted, so he opted for Japan.

His photo was everywhere. He even knocked the Giants off the front pages of the sports dailies for a while. The Swallows turned on the lights at Jingu stadium one off-night for three hours, at a cost of $30,000, just so Big Bob could take night-time batting practice.

Horner started playing in the first week of May. He hit six home runs in four games. Then the pitchers stopped throwing him strikes and the umpires started to squeeze him just like they did to all the new *gaijin* in town. It was a way of showing him his place, so to speak.

In early June, we played the Horner-ized Swallows at Jingu in front of 52,000 people eager to see what a big-time major league star looked like in the flesh. Horner hit a home run, his eighth, which made them delirious, and so did I, which didn't seem to have quite the same effect. Horner also struck out three times. The umpires rang his ass up. One ball was a foot outside. Strike. Another hit the ground. Strike.

I talked to him the next day in pregame practice. Approximately 200 reporters and photographers surrounded us, cameras clicking, tape recorders thrust between us, recording every second of our historic meeting.

"I don't believe this shit," he said.

Flash! Pop! Whirr!

"Horns," I said, "You ain't seen nothing yet."

Flash! Whirr! Pop!

The reporters were buzzing among themselves, trying to

figure out just exactly what it was we were talking about. They would take their tapes back to the city desk where an English expert would decipher them.

"Bob, give me a shout if your family needs help getting settled in."

Whirr! Pop! Buzz...

I think the mental strain was getting to Horner already. I was sure the writers and some of the fans wanted to see him fall on his face. Because whenever he struck out or hit into a double play, the credibility of the Japanese game, in their eyes, went up.

The next night Horner went 2-for-3, and I hit another homer, my ninth. I picked up the sports papers the following morning to see a page one story about the Great Battle for the Triple Crown. There was a picture of Ochiai facing pictures of Horner, Bass, and now me.

Under Horner was the caption, "Red Devil."

Under Bass were the words, "Blond Devil."

Under mine, "Black Devil."

Under Ochiai, "Ochiai."

SLUGGING IT OUT IN KUMAMOTO

I'd been hit by pitches in Japan more times than I can remember. That was an occupational hazard if you were a *gaijin*. The Japanese didn't do it much to each other, but they saw how we played. It was American pitchers who had introduced the high, hard, inside pitch to Japanese ball, and the Japanese turned it on us with a vengeance. The year before, I had led the league in "dead balls," as the Japanese said, with seven, and it was starting to wear on my nerves.

In Kumamoto, on June 12—a day that will live in infamy in Giants' history—a baby-faced pitcher for the Dragons named Miyashita drilled me in the back with a fastball. Something snapped inside me. A couple of screws came loose. I blew my cool in a major way.

I think what did it was the fact that Miyashita didn't tip his cap in apology, like a Japanese pitcher normally does when he hits a batter. Somehow it was this slight, this guy's bad manners, that really pissed me off.

I made a gesture as if to say how about tipping your cap. But Miyashita just stood there. I found out later that all Dragon pitchers had standing orders from their manager Hoshino not to do that sort of thing—no more apologies. For this was the new Dragon regime of "fighting baseball," and tipping your cap was supposed to be a sign of weakness. This might have explained the stupid look on Miyashita's face—half-smile, half-snarl. He was caught between two conflicting emotions—one, desire to placate me, the other, fear of what his manager might do to him if he did.

With the memory of last year's beaning still fresh in my mind, as well as the six brushback pitches I'd already received during that particular road trip, I decided enough was enough. No more Mr. Nice Guy. I dashed out to the mound and delivered a hard right cross to Miyashita's jaw. He just stood there and took it—like he was paralyzed.

Within nanoseconds, there was a mob of people around me, grabbing me. Suddenly I was down on the ground. I had a life-or-death headlock on somebody. It turned out to be Gary Rajisch, the Dragons' first baseman.

"Cro, Cro," he cried, "it's me. Stop it! Stop!"

I got up, my head spinning, dirt in my mouth, and somebody pulled me off to the side, pinning my arms behind my back. I didn't know who it was until I saw the video replay later. It was Kuwata. The little son of a bitch was even stronger than I thought.

Players from both teams were wrestling and shoving, yelling "*bakayaro,*" you bastard, at each other. Dragons' manager Hoshino was right in the middle, jumping around like a demented rooster, screaming something at me, his mouth flapping a mile a minute.

"Fuck you, Hoshino," I yelled.

Oh was trying to calm him down, but Hoshino grabbed Oh's shoulder and cocked his fist. Oh backed off. Punching people wasn't Oh's style, which was lucky for Hoshino. I found out later that it was the first time anyone had ever threatened Oh physically. But that was Hoshino for you. He was crazy. He'd already slugged a Carp infielder in Hiroshima, back in April.

Dozens of security guards finally made their way on to the field to break up the fight. I was thrown out of the game, naturally. But that wasn't the end of it. Not by a long shot.

In retrospect, I can say that almost everyone on the team supported me. On the team bus after the game, Oh came up and said, "*Naisu faito, Kuro.*" It was something that he couldn't say in public, because that would be condoning violence, and he was after all the manager of the Giants, who were always supposed to be gentlemen. That was why he never openly came to my defense in the days that followed. But he sure did in private. As did all my teammates—with the notable exception of Hara.

When I got back to the hotel that evening, there was a call for me from Tokyo. It was our new farm manager Sudo, a chunky, aggressive guy who liked to kick ass himself. He'd seen the game on TV and wanted to offer his congratulations.

"*Naisu faito,*" Sudo said, his gravelly voice coming over the fiber-optic cables.

Then his wife got on. "*Naisu faito, Kuro-san,*" she said, "*Gambatte ne.*" Hang in there.

Neither one spoke a lot of English but the message was loud and clear. I mean, it was hilarious, given the Giants' official position on ballpark violence. I went downstairs and told the guys about Sudo's call. They thought it was hilarious too.

Although fights did occur in Japanese baseball, they were much rarer and much less tolerated than they were in the U.S., even with the presence of Hoshino, because the society put such a premium on harmony. Moreover, an American player punching out a Japanese player was regarded as a much more serious offense than two Japanese going at each other. It reminded people of the Occupation.

The next morning the papers were all over me. I was page one news in every sports daily and I was definitely the villain. Miyashita had a badly swollen jaw that would keep him out for twelve days. He had not tried to defend himself. Therefore, it was all my fault. The fact that I had gotten hit first seemed to be irrelevant. And no one said anything about the influence of Hoshino and his "fighting baseball" slogans.

One editorial called me a "gangster"; another called me an "animal." Ochiai told a reporter that I had looked like a "crazed drug addict" as I rushed out to the mound to attack that "poor, defenseless young kid." He thought I should be banned from baseball in Japan for life. Osamu Higashio, a Seibu Lions' pitcher who held the all-time Japanese record for hit batsmen—and a man who had been slugged by American Dick Davis the previous year—was quoted as saying, "Why is it it's always the *gaijin* who are involved in something like this?"

Higashio had a point. The ratio of Japanese to Americans thrown out of games in Japan was about 3-to-1. But it was usually the Japanese manager who got the ax for manhandling an umpire. The players themselves were more subdued.

Everyone knew I was going to be penalized. Nobody was sure how, just yet, but the anger toward me was deep. When I got back to my Tokyo apartment at two in the afternoon, I had to push my way through a crowd of reporters outside the main entrance. They were grabbing my clothes and jamming pocket-sized tape recorders in my face.

"*Kommento? Kommento?*" they cried.

"*No kommento,*" I replied, and squeezed through the door into the lobby. I gave instructions to the doorman not to admit anyone I didn't know, under any circumstances. There might be a lynch mob from Nagoya on its way.

The *Hochi Shimbun,* the Yomiuri-owned sports daily—or house organ, if you will—was so concerned about the effect the incident would have on the Giants' sacred image that it printed an apology from me, which I hadn't made. The paper had me saying, "I was wrong in hitting him. And I'll never do anything like that again."

Hah! But I wasn't surprised. Iwamoto, a Giants' official, had given me the idea something like that might happen.

"I understand why you did it, Cro," he said, "but you are going to have to say you're sorry."

"Forget it, Iwamoto," I told him, "you can just forget it. That might be the Japanese way, but it's not my style. You do what you gotta do. But I'll never apologize because it's bullshit. Nobody apologized when I was lying in Keio Hospital undergoing a CAT scan, lying in a goddamn tunnel with rays going through my brain."

And so they had done it for me.

I stepped out of the elevator and into my apartment. I kissed my wife and my kids and my mother, who was visiting us. Perhaps Ma could help me ward off the lynch mob. Then I sat down to lunch—Kentucky Fried Chicken and potato salad from the mall across the way.

I decided I wasn't hungry. I got up and switched on CNN, which was airing the Bork hearings. I watched the man, not sure I wanted him for a judge either. Then I switched to one of the Japanese channels. There was Madonna, in Japan for a series of concerts, running around the Imperial moat. She was flanked by her bodyguards and followed by a convoy of Japanese press cars. One of the vehicles shot in front of her, then slowed, so the cameraman could zoom in. Madonna glared into the camera and gave the guy the finger. Then she yelled out in English, as clear as a bell:

"Fuck you, asshole."

My sentiments exactly.

The phone rang. It was Hirano, the interpreter, with the news of my penalty. The Giants had decided on a five-day suspension and a fine of ¥300,000, but the commissioner's office had extended the suspension to seven days. I wouldn't even be allowed to practice with the team. Hirano said I had gotten off lucky. The penalty could have been much stiffer, but the power of the Giants had saved me.

Well, I thought, when was the last time I'd had a mid-year vacation? I immediately called Trader Vic's in the New Otani Hotel and made arrangements to take my wife and mother to dinner. Maybe I'd even take them to Kyoto, the ancient capital of Japan, which I'd yet to tour in my three-and-a-half years in Japan. I'd been too busy playing—and practicing—baseball. Just think how the front office would like that. My teammates with their noses to the grindstone, while I inspected the temples of old Japan. Wouldn't the Japanese press have a field day with that.

In the end, I decided against Kyoto. Instead, I worked out alone at Korakuen everyday. I got up in the morning, went to the park, then at the end of the day, came home to my family like any other working stiff. I put my lunchpail on the kitchen table, pecked my wife on the cheek, and took a beer out of the fridge. Then I settled down to watch the ballgame on the tube. A black Archie Bunker in Japan.

With me gone, Hara started to hit with authority. His average soared to .363, with 13 homers and 29 RBIs, and the Giants went on a winning streak. They were in a dogfight with the Carp and the Dragons for first place. Shinozuka and Nakahata were one and two in the league in batting average. Kuwata racked up his eighth win. I was still leading the league in RBIs, but shit, I had to admit the Giants looked like world-beaters without me. I wondered if maybe I should stay out of the lineup more often. I wondered if maybe Oh wondered the same thing.

I began to feel a little antsy about sitting on the sidelines.

While I was sitting home in front of the TV, one of Japanese baseball's greatest record-breaking feats took place. On June 13, Carp third baseman Sachio Kinugasa played in his 2,131st consecutive game, surpassing Lou Gehrig's mark. It took him seventeen years of 130-game seasons. It took Gehrig fifteen years of 154-game seasons. What impressed me was that Kinugasa accomplished his feat while having to go through Japanese-style pregame practices every day. It was as if he had played 4,000 games in a row.

Kinugasa was half-black, half-Japanese—a war baby whose father had been in the U.S. military. I heard he suffered a lot of abuse as a child because of it. In this country, if you're not pure-blooded Japanese, you're a notch under everyone else. It's all or nothing. Ask Oh. Ask me.

Still, it was ironic—with all this business of Japanese racial purity, how many of the great record holders in Japan had alien blood in their veins. Oh, with his 868 home runs and one-season record of 55 home runs—half-Chinese; Masaichi Kaneda, with 400 wins—Korean; Isao Harimoto, the only person in Japanese baseball with 3,000 hits—Korean; Bass, who'd broken Harimoto's single-season batting average mark of .383 the previous year—white. I wondered what the thought of this did to the Japanese psyche.

MADONNA & ME

I served my sentence and, as the fates would have it, the Giants were scheduled to play the Chunichi Dragons, in Nagoya, on my first day back in action. I was not comforted by reports that the Dragons' front office had been besieged with angry phone calls, threatening me with all sorts of reprisals if I dared to appear in the Chunichi park. Nor was I encouraged by the statement of a Dragons' executive that his organization could not guarantee my safety.

The train carrying our team—and me—pulled into Nagoya station to be greeted by a battalion of railway security guards and about 500 photographers and reporters—all of whom accompanied me to the hotel and waited outside as I changed into my uniform. On the bus to the stadium, I began to feel a little nervous. A couple of my teammates tried to reassure me.

"No worry, Cro. You wear batting helmet."

"No punching today, Cro. You *daijobu*. OK?"

Somehow I didn't feel very *daijobu*.

Outside the park, more photographers—and angry Dragons' fans—waited for me.

"*Kuromatei—Baka! Baka!*" yelled one old woman, "*Yankee go homu!*"

It was the first time I had ever been called a Yankee. She kept yelling at me in a high-pitched wail:

"*Kurezi! Kurezi! Kurezi! Kurezi! Baka da! Baka! Baka! Baka!*"

On the field, there was another mob of media people waiting. They kept yelling at me, cameras clicking away—click! pop! whirr! Where did these photographers all come from? Was there a factory somewhere in Japan that produced them too?

It felt like World War III was about to break out. There were 340 guards in the park, a reporter told me, double the usual number. Every fan in the place had been checked for concealed weapons. "Is it safe?" I wondered. I thought of Laurence Olivier in *Marathon Man*.

Was it safe?

Nagoya Stadium was one of those tiny old structures with a

grassless infield and concrete stands so close to the playing field you could hear the fans spit. It seated 35,000, and the place was packed to the gills. The mood was very nasty. Fans were hanging over the railings, yelling insults at me. One group held up a huge banner that said MOTHER-FUCKING KURO in big black letters.

Oh turned to me and cracked, "You famous now. You number one star. Like Madonna." But Oh was nervous. So was the rest of the team. And with good reason. Dragons' fans had a history of hurling beer bottles, batteries, rocks, and other garbage onto the field to express their discontent.

Across the way, Hoshino was standing in the Dragons' dugout, arms folded, trying hard to look tough. He reminded me of a bulldog—a rabid bulldog. Miyashita was nowhere to be seen.

When I took my warmups, every camera in the stadium zoomed in. The fans were yelling at me as loud as they could, trying to get a reaction. In my first at bat, they went totally nuts. I could hear them screaming, "*AHO!*" Asshole! and other sweet Japanese obsenities.

On defense, it was just as bad. One guy in the right center field bleachers kept screaming at the top of his lungs, "*KURO-MATEI, NEE-GAH. SONNABEECHI. NEE-GAH!*" Some fans had climbed up onto the big screen out in right field and were yelling at me. I stood in center field, chewing bubble gum. I turned and smiled at them. I even blew a few bubbles their way. I don't know if I was being clever or just plain stupid.

In the middle of the game, Miyashita warmed up in the bullpen, just a few yards from where I was standing. But he didn't come into the game. I think Hoshino had just ordered that for dramatic effect.

I came to bat in the ninth inning, with the fans still screaming at me. We were losing 1–0, with a runner on second base with two outs. I would have given anything to hit a home run right then. It would have brought the place down.

But I popped out and that was that. Suddenly the game was over, and the foremost thought in all our minds was getting the hell out of the park as fast as possible. We grabbed our gear and raced through the tunnel to the bus. Nobody gave a damn about losing the game. They all just wanted to get out—especially me.

We were on the bus and on our way back to the hotel within seven minutes of the final out, which I'm sure was an all-time record. Oh imposed a midnight lights-out curfew. No one was allowed to leave the hotel.

The next day, I shared a two-page spread in one sports daily with Madonna. On one side was huge photo of her, taken with a zoom lens, standing on the balcony of her hotel in Tokyo. One breast was hanging out of her dress. On the opposite page was an equally large photo of me leaving the park. I wasn't sure what the connection was.

The lunacy continued. It rained in the morning, and I spent the entire day in the hotel with my teammates hiding out. At 3:30, when we boarded the bus to go to the park, a number of Dragons' supporters had gathered outside, including a young, very mean-looking character who came to the bus door and yelled:

"*Kuromatei—Konoyaro dete koi!!*" Cromartie, you bastard, come out.

I declined the invitation.

I stepped up to bat in the first inning, with a man on, to face a right-hander named Suzuki. The crowd was yelling crazily, just like the night before. In the background behind right field was one of the most beautiful sunsets I'd ever seen.

The sky was an orange pink, one of those terrific twilight skies you get in Japan after a rain and the wind sweeps the clouds away. A strong breeze was still blowing in off Ise Bay, and the air smelled clean and sweet.

I stepped back to suck some into my lungs and to admire the view. Was I nuts? Stopping a game to admire a sunset? It was breathtaking—a sight to move a man's heart. But the 35,000 people in the stands were not in the least bit interested. They were watching me instead, screaming insults, hoping Suzuki would brain me with a fast ball.

Aaahhh, baseball. What a great game it was. I stepped back into the box, and when the pitch came, a low slider, I slugged it, as hard as I could. The ball rose high and deep toward right field. I stood there and watched it soar through the sky, drop

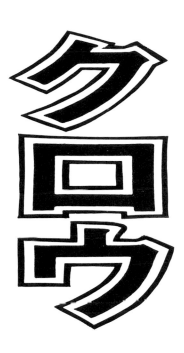

As the Cro flies.
(Nikkan Sports)

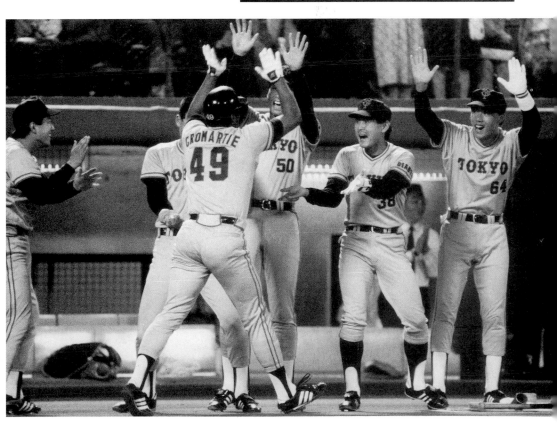

Japanese high-fives after winning *hitto*. *(Sankei Shimbun)*

The Pied Piper of Tamagawa. *(Nikkan Sports)*

Gattsu pozu, my trademark. *(Sankei Shimbun)*

Having the time of my life in pregame practice. That's Gully on the left. That's a no-smoking sign in the back. *(Sports Nippon)*

Afraid to touch home plate. I'd just hit my first sayonara home run, and my teammates are ready to pummel me senseless. *(Kyodo News Service)*

My first baseball kiss.
(Kyodo News Service)

Slaying the Chunichi Dragon *(Tokyo Sports)*, *right above*, and Kuwata, our mini-Tom Seaver, holding me from further combat *(Sankei Shimbun)*, *far right below*. Under police protection before our next game in Nagoya *(Tokyo Sports)*, *near right below*, at which I was greeted by a salute from hostile Dragons' fans *(Tokyo Sports)*, *above*. *Right*, usually there is mud on my face—this time it's my bubble gum. *(Sankei Shimbum)*

Carole and Marjorie, the Cromartie cheering section. *(Nikkan Sports)*

The kids Cromartie—Candice, Chris, and Cody—in Hiroo pool.

Me and Hara, the Giants' glamour boy. *(Nikkan Sports)*

The celebration. That's Nakahata, our captain on the left; Fujita, our manager, on the right. *(Nikkan Sports)*

Victory night in Tokyo. *(Nikkan Sports)*

Me, peaceful. *(Osamu Nagahama)*

down, and then disappear into the middle of the stands—right into the heart of all those people who'd been calling for my blood.

I shot my arm into the air in my triumphant *gattsu pozu*, my guts pose, and headed toward first. As I rounded the bases, I noticed how quiet the stadium had suddenly become. I could only hear one or two cries of "*bakayaro*" trailing off.

That put an end to it somehow. We won that night and when we left Nagoya, we were in first place. All in all, it wasn't such a bad weekend. But I still wonder: if my timing had been better and I'd slugged that home run the night before, what the fireworks would have been like!

THE RAINS OF TOYAMA

The rainy season was really doing its thing. From the third week of June on, we had a solid month of rain and drizzle. It just kept on coming. It was hot, muggy, wet, and awful. There was mold everywhere, bugs crawling out of the woodwork. Your skin would get all itchy and clammy.

The only place it didn't rain was Hokkaido, the northernmost island of Japan, where there is no rainy season—which was why we played an annual series there in July.

Hokkaido is everything the rest of Japan isn't—big, wide, open outdoors, rolling green hills, lots of farmland, and very few people, which is why nobody in Japan wants to live there. It's not crowded enough. Sapporo, the capital, is the only major city in Japan that resembles an American city. An engineer from the American midwest helped design it, and its streets are laid out in an even crosshatched grid. There are none of the twisting roads and narrow alleys that characterize Tokyo and Osaka.

We split two games with the Carp there, Kuwata throwing a 4–0 shutout to give us our win. Then we went home to sweep two from the Swallows. In one of the contests, Egawa left in the sixth inning, with a 14–1 lead, complaining of a blister on his finger. Everyone was suspicious as hell.

We got rained out in Hiroshima and Yokohama and then traveled to Toyama, a country town north of Tokyo, two-and-a-half hours away by train. It was pissing rain there too. We got off the train and onto a bus and rode for about another hour to reach our hotel. It was three in the afternoon. The game was cancelled, but we still had to practice. We were given about fifteen minutes to down a lunch of noodles, change into our uniforms, and file onto another bus for a half-hour ride to a high school field, where we would have our workout. It was still pouring like it would never stop.

The field was muddy and sloppy. Every time we hit, the ball would come down and make a huge splash. The coaches would pick it up, dry it off with towels, and throw it back to the batting practice pitcher. We kept this up for the next hour or so, getting soaking wet in the process.

But make no mistake, everybody was happy because we got to practice, and in Japan that's like getting your fix. It's a means of emotional fulfillment. They thought practice was the same thing as effort, and effort was the most important thing. I agreed with that last part, but to me, practice and effort aren't the same thing at all. That was the problem. Especially in Japanese baseball.

Our captain Nakahata, who was becoming a good friend, was in his element. He was out there running around. The press corps was snapping his picture, and he was loving every minute of it.

There we were, in the middle of nowhere, in the rain and mud, guys slipping all over the place. There was a dirt bank that was supposed to be the outfield fence. You'd see a guy leaping across it while looking up in the air and trying to catch the ball. He'd fall on his ass and slide about twenty feet in the process. Everybody would cheer his fighting spirit.

I stood back and took the whole scene in and started laughing. I couldn't help it. It was hilarious when you stopped to think about it. Marcano, standing next to me, started laughing too. Oh turned and looked at us.

"It's all right, Oh-san," I said. "This is quite an experience. When I retire, I can look back at all of this and write a book."

"You write book, Cro-san?" said Oh.

"That's right," I said. "This is chapter 74 right here."

Sometimes I think I wouldn't trade my time in Japan for

anything. So many unbelievable things went on. I could tell stories like this for the rest of my life.

After practice we went back to our hotel, which was yet another experience. A real country ass place. My room had a prefabricated bath and toilet so small that I had to duck my head to get into the bathroom and step on the toilet seat to get into the shower. If I stepped out of the shower with the toilet lid up, I risked putting my foot into the toilet bowl. That is no exaggeration. It was so small I had to stand on the toilet seat to open the door. It opened inward, and there wasn't any other way to do it.

The room itself was only about six feet wide. I could have put the entire hotel room into my bathroom back home in Miami. The TV was two feet away from the bed. I'd lie there with my feet sticking off the end and think, if I told the people back home about this room, they'd never believe me. You had to be there and see it with your own eyes.

We played a game in Gumma the next day, three hours away by bus, where it wasn't raining and and where I met my first umpire who seemed to be drunk. He called me out on a play at first base, in which I was clearly safe. I lost my temper and went face to face with the umpire, and I smelled alcohol on his breath. It was 90 degrees out there, and I bet he'd had a couple of cold ones before the game. Or three or four. Or something.

His eyes were only half open, he was so out of it. I pointed to his eyes. The announcers and the reporters thought I was saying he was blind. But I was saying something else.

Oh came out to argue, but only halfheartedly. Then he gave up and went back. We were ahead, 6–0; we were in first place by four games. What the hell did he care. Besides, it was too hot to argue.

THE GREAT SANCHEZ

Sanchez, Sanchez, Sanchez. What could one say but...Sanchez.

Sanchez had not been pitching very much that year, and on those rare occasions when he did, he did not do very well. His sore arm and his considerable belly had combined to limit his effectiveness. After he blew a big lead in Sapporo, Oh and the pitching coaches completely lost confidence in him. Instead Oh was using Katori, who had been magnificent. By mid-year, Katori was the ace of the bullpen and Sanchez was out of the picture. Sanchez didn't like this turn of affairs and decided to retaliate. In the process, he made an enormous ass out of himself.

Sanchez was a noisy person in the first place. He was loud on the bench. He was loud in the locker room. He was always shouting about something—delivering some insult in Spanish. He'd yell things like *"nohodé"* which means "don't fuck around," or *"nohoro"* which means "goddamn," or *"nohata"* which means *"bakayaro."* That's all he'd say. That was the extent of his vocabulary. After a while, even the Japanese players started saying those words—to the umpires usually—because that's what Sanchez was always yelling. After two years with Sanchez, they had learned how to swear in fluent Spanish.

By mid-season, his status on the team reduced to second-line reliever, he was getting worse. One day on the bullet train, he was growling about the way the Giants were treating him. Somebody asked him to be quiet and that pissed him off even more, so he got up and started waving his hands and yelling. Now, the bullet train, especially the first-class "green car" section, is a pretty formal place. A lot of wealthy businessmen use it and the Giants are supposed to conduct themselves with a certain decorum. But there was Sanchez standing up, his hair sticking up in all directions, and yelling in Spanish, behaving as if he were still back in school.

A few days later at Haneda Airport, while the Giants were waiting to board a flight, Sanchez criticized our pitching coach Minagawa in front of a group of reporters. Minagawa had been trying to get Sanchez to change his form, to pitch with a quick motion to keep runners on base and prevent them from stealing. Sanchez began complaining wildly about that. He was a fastball pitcher, he told the assembled press standing in the departure lounge. He had never thrown with a quick motion, and he wasn't going to start now.

Sanchez said he thought Minagawa was an idiot for making that suggestion. Minagawa had been a submarine-style pitcher and Sanchez threw overhand, so Minagawa had no business telling him how to pitch.

Sanchez tried to convey this to the sportswriters in English, which he barely knew. Gesturing, he pointed to Minagawa standing at a coffee counter nearby, then he pointed to his head and made a circular motion with his finger as if to say that Minagawa was crazy.

"Minagawa—stupid!" Sanchez spoke.

Now Minagawa was not all that well liked on the team. For one thing, the pitchers didn't think he was very good; for another, he was a front-runner. When Kuwata started winning, Minagawa was all over him, trying to be associated with his success. He made sure he was seen with Kuwata in pregame practice on a day Kuwata was scheduled to start, making like he was giving him advice. After, if Kuwata pitched well, he was there trying to share in the credit too.

Be that as it may, in Japan you were supposed to show the coaches the highest respect in public, regardless of your private feelings, and Sanchez was definitely not doing that. Marcano was trying to get him to shut up, but Sanchez kept babbling on. He just wouldn't quit.

Luis didn't have a lot of brains. He stood there, waving his arms. He was about 6'3" anyway, and he towered above almost everybody in the airport, so before you knew it, there was a big crowd around him with all the reporters taking notes furiously. Naturally the story was plastered in all over the sports dailies the next day. The big headlines read: "SANCHAY INSULTS MINAGAWA!!"

I was standing there with Yamakura, watching all this.

"Cro-san, Sanchay, no smart," said Yamakura, shaking his head sourly.

"You got that shit right, I replied.

Then there was the day Sanchez was doing his practice tosses with Minagawa standing in the batter's box as a batter's model, to put the strike zone in a game perspective, and I swear to god, Sanchez brushed him back. He threw a high inside fastball and almost knocked Minagawa on his ass.

Minagawa tried to ignore the beanball attempt and after Sanchez had thrown about forty pitches, he went out to the mound to give Sanchez some instructions on form. Sanchez stood there and made unpleasant faces, grimacing, rolling his eyes, making sure that everyone knew what he thought of Minagawa's efforts to coach him.

It was very hard for Bobby Marcano, as Sanchez's interpreter, too. Everybody liked Bobby M. He was well known in Japan and he had made a good name for himself. But poor Marcano was totally worn out, mentally and physically, trying to deal with Sanchez. Luis was not only making Bobby look bad, he was making me look bad too, because we were all *gaijin* and the Japanese tended to lump us together.

The Giants eventually fined Sanchez for insubordination: ¥300,000. The amount caused more than a little grumbling among the players because Nishimoto had earlier been fined ¥2,000,000 for essentially saying the same thing—that Minagawa was incompetent. It gave the impression that a *gaijin*'s misconduct was more acceptable than a part Korean's. Let's say 6.6 times more acceptable.

At the all-star break in late July, we held a four-game lead over the Carp and a six-and-a-half-game lead over the Dragons. Despite my stats of .285, 15 homers, and 54 RBIs, I was one of three Giants' starters who failed to be voted to the all-star lineup by the fans. Perhaps my slugging incident in Kumamoto affected my popularity.

The biggest vote getter was Kuwata, who was 12–1 with an ERA of 1.95 and throwing the ball at 93 miles per hour.

The more I saw of Kuwata, the more he reminded me of Tom Seaver. He had the same kind of body—heavy legs, the same kind of push off the mound, and the same kind of mental outlook. He was very quiet, but he had enough poise and confidence to shake off Yamakura's signs. It took a lot of fortitude to do that. He had a great fastball, slider, and change-up to go with his *sundaboru*, and was already one hell of a pitcher.

As a matter of fact, some of the guys were starting to get a little annoyed because Kuwata was doing so well. Little jealousies were surfacing. Nishimoto had about four wins and spent most of his time in the bullpen, while Kuwata got to start every four to five days, consistently. It was a fact that Nishimoto clearly resented. He mumbled to me one day,

"Next year, Kuwata's arm is going to fall off."

So the guys could be just as petty as players back in the States. When Hara was slumping, you'd hear some of them saying that Hara's heart wasn't in it anymore. Their jealousy over all the attention Hara got would show itself.

Horner, hitting about .320 with 16 homers, was also chosen for the all-star games. But he opted not to play. He'd strained his back swinging at a pitch and would be out of the lineup for several weeks.

A reporter mentioned to me that he had never, ever heard of a player hurting himself in that way.

Neither had I, I replied.

And I hadn't.

How could you possibly strain your bat swinging at a pitch—unless you were totally out of shape.

The press began to badmouth Horner, and questions were asked about his troubles in the States. He'd had a lot of injuries there too. He'd never played a full schedule. Now the Japanese were starting to write that their big import was out of condition. Stories circulated that he drank too much.

A few days later Horner appeared in a TV commercial for Suntory Beer, for which he received a reported $300,000. Thousands of lifesize Horner cutouts were erected in front of liquor shops all over the country. It was ironic when you stopped to think about it.

OH'S WAY

The rains stopped after the all-star break, to be replaced by the suffocating heat of the Japanese summer. Suddenly, everything started to fall apart. We lost two out of three to the Tigers and two out of two to the Dragons, getting no-hit the last game. The perpetrator of that foul deed was an 18-year-old rookie named Kondo, fresh from the farm. It was his first start ever in the Japanese pro league. And it was just his night, you know. The kid had a good fastball and a great curve. Also, nobody knew him. The game was under the lights, and therefore it was harder to see. The wind was blowing in. His mom was there in the stadium, and his girlfriend was probably watching on TV. He had everything going for him, including the fact that we stunk. We made him look like Warren Spahn.

Did Hoshino love it. He hadn't forgotten our brawl. He was standing over there, laughing his ass off, grinning like a madman. Still, you had to give him credit. It took a lot of guts to start an untried teenager in a tight pennant race. It was also a stroke of genius. Oh didn't think the Dragons had a left-hander to start. So he loaded the lineup with left-handed hitters—six of them—anticipating a right-handed pitcher. Talk about being caught with your pants down. Our lead dropped to two games over the Carp and two-and-a-half over the upstart Dragons.

We came back to Tokyo from Nagoya on a Monday, August 10, after seven days on the road without a rest. Yet we were herded right off the bullet train, onto a bus, and ninety minutes later we were at Tamagawa for a special three-hour workout. The temperature was about 95 degrees.

What we needed, again, was rest, not practice. We hadn't had a day off in three weeks. The guys were dead tired. But Oh and the coaches and the front office execs were all so humiliated by the no-hitter and our diminishing lead that they were desperate.

So we were all out there, running sprints, whooping and hollering, attempting to show the media, which were there as usual in great force, how determined we were. Nakahata was working harder than anyone, looking as though he was actually enjoying himself.

I may have been the only Giant who had gotten any sleep the night before. The others, I imagined, had all lain awake, sweating bullets over the adverse turn of events. Oh, most of all. He probably wouldn't get any sleep the rest of the year.

I was allowed to leave early that day, and skip batting practice, which Hara did not fail to note.

"You don't hit," he said, approaching me on the field.

"You don't need to hit either," I told him.

He nodded, stared into the distance for a moment and sighed. "I know," he replied in halting English, "I want to do like you, but I can't. Maybe Oh-san get angry."

I wanted to say, "So what if Oh gets mad. Why don't you stand up and go your own way for a change." But I didn't because I knew it wouldn't do any good. I just gave Hara a sympathetic pat on the shoulder and went home to have a cold beer.

The next might somebody sprinkled salt and *sake* on the floor of the Korakuen dugout, to bring us good luck and drive out the evil spirits that were dogging us. It didn't work. We lost again in stifling heat to the last-place Tigers, 6–4. It was our fourth loss in a row.

I was beginning to think Oh was losing it. He'd called a team meeting, in the second inning, in front of the dugout. The whole team formed a circle around him and the coaches—so he could tell us, "*Gambatte*," and so forth.

And he was yelling at the guys like I'd never seen him do before. A guy would come back to the bench, after making an out, and Oh would shout at him, do this, do that. So when the guy went to bat the next time, he was feeling the heat. He'd tighten up because Oh had yelled at him, and he'd do worse than before.

We had a postgame meeting where Oh got up in front of everyone and say, "We have to win," again and again and again. And the guys just stood there, staring at their feet. Frustrated by the lack of response, Oh said, "Do you know what will happen if we don't win this year?"

Of course, everyone knew exactly what would happen. Oh would get fired. That's what would happen, because you just didn't manage the Yomiuri Giants four years in a row and not win a pennant, even if you were the best ball player the country had ever produced. It was just one of those things that wasn't allowed, like eating American rice in Japan.

As soon as Oh had said that, a voice from the back of the room piped up, "*Hai*," Yes. The silence that followed was like a thunderous roar.

I truly felt for Oh. We'd gone into another swan dive, and everyone blamed him, especially for the fiasco in Nagoya. Our normally mild-mannered fans hurled insults at him at the park. He got a sack of letters from people, begging him to quit. He'd open up an envelope and inside would be a piece of paper with one word written on it in large black letters: "*Yameroo!*" Quit! Resign!

The sports dailies were forecasting doom: it would be impossible for the Giants to win a pennant with Oh at the helm. Nomura, the former great catcher turned baseball critic, rated Oh as the worst manager in the history of the Giants. But the most memorable line was this, by a TV commentator: "The fact that the Giants are still in contention, despite all the mistakes Oh has made as manager, is an indication of how low the level of Japanese baseball is."

It wasn't exactly fair. Sure, Oh made his share of slipups. He tended to leave his pitchers in too long. Only after disaster struck did he take action and bring someone fresh in. But we'd also been in first place most of the season—and had won more games than any other Central League team the year before—with Oh at the helm.

Trouble was most people wanted perfection where the Giants were concerned. And no one was willing to forgive the fact that Oh wasn't a perfect manager. Not when he lacked pure you-know-what coursing through his veins.

A DAY IN THE LIFE

I woke up late one August morning, with something biting me. Ticks. There were red welts all over my body. I changed the sheets all the time, but the little buggers wouldn't go away. The air-conditioning was on full blast, but I was still itchy and sweaty.

I got up, shuffled into the living room and gazed out in disgust at the blue polluted haze outside the window. Another scorcher. I slid open the balcony window. A blast furnace of hot air greeted me. Cromartie's inferno.

I put some coffee beans in the grinder for my morning cup of java and turned the tube on to CNN for the big league highlights. Some American players in Japan did not like to do this. They didn't want to be reminded of what they had left behind. But I always tuned in. I noted that Montreal had won again and was still in the pennant race. Too bad. I always felt better when they lost.

Next came a report on NFL exhibition games. I felt a surge of anticipation. The start of football meant I didn't have much time left in Japan. The Giants had forty games left, and I was counting. But if we won our league, I'd have to stay for the Japan Series in late October. A sobering thought.

I switched the TV off. The apartment was empty, as silent as a tomb. Carole and the kids had already gone back to Miami, supposedly to get ready for school. But they had left a week early.

Carole, it turned out, didn't really like Japan; she found it too confining. Most of the wives of the *gaijin* players felt the same. Ben Oglivie's wife hated it, because in Japan women didn't get much respect or recognition. Also, I think Carole felt left out—abandoned in a very foreign country—with me always gone.

I was on the road more than half the time, because the Giants played some of their home games in cities with no baseball franchises, like Sapporo and Sendai. But even when I was in town, there was always a practice, or a team meeting, or some other Yomiuri function.

I'd leave the house at 1:30 for a night game and I was seldom home before midnight because the games, which started at 6:00, would drag on for hours. In this country, baseball occupied a player's entire life. The wives were simply supposed to stay home and watch the game on TV. (Hara had recently gotten engaged, and when a reporter asked him if his bride-to-be was going to come out and see the new Dome that was being built for us, he replied, "No, her place is in the home.")

Carole had to be both parents to our children, a pattern common to all Japan. And while in Tokyo, she hadn't met one single Giants' wife. She felt frustrated and alone. We'd been arguing more than we used to. When Carole had Cody Oh, she'd gone back to the U.S. to give birth. She said it was because she didn't trust Japanese doctors. But I also think she just wanted to get out of the country.

Granted, there were nice things about Tokyo for family life. You could walk the streets anytime of night. It was amazing how safe it was. You'd see little kids, five or six years old, ride the trains by themselves. They'd have their train passes, and they'd walk to the station and get on the train and ride for an hour to school. Then when school was over, they'd come back. You'd see high-schoolers, even girls by themselves, coming back at 9:00 P.M. from cram schools. It wasn't your typical American scene.

The educational level in Japan was really high. My children had gone to school in Tokyo for one year, at the international schools of Sacred Heart and St. Mary's. They'd come early and enrolled for the academic year, which starts in April. And they found out how advanced Japanese schools were compared to the States. They had to catch up on a lot, and they got discouraged. But when they went back to Florida, they were way ahead of their classmates.

Yet, in other ways, it was very hard to raise children in a place like Tokyo. People talk about drugs in the States, but in Japan, there's easy access to alcohol. Although the drinking age is 20, nobody ever asks for ID. Besides, to the Japanese, American kids look older than they really are.

Our son Chris was at a difficult age then. He'd played little league and pony league in Tokyo, but then he started coming home late. We were worried that he was falling in with the wrong crowd.

It became apparent that Chris didn't really like living in Japan that much. He liked the Giants' players, Nakahata in particular, but the city was too crowded for him. He was used to the big wide open spaces of Miami. There was just no space in Tokyo to run around. I could see he was bored. He had that expression—"Give me a big skateboard and a big park, and let me go." That kind of life just did not exist in Tokyo. There was hardly any green. So after the one year, we decided not to send them to Japanese schools anymore.

Carole had put up with a lot over the years. I wanted to have kids at any early age to create the family I never had, so we had our first child when I was 22 and she was 21. Carole traveled with me all over the minor leagues with a U-Haul trailer attached to the back of our car, driving the Interstate, finding apartments to live in, barely making it on my salary.

It was not an easy life. My being an absentee father part of the year put enough pressure on her as it was. Then after each season was over, we had to pack up and move out and find another place to live for six months. When spring came, we'd load up the U-Haul again, head south for camp, and look for an apartment where we'd stay until I got my next minor league assignment. Carole stuck with me and she never complained, which wasn't easy because I gave her a very hard time. My friends used to say to me, "If a woman can stay with somebody like you for twelve years, well, she must be some kind of woman." They were right.

There is no question that I can be a real pain in the ass. I bitch and moan a lot. A ballplayer once told me that I'd bitch until the day I died. "Even when you're in your grave, Cro," he said, "people will walk by and they'll hear something. And it will be you in there moaning about it being too dark or wet or something like that."

But Japan was perhaps the hardest thing for her. She'd bring the kids over when school got out in June, and by the time she'd gotten used to it she'd have to pack up and leave again, to go back and get ready for the fall semester. The kids didn't understand. They wanted their mom and dad together all the time.

Ours being a mixed marriage was an added burden on them. My son had some problems back in Miami. If he clowned around with the other boys, he was the one who got picked out and blamed—or so he'd complain. He thought it was a racial thing, because all the other boys were white. So back in Florida, it was left to my wife to take care of such issues with the kids in school. And she handled them very well, because she didn't seem to look at the racial aspect of our marriage. I was the one who thought about it.

I liked having kids that were mixed. I called them coffee and cream. Chris was two coffee and one cream. Candice, the girl, was one coffee and one cream. And Cody, our youngest, was one coffee and two creams. Three beautiful children—people told us that all the time. They said we made good mixed-breed babies.

I tried to help my kids understand racial prejudice, because they were going to come across it in their lives. The old ignorance is still out there and always will be, not just in America, but all over the world. I'd tell my children that they were not going to feel comfortable in some black places and that that they were not going to feel comfortable in some white places. I wanted them to be ready for that. At the same time, I wanted them to be proud of who they were and not to be afraid of new and different things.

I'd tell them there might even be times when they'd have special privileges that others wouldn't have and that they should appreciate that as well. Going through customs at Narita, the agent would invariably say to them, "Aren't you Warren Cromartie's kids?" and then let them pass without checking their bags. But I didn't want them to get to depend on special favors. I wanted them to be able to find their own way and understand people better—both sides, white and black. And yellow too. I'd hoped that way they'd have more savvy than most folks.

But be that as it was, I was still sitting back in Tokyo, drinking my morning coffee alone and staring out at the photo-chemical smog.

I pulled out the English language daily, the *Japan Times*, which came every day, from under the door, along with a Japanese sports daily, the *Hochi Shimbun*. I scanned the standings. Despite yet another loss the previous night, our lead stayed two games ahead of the Carp and two-and-a-half ahead of the Dragons, because both teams had been defeated too. I noted my three hits and seventeenth home run in the box score and thought to myself, what a wonderful hitter you are.

Katori had gotten kayoed in relief, one of the rare times that had happened to him that year. But he was pitching every night. He'd pitch any time you asked him. He never complained. He never said anything. He just went out and did his job. He was the real MVP of the team, I thought.

I popped a coke from the fridge and ordered up some *gomoku soba*—a Japanese noodle soup with vegetables and meat—from the shop around the corner. Five minutes later, the delivery man was there. He produced the noodles and a sign card for me to autograph. "*Kuromatei wa dai suki. Watashi wa Kyojin no dai fuan,*" he said. I really like you, and I'm a big fan of the Giants.

After he left, I split open my wooden chopsticks and ate my

noodles in silence, trying not to slurp like the Japanese always did, even though I was alone. That was one thing that always bothered me about the way my teammates ate. They were so damned noisy. "Slurp. Shlup. Sloosh." You needed earplugs to be in the same room with them. I don't care if it was the Japanese way or if it kept you from scorching your mouth like I had just done.

I got dressed and went to the park where we beat the Tigers, 3–2, on Kono's home run and Katori's no-hit two-inning job. I had two hits and was so pleased with myself that I headed straight for Roppongi where I hooked up with some of the *gaijin* who were in town: Dick Davis, Ben Oglivie, and Bass. We had a pizza at Nick's and then stood in the center of Roppongi trying to decide what to do next.

Roppongi was frenetic as usual. It got me every time—the blaze of lights and color, the neon signs, the expensive cars, and the good-looking women. On one side of our group was a Mr. Donut, on the other, a McDonald's. Behind us was a two-story building which housed Spago's, Tony Roma's, and the Hard Rock Cafe. Suspended from the roof was a giant model of King Kong, made to look as if it was climbing up the side of the building.

Many of the passers-by turned to gawk at us oversized foreigners standing there with our hands in our pockets. One young Japanese man, wearing an Italian double-breasted suit and eye make-up, stopped in his tracks. His mouth dropped open.

"*Aahhh, Kyojin no Kuromatei,*" he blurted.

"*Kyaaa,*" screamed a teenaged girl, wearing jeans, a tank top and huge earrings. "*Basu da. Are wa Basu!*"

Before we knew it, we were surrounded by a big crowd of people. Even King Kong seemed to be staring at us. We started moving while we still could. We headed across the street, down an alley, and into a basement country-and-western bar. We sat down at one of the big square wooden tables in the center of the room and ordered huge mugs of draft beer, scanning our surroundings to see if there were any Japanese reporters present.

There didn't seem to be any gentlemen from the press, but

there were some groupies, girls who liked to hang around *gaijin* ballplayers. One of them, barely out of her teens, was wearing a T-shirt which read, "Passing Gas—It's Natural." She was chewing gum. As we walked by, she looked up and flashed a toothy smile. Then she blew a big bubble. A soul sister.

In one corner was a bar, on the other, a stage, on which a young Japanese man was trying to sound like Elvis. "Are you ronesome tonighto," he crooned. A few customers came over and asked for autographs. The American manager of the New York Pizza shop across the street, taking his evening break, gave us free pizza tickets. Then, one of the most beautiful women I have ever seen, a young lady in a white silk dress, approached and introduced herself to Bass in English.

"I admire your play very much, Mistah Basu," she murmured, flashing her long eyelashes and dazzling us all with her smile. I admired Bass's restraint. He shook her hand, gave her his autograph, and sent her on her way—to the accompaniment of oos and aahs and whistles from the rest of us. What self-control.

Some people worried about appearances; others didn't. Some of the married guys looked forward to the road trips, where they'd have a different girl in every town. Women were all over the place. Take your pick. If you were an American and you played ball in Japan, that automatically assured you that a certain category of woman would be at your beck and call. You'd see them at the stadium, in the stands before the games. They'd ask you for your autograph and hand you their phone number when they passed you a pen and "sign card." You'd see them waiting outside the clubhouse after the game and hanging around the hotel lobbies on the road. I knew of one girl, an organist at one of the stadiums, who had slept with every single American player in the Pacific League, and was working on the Central.

I knew of another who walked up to an American player in some Roppongi bar one night, wearing a black leather suit. She looked at him and said, "I'd like to tie you up." He made a date with her for the next night at 10:00. By 9:00 it was only the sixth inning, and it was obvious the game wouldn't be over in time. So he "injured" himself sliding into base. He limped into the clubhouse, changed his clothes, and called a taxi. A little after 10:00, while his teammates were still on the field, he was in a mirrored love-hotel room in the backstreets of Roppongi, his arms and legs tied to the bedposts, having the time of his life.

There were other roads to gratification as well: "fashion health" massage salons where bikinied young ladies with skillful hands and tongues would ease your anxieties; "lip service" parlors where scantily clad waitresses served you beer in dimly lit rooms, then crawled under your table to serve you in other ways; and special cabarets where the girls dressed up as stewardesses, uniformed high school students, policemen, whatever your fantasy was, then let you undress them and do your will right there in your seat. They had names like "Ahab," "Utamaro," "Nine-and-a-half," "The Red String," and "Silkheart." Altogether these places were as enterprising as any other Japanese industry.

It could cost you seventy bucks for forty minutes in some dingy hole in the wall, to five hundred bucks for the most expensive "soapland" in Japan. The soaps (or "turkish baths" as they were once called before the Turkish Embassy complained) in the old red-light district of Yoshiwara were supposed to be the best. You'd be greeted by some sweet thing in an elaborate *kimono*. She'd bow at your feet, then usher you into a room that looked like a private Roman bath—marble floor, sunken tub, gold fixtures, the works. She'd lock the door, remove layer after layer of her *kimono*, and for the next ninety minutes you'd receive a bath, a body-to-body oil massage, and other attentions that would leave you limp for days.

Not that I'd necessarily sampled them all, mind you, although I knew many who did. I do know of an American guy who bragged that he went to a soapland before a game and then went out and hit two home runs. But if you were a Giants ballplayer, you had to be very, very careful where you went. Scandal magazine photographers seemed to be hiding behind every tree, lurking in back of every parked car. They were worse than the CIA. And it wasn't just the photographers. The team kept tabs on you too; I frequently got the feeling I was being followed. I'd come to the park, and some official would say, "Did you have a good time in Roppongi last night?" Where the Giants were concerned, you didn't have any privacy.

Some Japanese coaches and managers said sex sapped your strength. They forbade players to have sex before important games, and sent instructions to the wives to lay off at such critical times.

There were guys who would be shut down completely until they started hitting. One veteran player I knew of, in the other league, complained bitterly about his restrictions: "No drink, no smoke, no sex. *Terrible!*"

But the *gaijin* were always exempted from rules like this, and the Giants never counseled me or Carole about activities in that area. The *gaijin* had bigger bodies and bigger dicks, the Japanese seemed to reason, so we could handle it better.

Besides the groupies and the sex shops, *gaijin* players would run into other women socially—airline stewardesses, disco queens, members of the Japanese media, and other assorted working women and ordinary girls, who, by some twist of fate, would come into their lives. Japanese women could be nice. They had a gentler brand of femininity than what Americans were used to. They'd clean your ears and clip your toenails and laugh at your jokes.

But, as the guys told me, there were also problems with this particular species. Once a young lady made contact, so to speak, she tended not to leave you alone. A night of passion wasn't enough. She'd hang around and cook breakfast, maybe clean your apartment for you. It seemed those were the first steps toward moving in. If you gave her your phone number, she'd never leave you alone.

"There's only one thing better than a blow job in this country," an American ballplayer said once, "and that's getting rid of it." That was a little extreme, but everybody understood what he was talking about—especially when you already had a wife back in the States.

After razzing Bass about the beautiful angel he'd just let go, we started in on baseball. The list of our complaints was endless. If it wasn't the umpires, then it was gutless pitchers, or the interminable length of the games, or coaches who wouldn't leave us alone, or nosy newspaper reporters. We were like hypochondriacs. Of course, hardly anybody squawked about the money he was making.

The big complaint that night was how hard it was to get your adrenalin flowing in the Japanese game, because there were so many restrictions. Davis, a muscular black who had played with the Kintetsu Buffaloes for three years and who loved to talk as much as me, was going on about how the Japanese didn't like it if you slid really hard into base to break up a double play. If you tried to play real major league–style hard ball, they'd say you played dirty.

Davis also complained that you changed as a player if you stayed in Japan long enough. You became Japanized. You found yourself doing things that you never did before—things you'd be ashamed to do in the States. He told us about a game in which his team was three runs down in the ninth inning, with one out, and their equipment manager was packing up all the gear. The players were helping him. And so was Davis! That was something you wouldn't see in the big leagues. You never relaxed your concentration until the final out was made, not if you were worth anything, because it was the good teams that always came back in the ninth inning.

In Japan, there wasn't the same intensity, Davis was saying. The players seemed too easily intimidated, too cowed by pressure, too certain that, since everyone would be watching, they would fail. To suppress those feelings, the Japanese tended to treat their game as a job; they adopted the attitude of a salaryman or a factory worker.

I sat there and listened as Davis went on, bluegrass playing in the background. I had to ask myself when was the last time the Yomiuri Giants had ever come back and won a game in the ninth inning. I didn't know the answer.

Then I asked myself when was the last time Cromartie had really slid hard into a second baseman. I didn't know the answer to that either. Hell, I'd lost some of my major league aggressiveness too.

Oglivie's complaint was that he still hadn't gotten used to

Japan. He said that since joining Kintetsu, he had started to talk to himself a lot. He kept asking himself, "What the fuck is going on?" The other night it had gotten so bad that, in the middle of the game, he threw up his glove in disgust—right there in left field in full view of several thousand fans. Oglivie was the quiet, deep-thinking type who read philosophy books. That was his hobby. He wasn't the kind of guy to blow up. But he did. That's how much the game had gotten on his nerves.

I can't remember exactly what it was that rankled him so much. It was something like runners on first and third with one out and the manager putting the bunt sign on. Or putting the squeeze sign on with two strikes. Or squeezing with runners on first and third with two outs. Or walking with the bases loaded.

Well, it did get to you from time to time. You would indeed shake your head and start talking to yourself. I'd done it myself, especially on the road, alone in my hotel room. That's why you needed somebody to bitch to. You could say that we were spoiled, considering all the money we were making. And you'd be right. Real men would have just sucked it up. But we were human and needed these sessions to get some perspective. They were group counseling, without the psychiatrist.

Oglivie, in his first year, had already left the country once, back in the spring. He'd OD'd on the grimness of it all, packed his bags, and left without telling anyone. He stayed away a couple of weeks, but somehow the Buffaloes enticed him back—with more money was my guess. Oglivie insisted that this season would be his last.

"I'm not coming back," he announced to us. "I've had enough." But he was hitting the ball well, at .300 with 20 homers or so, and he had another year on his contract. It wasn't easy to turn down three-quarters of a million dollars, or whatever it was he was getting. So we spent the next half hour telling Oglivie that it was useless to talk like that. He'd be back. He was doomed to stay in Japan for probably a good five or six more years. I knew. Look at me.

"You'll be here," I said, smiling wickedly. "You'll see. We'll be sending you telegrams from the States, telling you to keep up the good work. You'll see, Ben... You'll be back."

Oglivie was the one with the big name. He had won a home run title playing for the Milwaukee Brewers. But it was Davis and Bass who were doing the best in Japan. Bass, with his two consecutive triple crowns, was enormously successful. Davis had hit .343 with 40 homers in 1985. The next year, it was .337 with 36 homers. And as of that night, he was leading the Pacific League in batting with something like .352 with 14 homers.

That just went to show that there were a lot of good American players who never got a chance to demonstrate what they could do in the majors. If a man was not a starter in the major leagues, that didn't mean he didn't have the ability to be a starter—or even a star. A lot of it was timing and luck.

Cecil Fielder was the perfect example. A 25-year-old first baseman who was released by the Blue Jays, he would hit 38 homers for the Hanshin Tigers. The following year he would play for the Detroit Tigers and smash 51 home runs!

Davis had only gotten a little taste of the majors with the Milwaukee Brewers. He didn't have much chance to play on an everyday basis. Bass never really got a chance to play regularly in the major leagues either. He'd been on six different teams, but twice the manager was Dick Williams, who didn't like him. I really don't know why. Randy was too laid back, maybe. But Dick just didn't like him and when Dick doesn't like you, you're in trouble. And so Bass was screwed.

Bass could hit—better than all of us. But he was limited to that one particular ability. He didn't have a bullet arm. He didn't have blazing speed. He wasn't the guts-and-hustle type of player that Dick Williams looked for. But in the majors Bass could have been a fantastic DH—on the right ballclub, in the right park.

So that's why Japan was good. You got a chance to show what you *could* do. In a different environment, under different circumstances, you could learn, you could improve, you could come into your own. It wasn't easy or a lot of fun, but Japan represented opportunity. And a good-paying job.

THE O-BON DANCE

Tokyo was like one big frying pan. The sun beat down

through the smog, melting the asphalt pavement outside. I drove to the park in my air-conditioned car, halting and jerking in heavy traffic, on my way to a big mid-August game with the Carp. I rolled down the window momentarily to test the air. It made my eyes burn.

At stoplights, it seemed every cab within hearing distance had the radio on full blast, tuned to the national high school baseball tournament. On the sidewalks people were gathered around the storefront TVs watching the action. I recognized the pitcher. It was the same one as the day before, and the day before that, and the day before that too. The kid's career would be over before he ever got out of high school.

The Tigers had to turn their home park over to the high schoolers so they could play their tournament. Given the pre-tournament practice sessions, it meant the Tigers had to travel for three solid weeks. The Japanese called it the "Death Road Trip." And in this heat, you could understand why.

I passed a liquor store outside of which stood a large poster of Bob Horner—who was still on the sidelines He was posing with a young Japanese actress who was cute, toothy, and virginal. That was the type you found quite often on TV in Japan. That was the type you could take home to mama. I wondered what she thought of Big Bob. Was he that kind she'd take home to Papa?

I arrived at Korakuen at 2:00 and already our starting pitcher Kato was in the outfield with the rest of the pitching staff, running sprints as hard as he could. I could see him sweating and grunting out there through the shimmering waves of heat. The temperature on the artificial turf must have been well over 100 degrees. It was dizzying, the air so thick it was painful to breathe. Those guys looked dead already. It was amazing that no one out there had collapsed, I thought. All that practice was good for something.

I went in the clubhouse where the air-conditioning was, mercifully, working. The place was like a morgue. Our lead over the second-place team, which was now the Dragons, still stood at two, with the Carp three-and-a-half back. But we'd just dropped two in a row to the weak-sister Swallows and had the worst record in the league for the second half. It was only because the other teams couldn't put together a winning streak that we were still in first. Everyone looked so grim, you'd've thought the Reaper had come.

This was *o-bon* time, the midsummer season when you greet dear departed souls. Contrary to what you might think, it's not a somber time. Everybody in Japan was doing the *o-bon* dance in evening festivals around the country. There was an odd beat to the music that was catchy.

It was bouncing around in my head when I wrapped a bath-towel around my waist. I pulled out a *happi* coat that Oh had given me earlier in the year and put it on. Next I tied a *hachi-maki* headband around my head, and then I started dancing and singing around the locker room with that drag-and-lift *o-bon* step.

"*Wasshoi, wasshoi, wasshoi,*" I sang, mimicking the Japanese words. My somber-faced teammates, who couldn't believe what they were seeing, busted out laughing. Some of them even joined in. It was that rarest of occasions. For a brief few min-utes, members of the Yomiuri Giants had actually forgotten about baseball.

Kato, by some miracle, held the Carp to four hits over the first seven innings that night, before giving way to Katori. The Carp starter had checked us on six hits and no runs over the first seven innings, then departed in favor of their relief ace Tsuda. Tsuda was a big six-footer with a fastball like a Nike rocket and a 90-mile-per-hour fork. His ERA was 1.52, and the man was serious trouble.

Katori gave up a run, and we went into the bottom of the ninth, trailing 1–0. Our situation looked bad because Tsuda's fastball was really humming. But then Okazaki led off with a single, and as 50,000 people leaned forward in their seats, it was the Black Devil's turn to bat.

I'll say one thing for Tsuda: he challenged me. None of this dinky shit on the corner. He glowered in at me and threw seven straight smoke balls. I fouled off two, working the count to 3–2. Then he threw me a low inside slider and I whacked that sucker 400 feet into the lights.

I dropped my bat, threw my arms up into the air, and

turned to look at Oh as the ball sailed into the back rows of our lunatic cheering section. Oh was leaping for joy. *Every-body* was off the bench. Man, I'd my first hit *sayonara* home run!

My teammates swarmed out of the dugout and rushed across home plate to greet me—to pound my back and smash me on top of my batting helmet as was their custom at such dramatic moments. Sometimes they knocked the shit out of you, and I could tell by the looks on their faces they really meant business this time. So I came to a screeching halt a few feet from home plate.

"Get out of the way," I growled in mock anger. "Don't anybody dare touch me, damn it."

Yamakura parted the way.

"None of that hitting shit now," I cried as I went in and stepped on the plate. Then I started running to get the hell out of there. But it was too late. They caught me and pummeled the bejesus out of me.

Nakahata grabbed me and planted a great big kiss on my cheek—right there in front of God and everyone and all the folks at home watching on TV.

It was my first baseball kiss in Japan.

It was my first baseball kiss anywhere.

I didn't mind.

In fact, I was really touched.

You didn't see the Giants that happy very often.

In the clubhouse, we got the news that the Dragons had lost. That put us three up on them, and four-and-a-half up on the Carp. God damn, I thought, maybe we won't blow this thing after all. Oh came up to me, a wide smile on his face, and said, "We just started the second half all over again."

A reporter interviewed me later and told me that my mighty blast that night had been the Giants' 1,000th all-time home run versus the Carp, the 124th *sayonara* home run in Giants' history, and the first since August 7 the year before when Nakahata had hit one against the Dragons. What's more, he said, my lifetime average against the Carp had risen to .337—that was 35 hits in 107 at-bats, with 20 RBIs, in case I was interested.

You could say what you wanted about the Japanese sports press. But you had to admit—they were thorough when it came to statistics.

PENANTO RESU

The pressure really set in after that. Oh was taking vitamin shots every other day and was more fidgety and nervous than ever before. The guy couldn't sit still on the bench. He spit constantly. By the end of a game, there was so much saliva on the floor in his corner of the dugout, you could have held a swimming meet there.

And Oh was always calling meetings. Always. Before games, afterward, and during. It didn't matter to him what time of day it was. When we went on the road, we'd arrive in Nagoya or some place, get off the bus, and before we even had time to check in and put our gear in our rooms, we were having a half-hour meeting. It was a kind of ritual, like a prayer before a game.

But also something had changed. We'd stopped our slide and regained our footing. There was a feeling on the team that maybe our worst days were behind us. Our confidence began to return and we began playing better and better.

Egawa, the 100-pitch arm, pitched three complete games in a row—much to everyone's surprise. Hara upped his home run total to 28 by early September, and I took over the league lead in RBIs. Oh made some key strategic moves that were working, and the Giants were starting to look like a championship team.

In the a game with Taiyo Whales, with two runners on base and us leading 3–1, Yoshimura made a diving, sliding catch on the Astroturf. Somehow, he got up in time to double-up the runner trying to return to second. It was turning into that kind of year. The team was coming together, and it was a beautiful thing to watch.

I liked think my presence on the team gave them added spunk. In the nearly four years I'd been playing with my teammates, I had gone from being just another oddball *gaijin* who wasn't bad to being a fixture on the team. On a club like the Giants, which did not easily take to foreigners, that was saying something, I guess.

In the beginning, the guys had acted shy around me. But after four years, I could kid around with them just like I could with an American. Almost, that is. I could jump right into the middle of a conversation my teammates were having, crack a joke in broken Japanese, and they'd laugh at it. They accepted me. I could see it in their eyes.

They were also somewhat looser than they used to be. When I first arrived, they were the most uptight group of athletes I'd ever seen. When I started my little act, my fist-in-the-air *gattsu pozu*, they looked at me as if I was from Mars. They thought I was a big show-off, which I was, and which did not earn me any instant friends. Four years later, however, they were all imitating me—even Hara, our resident knight-in-shining-armor. Hell, even the opposing teams were doing it.

I was also plaing with a renewed aggressiveness, which rubbed off on them. The Japanese way was, and still is to a large extent, to play it safe, to avoid screwing up, and being singled out for criticism.

But I gave them a lot of flak about that. I'd always try to stretch a single into a double. If the outfielder bobbled the ball or made the slightest hesitation, I'd take the next base, sliding in headfirst. And if they didn't do the same thing, I would say something to them about it. If I saw a guy hit the ball into the gap and hold up on first base, I'd grab him at the end of the inning and say, "If that had been me, I'd have been on second base." And I'd point to the bag, just to make sure there was no misunderstanding.

There were guys on the team who began to copy me. That summer, at least, all of them were playing with more intensity than I'd ever seen—Nakahata, Hara, Yoshimura, the whole lot. Everyone was chipping in.

Shinozuka anchored our batting lineup, hitting around .330 all year. Hara was hitting over .320. Yoshimura would hit .322 with 30 homers. But Yamakura was the big surprise. He'd come through with numerous key home runs for us as well as caught most of the games. Our talkative batting coach

Yamauchi had helped Yamakura become a good hitter. Yamakura's lifetime average was about .230, but this year he was up in the .290s, with 18 homers.

The Giants still practiced as hard as they always did. It was as if they wanted to be certain they'd be exhausted. But it didn't make that much difference, because the Carp and the Dragons had stepped up their training in an effort to catch us. The result was that they were more tired than we were, and we slowly widened our lead.

Oh became more assertive than ever as a manager. In one game at Koshien, he took Kato out in the fifth inning with the score tied 2–2, a runner on base and Bass coming up, which took away Kato's shot at credit for the official victory. He put in Sumi, a tricky left-handed reliever, who got Bass on a popup. Ten days later, playing against the Tigers at Korakuen, Oh did it again. This time Kato was leading, 6–1, in the top of the fifth, but when he loaded up the bases and walked in a run, Oh yanked him. There were two out and any American manager would have left Kato in. But the specter of Bass in the on deck circle was more than Oh could bear. Sumi was brought in again.

Kato was really pissed, but being a Giant, he did not let anyone see his anger—not while the TV cameras or reporters were watching him. Kato walked off the field gritting his teeth, his second potential win in two weeks gone up in smoke. Only when he got into the privacy of the clubhouse did he dare to throw his glove.

With our lead at six games in late September and only fourteen games left to play (twenty-one for the Carp), the press was suddenly buzzing about "the new Oh." He was compared to Kawakami, the former manager of the V-9 Giants who was famous for the line, "There is no such thing as a manager who is too strict." Even Kawakami himself had seen fit to comment on the new Oh in a newspaper column. Said the godfather of Japanese baseball, as he was known, after watching Oh heartlessly deprive Kato of another win: "This is evidence that Oh has thrown his Chinese blood away and become a 'real

Japanese.' It is a sign that he has truly matured as a manager."

There is a saying in Japan that goes: "When you are on a pilgrimage to one hundred temples and you have passed number ninety-nine, making it to the last one is truly hateful."

Well, we were on the last leg of our pilgrimage and it wasn't that bad at all. We beat the Tigers 3–1 on September 27, with Oh using four pitchers—Egawa, who went seven innings, Mizuno, Sumi, and Katori. With runners on first and third, two out in the top of the eighth, he brought in Sumi to face Bass, once again. Bass lined what would have been a single up the middle, but our shortstop was playing him perfectly and grabbed it for the third out.

It was our fifth win in a row. It put us nine up on the Carp, who had lost four straight, and nine-and-a-half over the Dragons. With eleven games left for us, eighteen left for the Carp and twelve left for the Dragons, the roofline of that last temple was in clear view—and it was an easy downhill walk.

The next day, the Giants announced that Oh's contract had been extended.

We blew an opportunity to wrap up the pennant at home when we lost to the Swallows on October 9. It was an expensive defeat. The Giants had readied 1,600 bottles of beer and 100 kilograms of roast beef, among other goodies, for an on-field celebration, scheduled to be televised by NTV. Fifty thousand fans had packed the stadium, as usual, and many of them had stayed in line for seventy-two hours to get the few remaining bleacher tickets which had gone on sale the day of the game. There was even a full autumn moon in the sky directly overhead—an auspicious sign, one reporter had assured me before the game.

Despite the crowd, the moon, and the roast beef, the Swallows beat us 5–3. The second-place Carp defeated the Whales in Yokohama, and so our magic number was still 1. We had to pack everything up and head for a final series in Hiroshima two days later.

We flew in the next evening and checked into the Hiroshima Grand Hotel. There, we changed into our uniforms and assembled in a second-floor banquet room to await the result of a Dragons–Carp game being played that evening in Nagoya. If the Carp lost, then we were the champions, and we'd have our pennant celebration right then and there.

That's exactly what happened—there was speculation that the Carp had purposely blown the game so they wouldn't have to endure our celebration on their home field.

But no matter. When the news came in that we'd won the pennant, we went crazy, yelling and hugging each other all around. But we weren't allowed to touch the 1,600 bottles of Kirin Beer, the 100 bottles of champagne, and the three huge barrels of *sake* that were laid out for us on the far side of the hall. Not before a word from our manager.

The room buzzed as Oh climbed up on a makeshift stage and turned to face us. I felt a lump rise in my throat. He's finally done it, I thought to myself—after all the criticism, after all the abuse, after all the pain, the man's done it. I was so happy for him—for all of us really, but for him especially.

I produced the headband I'd been keeping in my uniform pocket and tied it on. It said, "*Yusho!*" Victory! I also pulled out a cigar I'd brought along for the occasion. I lit up, took a long, satisfying drag, and looked up at Oh as he stood there, smiling down at us, eyes misty.

I was struck once again by his fundamental decency and thought how glad I was to have known him and to be a part of this day. I'd been on championship teams before, but this, well, this was special.

"Thank you everyone," Oh began, his voice choked up. "I really don't know what I can say to thank you all for this. My heart is filled with emotion."

His voice welled up, and he fell silent. Tears filled his eyes, then rolled down his cheeks. No one had ever seen Oh cry before, ever. Not in all those glory-filled pennant-winning years, when he was a star. Not when he passed Hank Aaron's record. Not when he retired. Not even when his father died. They said that Oh was much too shy a man to cry. But he was doing it now.

I glanced at Nakahata, Oh's biggest critic over the years,

the man who had once contemptuously referred to Oh as *wan-ko*, a dog. And he was also starting to cry.

"We won by our ability," Oh began again, tears flowing. "We overcame many difficulties in winning this championship, and we did it all together. I'd like to thank you, every one of you, from the bottom of my heart for all you have done this year."

Nakahata was sobbing now, and the rest of the guys were not exactly dry-eyed either. Including me.

Then Shinozuka yelled out., "Let's get the manager." And we all swarmed up on the stage, surrounding Oh for the traditional *doage*. We grabbed him and tossed him up in the air, once, twice, three times, then a fourth, and then a fifth, and a sixth time. Someone told me later it was the longest *doage* the Giants had ever performed.

When Oh regained his feet, he exclaimed, "*Mechakucha nomoo!*" Let's drink to our heart's content!

I raced for the beer, shook one up, and sprayed it on the first guy I could get to, who happened to be Yamakura. "*Banzai!*" I screamed, "*Banzai!*" The celebration had started in earnest.

For the next hour or so, we drenched each other and anyone else who was foolish enough to get close, including the raincoat-clad NTV cameramen there to cover the festivities. I worked my way over to Oh and stuck a bottle of Kirin down his uniform. Then I hugged him for joy.

"Cro," he cried, pumping my hand, his smile stretching from here to China, "long, tough four years."

"That's what makes this day so sweet," I replied. Then I hugged him again.

In the days that followed, it seemed that everyone in the country was celebrating along with us. It struck me that I'd never seen the Japanese people so happy. It was as if they had just won a war. A cabaret in Sapporo where the hostesses dressed in Giant uniforms gave away free beer. A soba shop in Kagoshima served discount noodles. The Yomiuri Sogo department store in downtown Tokyo held a special sale. Even the announcers on the evening news, on all the channels, were smiling when they reported on our championship.

It was like a national festival.

The small matter of playing out the schedule, as it dribbled to a close, had to be attended to, even if we did all have serious hangovers. Shinozuka was leading the league in batting, and Oh benched him to help preserve that lead—a move everyone seemed to think was splendid. When the Carp second baseman Shoda caught up with Shinozuka, tying him, improbably, at exactly .333, he was benched too. Hiroshima fans thought that was an equally splendid idea.

In the wake of our winning the pennant, everyone on the team was beaming. The front office people were walking around with huge grins on their faces, heads held high. The Giants were back on top, and they were as cocky as could be.

But then suddenly, everyone became dead serious. It was as if we had started the season all over again. To prepare for the Japan Series, Oh and the coaches organized an intense, week-long "camp," which included practice six hours a day and meetings in the evening, during which they would show endless videos of our opponents, the Seibu Lions, and deliver detailed lectures on each player's weaknesses. One couldn't be too careful.

My teammates were put up in the New Otani Hotel, isolated from the rest of the world, to better concentrate on the task at hand. The Giants wanted me to stay there too, but Carole was coming back for the series and there was no way I would comply. I realized that my teammates had to be separated from their wives, but enough was enough. I claimed my *gaijin* exemption.

Our opponents, already winners of three Japan Series championships in the eighties, were owned by a man named Tsutsumi, a real estate and hotel tycoon who was one of the richest men in the world. The Lions played in a beautiful park in Tokorozawa, in the suburbs of Tokyo, surrounded by trees and hills. There were grassy slopes in the outfield stands where the fans could sit. It reminded me of the Kansas City Royals' stadium.

The Lions were managed by a man named Masaaki Mori,

Oh's former teammate and catcher on the old V-9 Giants. His team worked even harder than we did, if you can believe that. If playing for the Giants was like being in the marines, then playing for the Lions was like being in the Special Forces. They practiced all the time, and their players were not allowed to do endorsements or to engage in side businesses—it was considered too much of a distraction.

George Vukovich, who played for them, compared a year on the Lions to a year in a maximum-security prison. The previous season, he'd had hit only about .240 for them and was on the verge of being released, even though he had a year left on his contract. He didn't care because he'd get his money, about $800,000, whether he stayed or not. But then he'd delivered a big game-winning hit in the final game of the 1986 Japan Series against the Carp. Seibu decided to bring him back because it wouldn't have looked right to release the hero of the Japan Series.

"Of all the stupid things to do," Vukovich later told a fellow American player, "I just earned myself another year of misery."

The Seibu Lions were a class act—from their powder blue uniforms to the mini-skirted waitresses who sold cocktails in the expensive infield box seats. I had played against them in spring training games, and I had watched them on TV numerous times. They were a good, all-around team, well-schooled in all the fundamentals with a wealth of talented young pitchers. They had a kid named Kaku, from Taiwan, who had a 96-mile-per-hour fastball, the fastest in all of Asia.

They also had a 24-year-old center fielder named Akiyama who had hit 43 home runs and had stolen 38 bases; a third baseman, named Ishige, who led off, hit with power, stole bases, and was the team's spiritual leader; and a 19-year-old first baseman named Kiyohara, who had hit 31 out of the park in 1987. He was a big, strong 6'3" slugger and was still growing.

During our week-long preparations, I managed to run into trouble again. Seibu was loaded with left-handed pitchers, which was not a good thing for a left-handed batter like me. So I asked for extra practice hitting versus left-handers. Pitching coach Minagawa said no. He said I had no right to expect special treatment.

The press picked up on that one. How could they not? There were only about 250 of them present at our workouts, watching our every move. They also picked up on the fact that I had checked into the nearby Tachikawa Grand Hotel, with my wife, the night before the series opener, while the rest of the team were staying at a lesser business hotel, *sans* wives. That, combined with the media's awareness that I'd lived at home during "camp" guaranteed that I would get more than my usual share of negative publicity.

I sat in front of the TV on a Friday night in my room at the Tachikawa Grand, yet another of those tiny cubby holes with a pre-fab bathroom, wondering if I really was just another "selfish, spoiled *gaijin*" as one newspaper had described me. Then I wondered what kind of accommodations the Twins and the Cardinals had that fall during their World Series.

The 11:00 News sports report came on, and I was pleased to find—surprised actually—that I could understand what the announcers was saying: "No doubt many of you have just come home from a long day at work and are sitting down for a nightcap. You've been working so hard, you haven't had a chance to catch up on the news, so here's a summary of the day's happenings."

Well, one's lot in life is all relative, isn't it? It depended on what context you viewed it in. If the guys on the Cardinals could have seen me—lying on a bed so small my feet stuck out in a room so cramped I couldn't do pushups—then I didn't have such a good deal. But from the standpoint of the average working stiff in Japan, the salaryman who worked long hours, suffered terrible commutes, and didn't get home to his rabbit hutch of an apartment until 11:00 P.M., I probably did look "selfish and spoiled." What would those guys have given to trade places with me—or, for that matter, any of the Giants staying over at the business hotel which had to have had smaller rooms than mine.

That was the problem with hotel rooms. They made you think too much. I looked over at Carole who was sound asleep. Well, some people anyway.

When the sports report got to its interview with Minagawa, I turned the tube off.

DEFEAT AND SUPERSTITION

We lost the Japan Series in six games. And we were lucky to take it that far. Our only bright spots were a sloppy 7–3 win in game one, in which Kuwata was kayoed in the second inning, and a near-perfect four-hit shutout by Makihara in game four. The Lions took the rest, 6–0, 2–1, 3–1, 3–1. It didn't matter that we shut down their big hitters. They just kept throwing one good pitcher after another at us, and beat us with superior baserunning and fielding. We made six errors to their two. That they were the better team was clear to everyone.

I got eight hits in the series, but more attention was paid to a couple of high arching throws I had made from center field, on which runs scored. After the final game, coach Doi told a reporter that the Lions had obviously scouted my throwing deficiencies, which was why they ran the bases so aggressively whenever the ball was hit to me.

I couldn't find the words to express my appreciation to Doi for saying that.

If we had kept score by good-luck charms, however, the Giants would have won hands down. It seemed everybody on the team was carrying one. Someone had sprinkled salt in the dugout for luck at the start of the series and also before each contest. The wife of coach Yamauchi put packets of salt, collected from a nearby shrine and thus suitably blessed, in his back pockets before every game. Yamauchi kept his hands jammed inside those pockets the whole nine innings.

When Yamakura went hitless in the first three games, his wife served him octopus, a popular delicacy in Japan, to break the spell. *Tako* is the Japanese word for octopus. It is also baseball slang for going hitless.

There was also a lot of talk about blood type since a craze had developed for evaluating ability and personality by what kind of blood you had. Seriously. The TV announcers had started giving a player's blood type right along with his batting average. Type A was supposed to make good hitters, according to one theory. Type B, good pitchers and so forth. The coaches on the Giants took that theory seriously. They'd check a young boy's blood type out and had all of the Lions "typed."

"So-and-so is stubborn," they'll tell you. "He's Type O, and so forth."

I was asked for my blood type repeatedly. I couldn't count the number of times someone on the team or some Japanese reporter wanted to know that prior to the Series. But I always refused to tell them. I'd always say I didn't know. I didn't want to get into that at all.

In addition to all this, there was a great deal of astrology and fortune telling going on. Before the opening game, one astrologist did Oh's chart for a newspaper. She said that his moons were all in good order and that this meant good luck for him.

In another paper, however, a famous handwriting analyst—a man who made predictions based on the way people signed their names—did a study of a recent Oh autograph. Oh had written the word *doryoku*, meaning effort, signing his name alongside, and the analysis determined from this that our manager's personality was too split for his team to succeed. Oh's outside, said this man, was soft and gentle. But inside, he was hard, turbulent, and violent. This inner aspect, he concluded, made it impossible for Oh to communicate properly with his players.

I wondered if maybe that was why Yamauchi had stuffed so much salt into his back pockets.

REPORT CARD

After I returned to Miami, Yamakura was named the Central League MVP. He'd hit .273 with 22 homers and 66 RBIs, many of them game-winning hits. He barely beat out Katori in the voting. Kuwata won the Sawamura award, named after a former Giant pitching great named Eiji Sawamura who was killed in the war, for best pitcher. He finished with a 15–6 record and led the league in ERA with 2.17.

Rich Lancelotti hit 39 homers to win the home run title, while batting .218. Bass hit 37 with a .325 average. Ochiai hit .331, third in the league behind Shinozuka and Shoda, with 28 homers and 85 RBIs. Warren Cromartie finished with .304,

28 home runs and 92 RBIs, while his teammate Hara compiled a record of .307, 34 homers, and 95 RBIs. And how did I
like that?

Bob Horner, finished with .327, 31 homers and 72 RBIs,
then turned down a ten-million-dollar three-year offer from
the Swallows to go back to the big leagues.

Suguru Egawa made good his threat to retire, pleading a
sore arm, and thereby infuriating Shoriki and Oh, which was
no doubt part of his intention. Egawa was only 32. His record
had been a respectable 13–5, with 3.51 ERA, giving him a lifetime 135–72 mark. He could have pitched for a few more
years if he'd wanted to, even though his best days were behind
him. But Egawa was tired. He was going to be a commentator,
write a book, and probably make a lot more money than he
ever made as a player. He'd had enough of the Giants.

Also during my absence, the Giants and the Tigers played
an exhibition game on November 23, to commemorate newly
constructed Nishikyogoku Stadium in Kyoto. The temperature
was about 40 degrees. The place was packed. Standing room
only.

I know this because some Giant fan sent me a tape of the
telecast of the game. I wasn't sure why he had done that.
Maybe he thought that I missed playing baseball in Japan.
Maybe he thought I should have been there.

A commentator on the telecast remarked that the mood on
the Giants seemed lackadaisical. He wondered what effect that
might have on the 1988 season.

Some things never changed.

Another fan sent me the following translation of a "scout-
ing report" on me which had appeared in the *Sports Nippon*
daily on December 1. It was part of a preseason assessment of
our team. Pre-1988, that is.

This is how it went.

> GENERAL: Dependable on the one hand. Disappoint-
> ing on the other. Gets big key hits, but makes silly mistakes.
> Sloughs off in pregame practice and upsets the balance of
> the team. A former major leaguer whose days of first class
> play are behind him. This will be his last season.

BATTING: Swings from a crouching form. A low-ball hitter. Only swings at pitches he likes. Has a hard time with change-up low-ball pitchers like Obana of Yakult. Hits to the alleys when he's in good form. Grounds to second a lot when he's not. Nickname at those times, "Ground Ball Cromartie." Almost never hits down the lines.

DEFENSE: Coach Kunimatsu says Cromartie gets a bad jump on the ball, but he still manages to haul in those balls that go over his head. Weakness is tendency to make arching throws back to the infield, giving baserunner an advantage. Got burned in the Japan Series doing that. Maybe he's learned his lesson. Needs work on defensive positioning among other things.

RECORDS: Four consecutive years of batting .300 or more give him high rating, but home run total dropped. 1987 was his first year under 30 homers. RBIs dropped to 92. Inadequacies including defense remain.

I was a bum again.
But I was used to it.

1988

The Long Hard Reception

I sat there in the banquet hall with 300 other people and listened to the speaker drone on. "It's the destiny of the Giants to win," said the man on the podium, a major stockholder in Yomiuri, expounding on the glory of our team. I stifled a yawn and wondered if the speeches would ever end.

It was the custom in the Yomiuri organization to hold a reception like this every year, right before Opening Day. Nobody wanted to go. None of the players, that is. It was boring beyond belief. Yet, there we were, all present and accounted for, along with nearly everyone else connected with the organization, trying to look as attentive as possible.

The players were wearing their requisite dark team business suits, which I absolutely despised. It made everybody on the team look alike, which I guess was the idea—a squadron of dark-suited robots. After I wore mine the first time, back in 1984, I swore I would never wear it again. And I didn't. I even refused to wear the tie. People in the front office sucked air through their teeth. But I wouldn't give in, and finally they did.

However, they drew the line on my name tag. So I reported to the reception in my light gray, double-breasted custom-made threads, with my little name tag pinned to my lapel. "Warren Cromartie," it said in English, and, lest there be any mistake, the *katakana* equivalent was ink-brushed in below:

ウォーレン・クロマティ

I felt like a member of the Mickey Mouse club. If there was anybody in the room who didn't know who I was, he would have to have been deaf, dumb, and blind. Christ, I was the only black in the whole damned hotel. But there I was with my little tag that said "Warren Cromartie."

This year's affair was held in the New Otani Hotel, in central Tokyo. A hundred tables filled the room, and a brilliant red carpet covered the floor. On the podium, in front of a huge hand-woven silk screen, sat several stiff-necked dignitaries, each waiting his turn to speak. There were so many dark suits in the place—with white shirts, dark ties, and black shoes—that you'd have thought somebody died.

I glanced across the tables at my new American teammate, Bill Gullickson. The tablecloth was so white you needed sunglasses to dull the glare. Tanuma and Hirano were providing us with the running translations, and Gullickson couldn't believe what he was hearing.

On the dais, the speaker, an older man with thick glasses, was going on about how the Japanese had to be consistently better than the *gaijin*. Gullickson almost choked on the water he was drinking. I simply chuckled. There had been a time when it shocked me too.

Then it was Mutai's turn. Mutai was the honorary chairman of the Yomiuri Shimbun Company. He was the real power in the company and had been for years. He was about 90 years old, a contemporary of Yomiuri founder Matsutaro Shoriki, and, it was said, he had the power to fire Shoriki's son Toru, if he so wished. And he so wished, according to rumors—or he had until the Giants finally won a pennant.

Mutai stood there shuffling through his papers, arranging his speech. He cleared his throat for what seemed like half an hour before he began to speak. Everyone was being extra respectful. It was so quiet you could hear a one-yen coin drop.

Mutai talked for about forty minutes. He spoke about what it meant to be a Giant, about Babe Ruth's visit to Japan in 1934, and other important subiects. He exhorted the team not to rely on foreigners, as he had at every other team reception I'd attended, and he went on and on and on. I recalled the time he'd forgotten to put his false teeth in. He interrupted his speech, pulled his teeth out out of his pocket, and put them in, calm as you please.

After Mutai, Toru Shoriki got up to for his filibuster. By this time, half the team was nodding off. I glanced over at Gully. His eyelids looked like pretty heavy too, but, out of politeness, he was straining to stay awake—which was not easy because Toru rattled on for half an hour.

I was fortunate in getting Gullickson for a teammate. I didn't get along well with Sanchez, and I wasn't able to call Reggie Smith a true friend. But Gully was a buddy. We had played together on the Expos for several years, and I'd never had any trouble with him. Of course, when a guy is 6'4" and weighs 220 pounds, like Gully, well, then you tried your best not to have any trouble with him. Still, I genuinely liked and respected him. He was a generous person who gave time and money to charities. Not many people knew it, but he'd overcome diabetes on his way to becoming a success in the big leagues.

The year before he had played for the Cincinnati Reds and the New York Yankees, winning 14 games. He was only 30, and he had several more good years left in the States—if he wanted. But the Yomiuri Giants had offered him big money: two years at a million and a half per. He was a smart pitcher who also had a hell of a fastball when he was in top form. I figured he would terrorize them in Japan, once he recovered from the shock of being here, that is.

It made me laugh, watching his reactions when he reported for camp. I had gone to visit him at the legendary Miyazaki Grand. He was sitting on the bed in his little room, staring at a Japanese soap opera on TV. A young woman was screaming, her skirt was up around her neck, and she was getting raped.

He stood up to hug me, bumping into his suitcases, which were too big to fit into the closet.

"Jesus, Cro, " he said, "I feel like I've killed somebody and been sent to jail."

"At hard labor," I added, only partly in jest.

We stood by the window in his room and talked about the good old days. Outside was the same mountain I'd stared at for years. But we both couldn't look out the window at the same time because it was so tiny.

Gully shook his head and said, "Cro, what the fuck are we doing here?" Words I'd heard before.

Over the past winter, I'd told him on the phone a little about what he could expect. Now, I added detail. I told him about the dawn-to-dusk routine at camp and other fun things he would run into. I told him about how the umpires would squeeze him because of who he was, how they would test him to see if he'd get mad. I told him how the opposing players would try to embarrass him and how, if he faltered, the Giants' coaches would be all over him, trying to change his form. I told him about all the crazy things he'd see: all the bunting, all the running in the summer—especially the pitchers—all the crazy fans.

"There's a lot of things I can't even tell you," I said, "because there's nothing like good old-fashioned experience. You're going to have to go through it, man."

Gully was turning pale. He sat down on the bed and stared at his suitcases—still unopened. He was in a daze.

I must admit I was enjoying myself, getting a little sadistic pleasure out of spooking him. What the hell, Reggie had done the same to me. Then I slapped him on the shoulder.

"Buck up, Gully," I said. "Every time you start feeling down, just think of all the money you're going to make."

I also urged him to keep his composure, no matter what. That was for the sake of the Japanese, because if Bill Gullickson ever lost his temper, somebody was in for a lot of trouble.

TOKYO DOME

The star of the 1988 season was the Tokyo Dome, the new home of the Giants, and it was top of the line. It showed you what the Japanese could do now that they were rich and whipping our ass in trade. It was too bad the level of the baseball played in it wouldn't match.

The Dome was supposed to seat 56,000, which meant the Giants would be making a fortune; they charged outrageous prices for tickets—¥5,000, about $40, for choice infield seats —and, of course, all the reserved seats for the entire year had alrcady been sold out long before Opening Day. There were only two ways to get a ticket: one was to buy from the scalpers outside the Dome—they were easy to identify because they always stood in front of signs warning you to stay away from them; the other was to bring your sleeping bag twenty-four hours before game time and camp out by the bleacher ticket gate.

The most painful thing about the Dome for the fans, as well as the players, was the new no-smoking rule, because everyone in Japan is a chain smoker. The Dome was the first stadium in the country to have that rule, and if the fans wanted to light up, they had to go to one of the designated smoking corners near the back stairwell by the concessions. It was hilarious to see what happened during the course of the game. Whenever we'd get down to the bottom of our batting order, half the stands would get up en masse and head off to have a nicotine fix.

The Dome's official nickname was the "Big Egg." "Egg" was the acronym for Entertainment Golden Game. It sounded to me like Big Cojones, Big Balls.

THE RISE OF GULLY

Gullickson made it through camp with his sanity intact. He'd tried hard to adjust, and when the season started he was hot. He won his first four games, and he was just blowing it by them. We were in contention, and Oh was tickled pink. He predicted Gully would win 25 games.

The Japanese were overwhelmed by Gully's size. The guys were constantly looking at his body, feeling his arms and his muscles. They'd rarely seen a baseball player that hefty.

The Japanese press could not find enough good things to say about him. In one game versus the Carp, Gully stopped a line drive back to the mound with his shoe. The ball bounced up into the air, he grabbed it and made a jump throw to first to get the runner. "Great Fielding!" blared a headline the next day. "Gully Stops Ball with Leg. A Real Pro!"

Gully was really taken with Japan. He thought the people polite and kind beyond belief. He was fascinated by Japanese electronics and the whole high-tech aura of Tokyo, especially the laser displays in the Sony Building and the huge HDTV screens all over town. He kept a diary and carried a video camera to record his experiences: a walk in Ginza at night, ablaze with its hundreds of neon signs; his first trip on the bullet train; and joining Oh, me, and the rest of the team in a communal hot spring bath, sitting there with only our heads above the water.

By the end of April, he had gotten used to the Giants' routine. That was when I convinced him that it wasn't necessary to attend every single team meeting, because they kept repeating the same thing. One day, I talked Gully into skipping a pre-practice lecture. I had gotten a video, Led Zeppelin Live from Madison Square Garden, so we went into one of the rooms in the Dome that had a VCR and enjoyed ourselves, while our teammates were down the hall, studying baseball videos. I felt proud about corrupting him. He'd been getting too serious about Japan.

Gully was amazed at the way our teammates ate before a game. And so, still, was I, even though I'd been watching them stuff themselves for years. We had a cafeteria there in the new clubhouse, a buffet where you could dig in and take whatever you wanted. And they'd take it all, at a tremendous pace: noodles, rice, chicken, pork, tomatoes. There was pudding in the refrigerator. Fresh fruit in big boxes. You name it. Fans were forever presenting them with things to eat—mandarin oranges from the Izu peninsula, sweet cakes from the island of Shikoku—so mass quantities of food were always available.

This was 4:30 I'm talking about, an hour and a half before game time. It was spread time. Wagon train. Head 'em up. Stuff it in. Move 'em out. I think they had longer windpipes or bigger stomachs or something, but it was awesome what they ate. After that, they'd all light up. All of them. They'd sit there in a cloud of cigarette smoke.

And then it was time to play ball.

Gully took a liking to Kuwata, who'd been struggling again in the early going. Kuwata was pressing, trying to throw the ball by everyone instead of pitching to a batter's weaknesses. His fastball wasn't quite what it had been the year before, and he was getting knocked all over the place. Minagawa and the other coaches were punishing Kuwata with extra practice, and the sportswriters were making a big deal out of the fact that Kuwata had moved out of the team dormitory into an apartment in Kawasaki—which he was sharing with his sister. He was only 20 years old, sighed a reporter, and out on his own. Kuwata was also investing in some land. But since having outside interests was regarded as a sign of insincerity on the part of a baseball player, he was criticized even more by the press.

Gully tried to help Kuwata solve his pitching difficulties and the two worked together on strategy—how to set up hitters and so forth. In the process, they became great friends. When Gullickson's wife gave birth to a son later in the season, Gully gave him the middle name Kuwata.

GEDDY AND PHIL

Music was something I had always wanted to do, which was why I was about to cut a record, with my own band, with me on drums. As a kid, I was always beating on boxes and garbage cans. My cousin and I used to make drumsticks out of old pieces of wood and pretend we were the Beatles. I thought I could have developed into a musician if I'd had a pair of drums when I was young. But my family never could afford it. So I went to the local park and took up baseball instead.

Music remained a big interest, however, and when I went into professional baseball and started making money, I was able to buy my first set of snare drums. That was in 1978. And from then on, I was a dedicated drummer. During the winter, I'd practice six, seven, eight hours a day. In Japan, during the season, I'd practice at my Hiroo apartment, and also on the road in my hotel room, using sticks and a towel on the bed.

The drumming fool, that was me.

Even during games, I'd think about music. There was so much dead time during the average Japanese baseball contest—they were always changing pitchers or consulting with the coaches or otherwise delaying the game—that I'd be standing out in center field, humming to myself, playing a set of imaginary drums in my head. Keeping the beat with the nonstop trumpeting of the cheering section.

Through baseball, I'd been able to meet some heavyweights in the music business. Phil Collins was a baseball fan and we met in Montreal. I'd gone to his show, an outside concert near Jerry Park, and I went backstage to see him afterwards. We talked a bit. I gave him an Expos' jersey, and we hit it off right away. He was a real sweetheart of a cat. We got together several times after that. He listened to me play the drums, and he thought I had ability.

I also met Geddy Lee of the band Rush, which was based in Toronto, and we became really close friends. Geddy was a stone Expos' fan and also one of the best rock bassists in the world. When Geddy first heard me play, he told me that I had "good meter." It was the ultimate compliment. He and Phil Collins. It beat being named MVP any day.

Geddy became my teacher from then on. We talked often on the phone, even when I was in Japan. In the winter of 1987, I began putting together a group: five guys plus myself on the drums. I called the group Climb.

Geddy helped me through the various phases of getting set up. When I wanted to learn something, I'd ask him. If I wanted a professional opinion on our work, I'd play it for Geddy before anyone else, to get his stamp of approval. I was fortunate to have somebody like him to help me. He was very shrewd about the music industry. It was a very swiny business in many ways, and he helped me stay clear of that side of it.

The one thing he told me was to try to keep everything in perspective, to expect to be turned down when I sent my demos to a record company, and when that happened, to go out and bust some more. I knew what he was talking about. I'd been in the minor leagues before.

I built my own studio in Florida, which cost about $110,000, and it was there that Climb recorded its first demo tape. We made five or six good demos and sent them to the record companies in Japan. One of them, Toshiba-EMI, offered us a recording contract in the spring. Climb recorded nine songs later in the year, with some of the songwriting done by me. The album would be released in the fall, and a tour was also in the works.

COFFEE CUP, ANYONE?

In April, I announced my retirement—yet again. My two-year contract would be up at the end of the year, and enough was enough. I had my music to look forward to, and I thought five years of playing baseball in Japan was as much as you could ask from any man. That was medal-winning service—above and beyond the call of duty.

Despite the fact that I usually led the team in most categories of batting, I began to think that I would finish my career in Japan without ever having a commercial—which was a sign of having made it on a mass level. My teammates continued to flood the air waves with endorsements of a wide variety. Young Yoshimura, who'd hit .322 with 30 homers in 1987, was plugging three products. His face was all over the subway posters, whereas I, the real spark plug of the team, one of the most famous *gaijin* in Japan and not bad looking to boot, could not get a second glance from the sponsors.

What was the problem?

Maybe I wasn't modest enough.

Maybe that was the problem.

Within Yomiuri, it was just as bad. The Giants had put Hara on the cover of the guidebook, even though he hadn't played a full season in two years. They'd used Okazaki and Yoshimura on the printed schedules. When were they going to get around to me?

I went to see the man in charge of Giants' PR and asked him about the matter. But he was lukewarm. There was resistance. It wasn't open, exactly, but it was there. I couldn't quite figure out what was going on.

My contract for the 1987 and 1988 seasons supposedly

allowed me to control my own destiny—that is, to do newspaper interviews and negotiate commercials on my own, without the approval of the front office. No one else in Giants' history had ever had a contract like that, except Reggie Smith. But nothing was happening.

Part of the problem, I knew, was that people in the business community were reluctant to deal with me if they thought they didn't have the Giants' wholehearted approval. But also there were business types in Japan who hated working with Yomiuri because the front office gave them such a hard time. The Giants wanted to be able to call every shot, as far as when the player had to show up, when he'd be allowed to leave, and what he would and wouldn't do in front of the cameras. The Giants made sure they had two representatives present when the player was filming the commercials, watching over everything. They'd interfere so much that in the end the commercial became one promoting the Giants, not the product the sponsors were hoping to sell. If a *gaijin* player was involved, that would make it doubly difficult.

A few weeks after I had talked to the Giants' PR man, the traveling secretary handed me some money and said, "Sign here. This is for the coffee cups."

"Huh? What coffee cups?" I said.

It seems that the the Giants were making some coffee cups and other things—T-shirts, baseballs—with my name on them, as well as the names of other players.

Great, this is a start, I thought.

But then he said that the team had been making and selling these things for a "quite a while"—and taking a 20 percent cut too.

"Hold it," I cried. "You've been making these things, all this time, using *my* name and *my* face without *my* permission?"

"We didn't think it was important," he shrugged.

"Not important?!" I sputtered. Jesus.

I told him that I wasn't signing anything until we had a serious conversation about why they had never consulted me about this in the first place. And we did, later—the Giants continuing to peddle their illicit wares in the meantime.

We eventually reached an agreement. But I had been

taught an important lesson: I didn't have the foggiest notion what was going on in the organization I'd spent the last five years with.

Neither, probably, did my teammates. They were no doubt the last to know too. Their lot was to put in ten underpaid years of drudgery and unquestioning obedience, and then maybe wind up running a *yakitori* shop or shuffling papers in some crowded office in the Yomiuri organization. That was their reward for being allowed to play for the Giants—and enjoying the social status that went with it.

It was times like that when I asked myself if those guys were really happy. And then I'd wonder if maybe "being happy" was a purely Western concept. Those guys just did their duty. They put in their time and did what was expected of them. And that was it. They just *did*. If you were Japanese, maybe you weren't necessarily supposed to be happy. Maybe *life* was duty, period. Maybe that was why my teammates didn't normally get excited whether we won or lost or tied. Maybe that was why they approached practices and games with exactly the same frame of mind. They were salarymen.

GULLICKSON'S TRAVAILS

Gully was chosen the Central League Player of the Month for April on the strength of his 4–0 record. Then he got pounded and lost four in a row in May. The opposition had started bunting on him—and it worked. He was so big and hefty that he had a hard time coming down off the mound. Moreover, the batters were getting used to his fastball. They were reading his pitches, and the base runners were beginning to steal off him.

The pitching coaches, who had left him alone until now, started to correct his form. They took him out for special practice several days in a row. They had him doing sprints and laps, as well as working out in the bullpen. In April, when he was winning all those games, they had loved him. They'd be standing next to him when the press was taking his picture, just like Minagawa with Kuwata the previous year. But now, it was as though Gully had a social disease. The big chill had set in.

The newspapers also turned on him. In a game versus the Carp, Gully had tried to spear a line drive over his head bare-handed and wound up sprawled on the mound instead. A columnist for the *Nikkan Sports* moved in to attack: "Gullickson should have been fined, because if he had injured himself, the team as a whole would have suffered... Why did he even try to catch the ball with his right hand? The reason is simple. Because his fielding is poor." It was quite a turnaround. In less than two months. Gully had gone from a great fielder to a poor one.

Gully wasn't the only thing wrong with the team. We fell into a horrible slump in May and dropped six games out of first. We'd lost seven one-run games and were 5–8 at the Tokyo Dome. We were looking like a very small team in that big major-league–sized park.

Oh was starting to lose it again too—acting fidgety in the dugout, calling "emergency" practices, ordering special bunting drills—in general, succumbing to the pressure that was always there on the Giants.

We beat the Carp one night in Hiroshima, 5–4, for example, but Oh got bent out of shape anyway because we had let them score twice in the bottom of the ninth. "Why in hell did you let them do something like that!" he screamed at us.

It was panic time, and it was only May.

There were 100 games to go, but the guys were already beat, especially the pitchers. They were in the training room every day, getting massages on their arms. The trainer was always sticking needles in their shoulders and elbows. Or doing acupuncture. There were more needles flying around the training room than in a blood bank.

The mood then was as bad as I'd ever seen it on the Giants. The guys were so down that one evening in mid-May, a coach asked me to talk to the players. So I called a meeting in Nagoya, behind closed doors, with only players present, and gave a little speech, which Hirano translated.

"We all know that Oh is so tense he's not showing any leadership," I said, "and we don't understand the coaches either. None of us do. But let's forget them and go out and play the best game we can. Let's try to score a lot of runs because then the coaches won't have to make any decisions. That will make it easier on them—and easier on all of us."

We lost anyway. So much for me as team leader. But at least *I* started hitting. I wound up with nine hits in nine straight at-bats. It seemed the only one I'd inspired, with my little speech, was me.

The next day, a famous singer named Hibari Misora came to watch us practice in Giants' land. The photographers went berserk. Flashes were popping all over the place. She was one of the most famous postwar singers in Japan. She had been a child star, Japan's Shirley Temple. Now they called her the Queen of Song. People adored her.

It was a rain-soaked day. She arrived in a chauffeur-driven Cedric, wearing a mink stole over her kimono, and sat in a chair in front of the batting cage, under an umbrella. She was a Giants' fan. She knew the team was in trouble, and she had come to encourage us, to shake us out of our slump with her superstar presence. Oh went over to talk to her, and the cameras went even more berserk. It was like a visit from the Imperial Family.

The next night we beat the Whales 10–7, and the sports papers were saying it was all because of Hibari. But then we lost the day after that. Gully got pounded again, and you could hear the boos. Oh got so mad, he even pulled Yamakura out of the game in the eighth inning for calling the wrong pitches and gave him a ten-minute lecture behind closed doors afterwards.

ON THE ROAD AGAIN

YAAAHHHH!! Slash! Splat! AAAARRRRGGGGHHHH!

The Yomiuri team bus rolled down the inland Kyushu highway, curtains drawn, lights dimmed, its occupants totally absorbed by the *samurai* movie being shown.

AAAAAAHHHHH! Slash! Splat!

A *samurai* with two swords was lopping off arms and heads left and right, splattering blood everywhere. He was up against about fifteen guys, but it seemed to be an even match.

Slash! Swish. Whoosh. Slash. A bad guy's back was laid open. Slash, swish, whoosh. Someone's jugular was severed, sending a thick stream of blood shooting into the air. I couldn't tell exactly how many had been killed thus far from my seat near the back. The haze of cigarette smoke was obstructing my view.

Slash, Splat! AAAARRRRGGGGHHHHH!

It was late May, and we were on our way from Fukuoka to Kumamoto, the second leg of our anual three-game Kyushu series. The ride normally took two-and-a-half hours, and our team passed the time by watching movies. Team officials had stuck a screen up there at the front of the bus, drawn the curtains on the windows, and put a flick on.

We made these trips in two different buses. Bus no. 1 was headed by Oh, who liked the volume turned way up. Bus no. 2 was headed by Nakahata, our team captain, who liked the volume slightly less loud. Oh and Nakahata got to chose the films. Oh liked *yakuza* gangster movies. Nakahata liked *samurai* movies. Both liked flicks with a lot of violence, people getting stabbed and sliced to bits, women, preferably nuns, with their clothes being ripped off, and lots of screaming and yelling. The more blood and guts, the better.

Every year it was the same. They chose the same sort of movies, and I had to sit there and watch. No choice. I'd watch a movie in a language I couldn't understand while choking on the smoke that filled the bus. You weren't supposed to open the window because that interfered with the sound of the movies. The bus didn't stop either, because that would be against the rules too. You couldn't get out and stretch your legs or breathe some fresh air or take a leak. Team rules didn't allow it.

Slash! Splat!

Gully couldn't take his eyes off the screen. Me, I tried to ignore it. I think I'd already seen this one. So I sat and pulled back the curtain to peer out at the countryside rolling by. Raindrops slapped against the window, the sky was a melancholy gray. We were in the lowlands of rural Kyushu—green rice paddies, red *torii*, and mist-covered mountains in the distance.

It was a scene of rustic beauty, interrupted only by power lines everywhere and blood-curdling screams coming from inside the bus.

We passed a farmer working in his field, an older guy. He noticed me looking out the window and he took off his cap and waved. A Giants' fan, no doubt. I wondered if he liked *samurai* movies too.

YAAAAHHH! YEEEEEHAAAHHH! AAAAAARRRRGGGGH-HH!

Our Kyushu trip south was followed shortly by our annual visit to northern Honshu. That included a three-hour train ride to Sendai followed by a two-hour bus trip to Toyama for our first game, a ride back to Sendai for game two, then a two-hour bus ride to Morioka for the third and final game. When that was finished we'd return to Sendai to take a plane to Osaka.

On all those bus rides, the movies were on. One of Nakahata's choices was *Rambo II*, the one set in Vietnam. The film had come out about three years earlier, and since then I would guess I had seen it at least ten times, maybe twelve, each time on the Giants' bus and each time dubbed in Japanese. Now I was trapped again. I was getting pretty good at reading Sylvester Stallone's lips. I knew all the lines by heart, just from lipreading. I even translated for Gully. I wondered if my new talent could make me useful to the CIA. Maybe I could even become a reporter for a Japanese scandal magazine.

On the trains, there were no movies, so my teammates read comic books instead. *Manga* comic books for adults—which have lots of sex and violence in them—are a huge business in Japan, and the members of the Giants are among their most avid readers. They'd be sitting in first class, wearing suits and ties as required by the Giants' dress code, speeding across the countryside at 95 miles per hour with their noses buried in these comic books. They were the idols of the entire nation, heroes of every school kid in the land, the love fantasy of every young woman, the topic of nightly conversations in bars all over the country. And they read comics.

It really irritated Oh. "They are supposed to be professional players," he told me once, "yet they go on the bullet train, sit in reserved seats, and they read *manga.*That's not professional at all."

If you asked any of them what was happening in the world—who was the prime minister of England, what was the difference between the PLO and the PGA—they wouldn't have been able to tell you. Their sphere of interest did not extend that far. Real life for them was that night's game and their favorite comics. And their Louis Vuitton travel bags in the overhead rack. They lived in a kind of fantasy land. It was understandable when you consider that most of them had never studied in high school. They had gone to school to play baseball; in fact, "baseball factories" is what their institutions of learning were called. These schools were like some big-time colleges in the States in the sense that all the athletes did was play sports.

About the only guy on the team who'd actually studied was Kuwata. At one time, he had wanted to go to college and major in English, before he decided to turn pro. On the train he would read an English textbook. He would come over and ask me the correct way to say certain phrases like "I'm going to the ballpark" or "I'm going back to my home." I got the feeling the other players were a bit jealous of him.

TATSU & CO.

I liked all the guys pretty much by this time, and they had all accepted me—aside from a guy named Hide kato, who had joined the team in 1986, coming over from the other league. His locker was next to mine, and I didn't get along with him at all. He had a bad attitude, and he was a selfish player. He had been a big star for the Hankyu Braves for a long time, and it seemed he really didn't care for being on the Giants—hard as that may be to believe.

Perhaps it was because he was only a part-time player when he came on the club, but he was really bad news. He wouldn't congratulate people if they did well, and one time, when we'd had a scuffle with the opposing team, he was the only one who stayed in the dugout. One day I lost my temper with him. In my broken Japanese, I told him to shape up. We didn't come to blows or anything, but I made my point clear. At the end of the year, the Giants shipped him back to the Pacific League, which was where he belonged.

But besides Kato, they were a good group of guys, all pretty friendly.

Hara remained the golden boy of our team because of his wholesome good looks and the fact he was Nagashima's successor. But as a ball player, he was only so-so, in my opinion. He might have hit .300 and 30 homers every year, but he didn't hit well in the clutch, and statistically we played better without him. The worst thing about Hara was that the press loved him. He was always in the news, no matter what he did, and he took all the attention away from the other players. It hurt the team to have the limelight constantly focused on one man.

The guys were jealous—that was clear. They read the sports dailies every day, religiously. You'd walk into the clubhouse, and they'd all be sitting there reading the sports newspapers—and Tatsu's picture was usually there, a hell of a lot more often than theirs were. Nakahata didn't like it. Neither did Shinozuka. And it bothered me too, to tell the truth. If Hara and I both hit home runs in a game, it was always Hara's that got the headlines, not mine. I was as jealous as the next guy.

Hara was a real piece of work. I'd still catch him primping for the photographers. In 1986 he'd hurt his right wrist, and it was all taped up. I spotted him in the clubhouse, brushing his hair in the mirror with his left hand, patting it carefully into place. It was still early. There was nobody on the field, and Hara wasn't even playing. But he knew all the cameras would be there, and so out he went.

I followed him just to watch. Hara stood in the front row of the dugout and posed as the photographers zeroed in, like a movie star or something.

"Tatsu," I jibed, "what is this? A screen test?"

It didn't faze him at all. He just nodded as if to say, "Well, who wouldn't want to take my picture."

The women were crazy about him. The Giants realized this,

so they built him up accordingly. Up until Hara announced his engagement the previous year to a girl he'd known in high school, he could have had his pick of any woman in Japan. One time he brought an album into the clubhouse with him. It was filled with photos of young ladies, along with their personal histories. They had sent them to Hara in the mail, presenting themselves as prospective marriage candidates, and Hara had them all in this album. Japanese mail-order brides.

Not that Hara's marriage stopped him from fooling around. He had his mistresses, but he had lousy technique. I mean the scandal magazines kept finding out about his love life. Every now and then he'd be photographed coming out of some girl's apartment. And that would be a big topic of conversation for a while.

Hara was the type of guy who avoided fights. Perhaps he was worried about his looks, or perhaps he was worried about his hand, which he had broken twice. Or perhaps it was just his nature. They say his father, a famous high school and college baseball coach, used to whack Hara Jr. around a lot, which, they also say, accounted for his passive, submissive attitude. To be fair, he also took his image as the Giants' shining star seriously. He didn't think it was right to be seen punching an opposing player in the teeth.

But whatever the reasons, when I was watching the video replay of our brawl with the Dragons to see who on our team had participated, Hara was not one of them. He was running back and forth on the fringes of the melee. So I needled Hara about it on the bus that night, like we used to do on the Expos. We'd call the guys who wouldn't get in there and fight pussies.

"Hara," I said, "Why you running?...*Doshite?*"

I began imitating the way he had been running around as if to say, "Don't hit me, don't hit me."

Hara thought I was trying to be funny. But I wasn't exactly joking. A couple of young boys, Mimura and Yamazaki, had gone flying through the crowd to help me. Yoshimura too. But Hara was just making sure he didn't get hurt.

This is not to say that Hara was a coward. Years later, in an another Dragons-Giants set-to, he grabbed onto Hoshino to stop him from punching one of our players. That took some guts, I guess. But all things considered, Tatsu would rather be a peace negotiator.

In the first two months of the 1988 season, Hara wasn't hitting the ball at all. He was down around .225 with only 3 homers. Yamauchi, our batting coach, had been working with him in extra practice and, as usual, the focus was on technique and form, not reflexes, with Hara watching videos of how he'd swung the year before when he was hitting well. In my humble opinion, all of that just psyched Hara out. He'd become so concerned with his form that he just forgot how to hit the ball.

So during one game, I stopped him before he went up to bat.

"Tatsu," I said, "forget your form. If you're going to make an out, at least do it swinging the bat hard. Just go up there and swing like hell. Swing the fucking bat."

I didn't use an interpreter, but Hara got the message. He stepped up to the plate and hit a three-run homer that won the game for us.

The next day, he called me "*sensei*," a term of respect that means teacher or master, all day. I got a big charge out of that.

If Hara had lifted weights, he would have hit a lot more home runs. He could have gotten more "oomph" on the ball. Nakahata and Shinozuka too. With his shirt off, Shinozuka looked like a junior high school student. A number of American stars like Steve Garvey, Joe Morgan, Davey Lopes, and Ron Cey were smaller than Hara, but they built themselves up with weights. Unfortunately, the coaches in Japan didn't like weights, because they thought it tightened you up. Their tendency was to say, "We're small—it can't be helped." But with the new Nautilus machines, you could build strength on the forearms, wrists, biceps, triceps, and so forth, without affecting the flexibility ballplayers need in the chest and neck.

The Japanese were strong in the legs because they did a lot of running—you didn't see a lot of pulled muscles in Japan—but they simply didn't have the upper body strength. And that was the pity. Good weight training can also keep a player around longer because it not only builds strength, it helps decrease injuries as well. My high school coach was a fanatic about it.

The Japanese coaches were just too leery of anything new, however. Their attitude toward the players was, "Do what we did—stick to the old ways."

The player I liked and admired most was our captain Naka-hata. He held things together on the team with his attitude, even when he wasn't playing well himself. I remembered the horrible year he had in 1986. His batting average was down in the low .200s—about a hundred points below where it normal-ly is—and he wasn't hitting home runs either. He was usually good for 20 or 30. He'd had good reason to get mad at him-self and lose his temper. But he never did, even during one stretch when he sunk to about .160. He always found time to encourage the others on the team, to pat them on the back. He always kept his poise, even in private.

Nakahata was a showman, like me. He'd mug for the cam-eras. He'd goof around on the field, which was unusual for a Japanese. But he never lost his cool, and he had guts. He played every day, hard, whether he was up or down or sore or not. He kept the same intensity all during the course of the season—from spring training on until the last makeup game in October—no matter what the standings, or the score. He was special, and I tip my cap to him.

It was ironic that although Nakahata probably disliked Oh more than any of the Giants' players, he also tried the hardest under Oh.

Shinozuka was much less intense. He was a sure .300 hitter, a good fielder, and a nice, mild-mannered, quiet type of guy. But he also had a lot of mysterious injuries. We called him "Shammyzuka." "Shammy" was a word we used for a ballplayer who pretended to be hurt, but really wasn't. In the U.S., we called a guy like that a pussy, a wimp—a "wusp." "He's wusping out today," we'd say. But Japanese players said "shammy." It came from the term *shamisen*, an ancient Japanese musical instrument that looks like a banjo and sounds even worse. So if a player took himself out of the lineup, the guys would say,

"He's playing the *shamisen*." It meant he was lazy, he didn't want to play. He'd shammied out.

We called Shinozuka the no. 1 shammy, because he missed so many games over the years. If he didn't want to face a particular pitcher, Shino would come up with a sudden back injury, and Oh would have to take him out of the lineup.

Yamakura was another shammy, but he had a good excuse. He caught pregame practice in the bullpen, he caught the games themselves, and he caught during off-day drills. Yamakura, understandably, looked hard for reasons to sit down, and when he did play, he was somewhat lazy. He also didn't call his pitches very intelligently. He was probably too tired to think.

The top five shammies in my years on the Giants were Shamizuka, Shammykura, Shammygawa (since retired), Shammyhara, and Shammymartie. I said Shammymartie because, if the truth be known, I, too, sloughed off on occasion. There were day games after a night game when I had nothing. I just went through the motions. But you try playing baseball every day for nine months, and you would be a shammy too.

Shammy wasn't the only nickname on the Giants. Kato, our fifth starter, had a poker face which somewhat resembled Frankenstein. "Mr. Frankie," the guys called him. And Komada, our big, 6'4", raw-boned outfielder, was nicknamed "Horse," because the guys thought he had a horse's face. In fact, when he came to bat, the cheerleaders in right field would even start imitating jockeys, yelling out "*uma, uma*" —Japanese for horse.

But you had to be careful about things like that in Japan. The Japanese didn't like needling very much. They didn't get on each other anywhere near the way we did in the States. So I had to watch what I said.

I took a special liking to Junki Kono, one of our shortstops. Junki spoke some English, and he was the only Japanese player I knew of who chewed tobacco. Everyone else thought it was a filthy habit. So Junki would sit on the bench and chew, but he wouldn't spit. Not even into a cup. I think he swallowed the stuff.

Junki didn't say much. He was Korean, born in Japan, but

wasn't like Nishimoto at all. Perhaps it was because he was just a part-time player, but he didn't say shit and the guys left him alone. Junki was cool. I admired him because although he was in a place where they got down on Koreans like him real fast, he never made a fuss. When he got hot, they barely gave him credit. Then when he cooled off, they'd knock him around. They'd take him out, and they'd make him work extra hard. Once Junki dropped a pop fly that cost us a game. The next day he was shipped to the farm for two weeks. He took it all without a word.

Another guy I really took to on the team was Nimura, a reserve outfielder who'd been with us the year before. Nimura was the only guy on the team who had a mustache—in violation of the Giants' policy against facial hair. But Nimura kept his mustache somehow. How he managed that, I don't know, but it was probably one reason why he sat on the bench all the time.

I always teased him about his mustache. I'd tell him to shave if off almost every day. I'd ask Oh, in front of Nimura, "Oh-*san*, *doshite?* Why you let mustache? He bench-warmer. He pine-rider."

Oh would just laugh. I guess that maybe Oh considered Nimura a good-luck charm, because we'd won the previous year with Nimura on the squad.

It seemed, at times, that the Japanese were trying to be a little more liberal. There were a lot of non-*gaijin* guys who had mustaches on other teams. You could even see an occasional beard—a rare beard, actually. But never on the Giants, and when Nimura was traded to the Dragons in the off-season, I wasn't surprised.

My teammates had always professed a lot of respect for the major leagues, and one day in the clubhouse, I asked Yamakura if he would play there if the opportunity ever presented itself.

"No!" came the resounding reply.

Then I asked the same question to Shinozuka.

"No, thank you," he said, "I don't like."

They told me they had it too good in Japan, so why on

earth would they want to give up their stardom and their stature to play in the U.S.? Besides, they couldn't hack the food, they said. They'd have to eat Cup Noodles all the time.

That made me laugh.

"How do you think *gaijin* feel here?" I asked.

Yamakura and Shinozuka looked at each other. They shrugged. You could tell they hadn't given that particular subject a great deal of thought.

THE DRUGLORD

I walked into the hotel coffee shop and squeezed myself into a chair across from one of the interpreters. Ordering my morning cup of *kohi* and *tosuto*, I picked up the sports paper to see a picture of Dick Davis, clad in his polo shirt and slacks, being led from his house in handcuffs. The cuffs were tied to a rope that was knotted around his waist and held at the other end by a grim-looking policeman. But if the cop looked grim, Davis looked absolutely shell-shocked.

He had just been arrested for drug possession, the interpreter explained, showing me another large photo in the paper of Davis's living room where the incriminating evidence had been found, hidden inside a camera case. On the opposite page was a photo of the new commissioner of Japanese baseball, Takeuchi, announcing to reporters that Davis was finished forever as a baseball player in Japan. He looked very angry.

Smoking grass, or even possessing it, was a major crime in Japan. To the Japanese, it was no different than shooting heroin, and the penalities were very stiff. Several years in jail was not inconceivable for what Davis had done.

The police had apparently been tipped off. They showed up at his house with a search warrant, located the hash, put the cuffs on him, and took him downtown, so to speak.

Davis protested he didn't know what he had was marijuana. He told the police that a friend had given it to him as a salve or balm for a bruised heel. But I don't think the cops believed him. I don't think anybody believed him. I know I didn't.

The Japanese press went nuts over Davis's arrest. They were

treating it as The Crime of the Century. It was the top story in all the sports dailies, accompanied by articles about Davis's past "history" of violence and photos of him punching out a pitcher two years before in a brushback-pitch brawl. There were also close-up shots of a stadium refrigerator he had once demolished with his fist and pictures showing him pushing an umpire. The man was evil.

One writer surmised that when the American players got together, they no doubt smoked dope and fornicated with women and did god knows what else. It was common knowledge, he said, that foreigners had lower moral standards than the Japanese.

Suddenly, I became aware that everyone in the room was staring at me, including the reporters who were furiously taking notes. I smiled my brightest smile, then chuckled loudly to myself, like Eddie Murphy, shaking my head as if to say, "What will these crazy *gaijin* do next?"

On my way to the park, a writer asked me if I had ever smoked marijuana. I chuckled again, shaking my head. What a silly question.

I sat out the game that day. My back had stiffened up, and I couldn't swing the bat. So Oh kept me on the bench and we got clobbered 8–2. This, coming on the heels of an 11–2 loss the previous game in which Gully had been kayoed yet again (his ERA was disappearing into the stratosphere), was enough to put me back on the *gaijin* enemies list in some people's eyes.

I had played in forty-five straight games until that day, despite all the traveling, and that was nine innings every time out. But that didn't matter to one evening tabloid. It accused me of sabotage in a big headline, running my picture on the back cover right next to a photo of Dick Davis.

ODDBALL

By mid-June it had become obvious to me that the Giants did not have what was necessary to win again. It was equally obvious to me that the team was going to have to make a change and that Oh was on his way out along with all his coaches.

Oh was severely tarnishing his image by the way he managed. The deeper we got into the season, the more edgy he seemed to be. He was nervous before, and now he was positively neurotic. During the the course of a nine-inning ball game, his face would wear a hundred different expressions. If one of our batters struck out, he'd scowl. If our pitcher gave up a walk, he'd grimace. If we got the lead, he'd smile in ecstasy. If the other team took the lead from us, he'd look like a man on his way to the gallows.

There was no reason why he should have displayed that attitude in front of the team when we'd won the pennant the previous year. But Oh, and everyone else from the V-9 era, was still living in the old days. There was no way the Giants were ever going to win nine Japan titles in a row again. Things were different. There was a draft system. It was impossible.

The players were getting sick of hearing every day about old Shoriki's deathbed wish that the Giants win every game. The pressure was just too much. If a player did one little thing wrong, they'd farm his ass right out, like they did to Junki Kono. They were always sending players down and bringing players up. It was like the Grand Central shuttle. A young pitcher named Saito came in one game, pitched to one batter, and gave up a home run. They yanked him and packed him off to the minors the very next day. That happened to him more than once. He was like a yo-yo, and it got so that he hated to come up to the first team anymore. It was embarrassing, mortifying. He knew that one false move on his part and he'd be history. He vastly preferred the farm team. A lot of guys on the farm team felt the same way. They hated coming up.

Oh simply had no confidence in his younger players. He didn't believe in them. He wanted to win every damn game. But our veterans were getting old. If we wanted to stay in competition, we'd have to bring up some of the young blood they had on the farm—guys like Suguro, Kawai, and Roh, a kid from Taiwan who was hitting homers all over the place. Roh, unfortunately, was classified as a *gaijin*, meaning there was no place for him as long as Gully and I were there.

Oh's managerial moves became harder and harder to fathom. I'd say that nine times out of ten, he didn't make the correct decision—or his coaches didn't. Whatever, we were sinking into oblivion.

BAD MEDICINE

We moved into the Tigers' stadium in Osaka on June 13 for a series that would prove fateful to me. The Tigers were minus Bass, whose eight-year-old son Zachary was diagnosed with a tumor on the back of his neck. It was hard as a rock, water was building up on the brain, and his life was in danger. The doctors in Japan didn't want to operate because it was right on the spinal cord, so Bass took his son back to the U.S. for surgery by a specialist in San Francisco.

Zachary eventually recovered, but Bass's leaving his team was a decision that would lead to his release two months later and ultimately to his being blackballed out of Japanese baseball. In Japan, you weren't supposed to put your family before work. Your wife was supposed to handle such matters.

I don't know whether Bass's absence affected the way the Tigers thought about me—whether they thought they had to shut me down to balance the scales—but their pitchers began throwing at me a lot, high inside, much more than they had done before. In one of the games, a guy threw a pitch at my neck. I raised my hands in self-defense, and the ball hit me on the right thumb.

I saw red—not from anger but from the thunderbolt of pain that struck me. Hot flashes of red and white. I doubled over, gritting my teeth and grimacing in agony. My thumb began to swell immediately.

"The goddamn thing is broke," I cried, to no one in particular.

Oh came dashing out of the dugout along with the trainer. He took a look at my thumb, then, incredibly, he patted me on the back.

"*Gambatte*," he said.

I turned and looked at him.

"*Gambatte?*" I gasped, not sure I heard him right. "*Gambatte?!*"

I was certain my thumb had been broken, and Oh was

telling me to hang in there? Then a wave of nausea hit me, and I needed help getting back to the dugout.

Hirano called a taxi for me, and we went to the hospital. There was Hirano, the trainer, my son Chris who'd come along on this trip, and me, all packed into this tiny cab. I watched in three parts pain and one part fascination as my thumb continued to swell up. By the time we reached the emergency entrance of the hospital, it look as big and as round as the handle of a baseball bat.

X rays showed one fracture, the doctor said. He wrapped it up and told me to forget about playing for a month.

"Well, now Roh gets his chance," I declared to everyone.

I caught the last bullet train back to Tokyo with Chris. I was doped up and feeling no pain, and I jabbered nonstop all the way back, the lights of Kyoto, Nagoya, and the other cities along the old Tokaido line whizzing by.

We pulled into Tokyo station at midnight, and a crowd of reporters were waiting to greet us. What they wanted to know most was what was I going to do to the Tigers' pitcher who'd hit me. Would I bust him in the jaw the next time I saw him, as I'd done to Miyashita of the Dragons in Kumamoto?

But the painkillers had put me in the twilight zone. I was really up there. And suddenly, I was feeling generous.

"Of course not," I said, chuckling. "Everybody knows it was an accident."

I couldn't remember when I'd ever felt so good. I was filled with goodwill, compassion, and love for my fellow man. Why, the next time I met that pitcher, I'd shake his hand and wish him good luck. Hell, I might even invite him to dinner. The poor kid was probably worried sick about what he'd done. Maybe I'd call him tomorrow, just to reassure him. I started giggling as I made my way to the taxi stand.

My thumb wouldn't stop swelling, however. By the next morning, it was a big as a balloon. So I went to my Tokyo doctor, first thing. He took another X ray and found two breaks. He said I couldn't play for at least two months. Two breaks. Two months. Maybe more. Because I also had severe ligament damage.

This was serious business. That was my right thumb, my

drumming thumb, my writing thumb. It was by far my favorite thumb. And I didn't want to take any chances with it.

"Roh's going to get one helluva chance," I told Hirano, "in fact, he might be playing the rest of the year, because I ain't going near a bat until I'm a thousand percent sure this thing has completely healed."

Hirano looked at me, as if he wasn't sure what to say. He was a good man, but he was a Giants' employee after all. His interests were first and foremost seeing me play again. Unfortunately, for him, he was going to have to wait a long time.

I was leery of medical treatment and rehab methods on the Giants. They were not very advanced. Nor were they on other teams either. They all tended to stay with the same old methods. We'd lost Nakahata for a month in mid-1987 when he hit himself in the ankle with his own foul ball. He would have been back a lot earlier if a good orthopedic surgeon had looked at him.

But that didn't happen. The Giant trainers treated Nakahata's injury by punching little holes in the bruise with a needle and then putting a suction cup over it to draw out the blood and relieve the pressure—instead of letting it clot. That was supposed to enable a player to play the next day, but in Nakahata's case, it didn't work.

In the States, they would have immediately gone to ice. But the Giants didn't believe in ice. They were great on massaging. Acupuncture too. But no ice. No whirlpools. And no electric machines.

It was possible that Nakahata had bruised a tendon, or broken ligaments, or even cracked a bone. Maybe there was something seriously wrong. The Giants didn't know, and because they didn't check it out properly, it took a long time to heal.

When I hurt my wrist in the fall of 1985, the first Giants' doctor misdiagnosed me. Then I saw a second doctor who told me I had two hairline fractures. Two front office executives asked me to keep quiet about that first diagnosis. They didn't want the word to come out that their doctor had made a mistake.

In my opinion, the Giants did too much unnecessary damage to their players. I've seen players passed out in the clubhouse, lying on the bathroom floor, done in by the heat and the practice. One coach told me, "Don't worry, so-and-so just drank too much water."

The Giants injured too many pitching arms too. Including Mizuno's. Mizuno had come to the team when he was 18, as an overhand thrower. By 1987, he was throwing from the side, or three-quarters, out of necessity, and there was a big zipper on his shoulder from surgery. In his first year, he had ripped his arm out of joint from lugging the team suitcases around all season. Carrying the team bags is one of the duties rookies must perform on the road. They have to haul the luggage from the bus to the hotel, as well as pick up the balls after practice and run other errands. It's considered part of their "education."

Well, that was one reason why Mizuno wound up needing an operation on his arm. Another reason, of course, was the way the coaches kept making him throw every day in practice. To me, it was a miracle he could still pitch four years later, that he still had anything of a fastball left.

I remember seeing Mizuno throwing on the side even when his arm was hurting him. Oh was out there looking him over, the trainer too, and the pitching coach. His arm was so sore that he couldn't lift it above his shoulder, and yet they had him throwing on the side. Unbelievable.

They overworked a pitcher named Miyamoto, too. He had a bad start one year, so they made him go through a second spring training. A mini-camp. All that boy did was run, run, run, run, run—and pitch, pitch, pitch, pitch, pitch. They'd slap him on the head, for good measure. When he finally came back to the first team, he had a 5-mile-an-hour fastball. So they sent him back down to the farm team.

Because of our medieval training and coaching methods, we had seven guys on the team with zippers on their arms. Frank Jobe, the famous orthopedic surgeon in Los Angeles, had operated on everyone of them. Having your shoulder cut open by Jobe was becoming the thing to do on our team. Jobe should have opened an office in Tokyo and paid the Giant coaching staff a commission.

Roh was an overnight sensation. The boy from Taiwan, who had once batted against Dwight Gooden in the Little League World Series, hit seven homers in his first eleven games. He became the new darling of the media and now the press was, predictably, saying that the Giants didn't need Americans anymore—not old Cromartie (.344, 10 home runs, 36 RBIs), who was broken down and washed up anyway, or Gullickson, who was just another flash in the pan. Hell no. From now on, they could get their foreign players from Taiwan. They pointed out with glee that Taiwanese were more obedient, caused a lot less trouble, and were much, much cheaper. So *sayonara*, Cro and Gully. You get the idea.

It didn't help that Gullickson kept getting bombed. He was more depressed than ever, and nobody was talking to him except me and Kuwata. I didn't think Gully had a dead arm. I thought he was just dead, period, from all the running they were making him do.

I felt truly sorry for him, but I also had problems of my own—my wife and my kids had just left Tokyo. The year before, my family had gone back to the States in early August. This time, it was late June. Next year, they probably wouldn't even come.

Well, I could joke about it but my family was something I had to start seriously considering. I had a three-year-old growing up and a twelve-year-old who was going through a rough period in school, and I spent entirely too much time away from them.

I could have gone back with them, but I had commercials in the works, finally. Two of them. They were aimed at little leaguers, but what the hell. They were still commercials. More important, there was my record album, now in the middle of production, to think about.

Climb's producer and engineer was doing the mixing at a studio named Tara, owned by Toshiba-EMI, in central Tokyo. Now that I couldn't play ball I intended to be there for it. And for the next four weeks, I was—from eleven in the morning until eleven at night. In a way I was glad I'd been hurt. Otherwise, I'd have been standing in center field at the Dome every night, humming my songs to myself, while the guys were in the studio having all the fun.

For the first time in my entire adult life, I was free for the summer. And for the first time in my career in Japan, I had time to look around, to prowl the streets, and to go to different places at different times of the day. Since I didn't have to be at the park, I could walk around during rush hour like all the other Tokyoites. I could go into a bar at six for an end-of-the-day drink, as the salarymen did, and I could eat dinner at a decent hour, like a civilized human being, instead of having to wait until eleven o'clock at night after a game.

I learned a lot of things that summer about Tokyo. I learned to walk in rush-hour crowds at 1/30 musical time —just to keep up.

I learned that Tokyo had more different and interesting places to eat than any city I'd ever been in. I was taken to restaurants that I didn't know existed—places that closed before the games were over. There was German, French, Swiss, Czech, Mexican, Hungarian, and a zillion kinds of Japanese. There were *fugu* blowfish, *robata yaki*, sitting around an open pit where your food was cooked in an open pit, and restaurants where they'd pull a live fish out of the tank, slice it open fin to dorsal, and serve it to you while the fish's tail was still moving.

I felt like a tourist. It was really a high. The rainy season had started, but Tokyo in the rain, especially in the early evening when all the night spots were opening and the neon signs had just been turned on, was one of the most romantic places in the world.

I began to look at Japan in a whole new light. I remembered a talk I'd had with Bill Madlock, the man who replaced Leron Lee on the Lotte Orions. He didn't care for Japan very much at all. He spent all the time he was away from the park in his apartment. He said he had been out twice all year: once to Nick's, and once to a nightclub where they had charged him a thousand dollars for two drinks.

He seemed intimidated by Japan. He'd go straight home

after the game, a cook would make him a steak, then he'd turn his video on and watch movies all night. He usually fell asleep in front of the TV. The fact that he'd been hitting in the .230s all year didn't make it any easier, I'm sure.

It was too bad, but you had to give Japan a chance. It wasn't just another version of the U.S. My friends would visit from the States, and we'd go out to eat at some restaurant, and they'd order a Diet Pepsi. The waiter would say, "*Nani? Dieto nani?*" What? Diet what? He'd never heard of a Diet Pepsi because they didn't sell them in Japan.

You would think that if you fly fifteen thousand miles to get to Tokyo, you might order something Japanese. Anything but a Diet Pepsi. It was like a Japanese going to the States to eat *sushi* or noodles. But my American friends would look at me like I was the one out of my mind because I'd order green tea and also because I'd do it in Japanese.

You had to realize that life wasn't a bowl of fucking cherries. You had to give a little bit to get something out of life. I was one to talk, I know, because I'd complained about life in Japan as much as anyone. But I was learning. I'd picked up some Japanese, and I could walk into just about any place alone now and make myself understood enough to get what I wanted.

At first, I'd rebelled about almost everything Japanese. Even the language, which I refused to study seriously. Now I was happy to have picked up the little I knew. I didn't think I'd be saying this, but I should have learned more.

I was getting to like Japan a lot. It had its problems, but it didn't have a Jerry Falwell begging for $190 million in the name of God. It had as much to offer in its own way as the U.S., and I had begun to understand that. The Japanese had their own way of thinking, and in most respects, it was no worse than ours.

Take the trade thing, which I'd actually begun to do some thinking about. On the one hand, you could understand the Americans' point of view. It seemed like the Japanese could buy and sell anything they wanted in the United States, but the reverse wasn't true. The Japanese owned half of Hawaii. They bombed the son of a bitch, then they bought it. It didn't make any sense. And when the Americans came to Japan to do business, the Japanese made it hard as hell. For years, they had a 100 percent tax on imported cars.

But then you had to look at the situation from the Japanese point of view. The Americans were bitching over the new Osaka Airport. They said their construction companies were shut out of the bidding. But why should Japanese use Americans? They didn't need Americans to work on the damn things. They knew that the Americans were going to bitch and take their sweet old time, arguing, screwing around, and whatever, until they finally wound up actually getting some construction done. That was the American way.

The Japanese would just do it. No hassles. I've seen buildings in Japan go up in a few weeks. In the States, it takes months, even years, because of labor strikes, guys not showing up for work, doing half-ass jobs and what have you, pissing and moaning all the while. The Japanese would come in and do the job. You'd never hear them complain. What they should have been doing was helping us build our airports, not the reverse.

A lot of Americans think that the Japanese got to be so successful because of us, because of our generosity. They say that if it hadn't been for Douglas MacArthur, the Japanese would be speaking Russian. But the Japanese don't look at it quite that way. They say American kindness might have helped, but more important was their hard work.

And they did work hard. This country was ashes, and they worked twenty-four hours a day to rebuild it. Even now, you walk in the financial district late in the evening, and all the office lights are still on. That hard work is what helped make Japan powerful and wealthy—a lot more than anything we did for them. You had to respect the Japanese for their perseverance. I just wished the Americans would be more like the Japanese at times.

Take a look at the small old Japanese ladies walking with this terrible stoop, all bent over. They're the *real* Japan. Think about all the work they did, about all the sacrifices they made for their families. Because of them, the salarymen have stable lives and those kids are running around Roppongi.

Of course, the Japanese are very shrewd people. Don't let their smiling faces fool you. They know how to set up a good deal for themselves. They'll slide yen under the table to get things going, to motivate the other party. But, at the same time, they're not afraid to put out when it comes time to go to work.

Living in Tokyo, as I did, you could see the pride people took in their work. You'd see that dedication everywhere you looked. You bought a tape—a music tape or a video in Japan—and there'd be no hiss on it. The taxis were immaculate. The factory floors too. If there was a speck of dirt on the floor, it'd be a contest among the workers to see who could clean it up first. Their approach to baseball was the same with their endless practice. You could argue that they were out of their minds, training the way they did, but—and I can't believe I'm saying this—you had to admire their devotion.

I remember one night in Miyazaki, walking by this young kid's room. He was in there listening to music and shining his baseball shoes. I immediately identified with that. I thought back to my young days—in one of those rundown apartment buildings we used to live in. I used to get up at four or five o'clock in the morning for a 10:00 day game to iron my uniform. My mom used to wake up and ask me what the hell I was doing. After the game, I'd wash my uniform and hang it up. I got this warm feeling watching that kid. He was hungry, I thought, just like I had been.

Some Americans would complain that the Japanese were dishonest, that they reneged on deals. But I never found that to be the case in my dealings, especially with the Giants. The Giants were no dream, but they honored every clause of every contract with me. And they did it with Reggie too.

Of course, the longer I stayed in Japan, the more and more materialistic it seemed to get. They placed so much value on the things people possessed—Gucci bags and Benzes—even if they did have to pay outlandish prices. But then so did Americans, including me. Maybe they learned that from us?

LETHAL WEAPON

In early July, a story came out in the papers that I was going to
be traded—now that the Giants had Roh. It wasn't true, but it
still made big waves and the press was after me again. My
phone started ringing at 8:00 A.M. the day the story broke.

It rained like hell that day. I went out at ten and came back
late in the afternoon. Standing outside my apartment building
was a magazine reporter. The guy had been out there for
seven hours, waiting to interview me. He was soaking wet.
Drenched. I had to turn his request down because I had to get
back to the studio. But I admired his persistence, and I told
him so.

Dick Davis had been released at the end of June, twice in
the same day in fact. Once from jail and once from the Kintetsu Buffaloes. It was a world's first. The police had questioned
him for twenty straight days. They'd bring him to the interro-
gating room every morning and work him over for eight
hours. Then they'd send him back to his cell, a three-foot-by-
eight-foot affair with a *tatami* mat floor, a sink, and a Japanese-
style squat toilet. He was forbidden to talk or to read. He had
to sit in there on the floor, facing the wall until lights went out
at nine. Once or twice a week, he was allowed to take a bath.

But Davis stuck to his story about the hash being a balm,
and so in the end the police gave up and decided to let him
go. They gave him just enough time to go home and pack his
bags, then catch the next plane out. He was gone from Japan
within twenty-four hours of when they opened the cell door.

Bass's release was announced at about the same time. The
Tigers said they couldn't wait for him any longer and signed
up Rupert Jones.

A team official said that the club felt justified in its actions
because a Japanese player would have never left his team as
Bass did. According to one magazine survey, 70 percent of
Japanese company workers thought Bass had done the wrong
thing.

That was the Japanese work ethic for you.

Nobody seemed to mind that a two-time triple crown winner was gone. Every *gaijin* was disposable. It was like replacing

a part in your car.

Gully was still there, however, and in the process of making a comeback. He'd resorted to the inside pitch, the high hard one—which he'd avoided in the beginning perhaps out of a weird sense of fair play—and it seemed to be working.

One night on a television in the studio, I watched Gully mow down the Tigers one after another. It really did look like he had gained his second wind or something because he was firing pellets. During the course of the game, Gully hit one of their guys on the shoulder. Whether that was intentional or not, I don't know. But he smoked the guy and so the next time Gully came up, the Tiger pitcher threw at his head.

That was a big mistake.

In the States, Gully had been known for drilling guys. The last thing anybody wanted to do was throw at him with a fucking baseball.

I sat there in my control booth chair and said to myself, "This guy has had it." Gully got up out of the dirt. On the next pitch, he swung at the ball, popping it up on the first base side. As he ran down the line he yelled at the pitcher. You could see his lips moving. You didn't even have to be an accomplished lipreader, as I was, to know that what he said was "Fucking Asshole!" It was clear as could be.

I turned to the other people in the booth and said, "Take five, because Gully's going to smoke the first batter that comes up next inning."

Sure as could be, Gully uncorked a heat ball right at the batter's head. The batter ducked, and the ball hit his bat. Foul. Their bench stood up. Our bench stood up. Their manager Murayama started yelling. But nobody came out to fight. A wise move. I wouldn't have either.

Gully pitched inside a lot during that game. And he shut them out, 7–0, on three hits, to move his record to 6–7 for the season. After that, he was back on track (he wound up at 14–9), and he was also back in the Giants' coaches' favor, which was good because he caused a stir a few weeks later when he asked for a three-day "paternity leave" to be with his wife during labor. The Giants granted his request—with great reluctance—making it the first such leave ever in the history

of Japanese baseball. Naturally, the media went apeshit, but
everybody calmed down a little when Gully revealed the middle name of his newborn son.

PASSAGES

I was having the time of my life. The night after we finished
mixing, I was out with two studio executives, making plans for
the record's release in the fall. The next night, I was having
dinner with Boz Scaggs, who was in Japan touring for EMI.
The night after that, I was out with two video executives.
Then, in the third week of July I headed back to Miami, for
summer vacation with my wife and kids—our first ever together.

While I was gone, Yoshimura badly injured his leg crashing
into Komada in a game in Sapporo. The Giants sent him to
Dr. Jobe in Los Angeles where he underwent surgery and
stayed for a lengthy period of rehabilitation. That meant two-
thirds of the Giants' starting outfield was on the disabled list
and in the United States.

During a nationwide telecast of a Giants game, someone told
me later, the NTV announcer turned to guest commentator
Suguru Egawa and asked, "Egawa-san, tell us, who is the person
overseas who is hoping most for a Giants' championship?"

Egawa, with his usual insolence, replied, "Cromartie?"

The announcer was startled. This was not the answer he
had been looking for. But he recovered quickly.

"No, no, no," he replied, adopting his best lecturer's tone,
"It's Yoshimura."

Egawa didn't quit easily.

"I think Cromartie feels the same," he said.

The announcer changed the subject.

But he had been more or less right.

I didn't even think about baseball anymore.

In Miami, my wife and I had come to the conclusion that it
was time for a divorce. Actually, *I* had come to the conclusion
that it was time for a divorce. I didn't believe we had anything
in common anymore, except for our kids. She didn't seem to

care anymore for baseball, or for my music, or for me, for that matter. She didn't appear to have a great deal of difficulty agreeing to the split, although I couldn't exactly say she was delirious with joy either.

To my mind, the divorce had been coming for a long time, and we had grown in different directions. We'd gradually drifted apart without really noticing it, and one day we looked up and saw we were leading two separate lives.

We'd been married for twelve years, and much of it we'd been separated, with me on the road. Carole basically raised the kids by herself. And we'd lost touch.

My going to Japan was the final strain on our relationship. I'd been toying with the idea of opening a business there—a boutique or a restaurant or something. Carole did not want to be a part of it. She was still just a small-town girl at heart, while I was becoming a man of the world.

I remember when I signed the contract to come to Japan, Carole said to me, "I hope this doesn't lead to a divorce." Well, it did. We were fighting all the time. And it was time to put an end to the misery.

That's a self-serving argument, perhaps, and she would have her own reasons for the breakup of our marriage—my selfishness, my petty mean streak, my gigantic ego, my big mouth and so forth, which would not be without a certain amount of truth.

But whatever the reason, I asked for a divorce and she said OK, *provided* we could agree on the matter of alimony, which suddenly put my plans for retirement in a completely new light.

I would need to play another year to straighten things out financially. I'd need to get a good contract for 1989. So, in early September, I flew back to Japan to pick up the pieces of my baseball career.

THE RETURN OF A MAN CALLED CRO

The day after I arrived, I headed out to the Dome to say hello to my teammates, who had disappeared from view in the Central League standings. The night before, after a 6–1 loss to the

Dragons, Oh had held his eighth consecutive postgame "emergency" meeting. It had lasted thirty-two minutes, according to Hirano, which was a new record. The Giants were trying to talk their way back into contention.

Shoriki was panicking. He publicly declared that the pitchers should throw on consecutive days. Everyone was saying that Oh's days were numbered.

At the park, I was swamped with reporters' questions about my future plans. So I held an impromptu news conference in the Dome press room. Wakabayashi, our new PR director, had a fit. He tried to stop it. But there were already some sixty people assembled around me, so I went ahead anyway.

Wakabayashi reamed Hirano right there in front of everybody for allowing this breach of form to happen. I couldn't understand what he was saying, but I got the general message. He was pissed that someone had arranged a meeting with the members of the press without getting his permission. All player contact with the press, on and off the field, had to have the Giants' approval. Although my contract allowed me to talk to the media anytime I wanted, Wakabayshi's sense of authority had been offended and someone had to pay, meaning Hirano, since he couldn't do anything to me.

Gully had become totally fed up with the Giants in my absence and was already talking about going back to the States the following year—which he couldn't do because he had a two-year deal. It was a familiar phenomenon among rookie *gaijin*. Call it the Japan Syndrome or the Tokyo Giants Syndrome.

Gully had recently given up a home run in Yokohama to Carlos Ponce, who was Hara's main competition for the home run title (Ponce eventually won it, 33–31), and Hara made a sarcastic remark to Gully about it.

"Ponce...*furendo*?" A friend? Hara had said.

Gully said he suppressed the urge to answer yes.

Roh had cooled off, as I knew he would. He finished with 16 homers and a batting average of .255, which helped renew interest on the part of the Giants in the future of Warren Cromartie.

THE LAST OF OH

I was doing exercises in the outfield at the Dome, my hand still too sore to take batting practice, when I got the word that Oh had been fired. Actually he'd been asked to resign, which he did. But he wasn't at all happy about it because the Giants had made the decision to replace him before the season was over, something that was very unusual for Japan. The team still had five games left, making Oh a lame-duck manager.

I'm sure he knew it was coming. Shoriki had wanted to keep him, but chairman Mutai was against it. He wanted Motoshi Fujita, a former manager of the Giants, and whatever Mutai wanted, Mutai got. Oh was not eager to go, despite all the criticism and scrutiny he had been subjected to. He'd never won a Japan Series championship as manager and that bothered him, being the perfectionist that he was. Besides, whether you were asked to resign or just simply fired, it was always embarrassing, especially in Japan, where face was so important.

I was both sad and happy. I was sad that I wasn't going to play baseball for him anymore. With all his managerial short-comings, I'd rather have played ball under him than anyone else I knew. But also, I was happy that he'd finally be able to take a rest. He'd spent thirty years in a Giants' uniform. And there were a lot more worry lines on his face than there were when I first arrived.

I walked across the field, down the runway into the club-house, and knocked on the door of his office.

"*Hai*," said a voice from inside.

I opened the door and walked in. I expected the place would be jammed with people, but surprisingly, it was empty. There was just Oh, sitting alone behind his desk, the tiny, gray room bare of any mementos except a photo on the wall of last year's pennant-winning team.

Oh was smoking a cigarette and holding a cup of green tea. His face wore an expression of resigned calm. I patted him on the shoulder and sat down. I told him I'd heard the news and how sorry I was. He shrugged, smiled, twisted his head to the side in that shy way the Japanese have of saying they don't know what to say.

I told him that I wanted to thank him for everything he had done for me. I told him that he'd had more influence on my life than any other man I'd ever met, that he would be a friend forever, and that I really didn't have the heart to play for the Giants without him on the bench. We'd come such a long way together.

He told me he appreciated how I felt, but said that the Giants needed me too much for me to think that way.

His English was not great, to be sure, and my Japanese was certainly nothing to brag about. But we communicated just fine without an interpreter. We sat there and talked for a long time about the team, about the pennant we'd won, and the high points of the past five years. And then someone knocked on the door and stuck his head in. Oh was being called by the press.

We stood up. We shook hands and I felt my eyes getting wet. I hugged him, hard. I mumbled, "Good luck," and then I left. I went back to the dressing room, changed back into my street clothes, and went home. I didn't feel like hanging around to watch the media descend upon him.

I suited up for the Giants' last game a few days later in Yokohama. I still couldn't play. But I wanted to be in the dugout with Oh for his last game.

Afterwards, Oh talked for the TV cameras. He thanked the fans for their support, he thanked the players in the club-house, and then he departed. One of his last acts as manager was to recommend strongly to new Giants' manager Fujita that Warren Cromartie be signed to play for another year.

The Giants finished in second place, twelve games behind Hoshino's Dragons, and announced a new all-time attendance record of 3,391,000, thanks to the new Dome.

Bill Madlock, who finished at .260 with 19 homers and 61 RBIs, was released. So was Oglivie, who'd hit .311 with 22 home runs, proving my prediction that he'd be around for a long time wrong. Bass finally reached a settlement with the Tigers. He had threatened them with a lawsuit when the Tigers tried to back out of paying the money they owed him on the remaining year of his contract. Things got very touchy when the Tigers' executive dealing with Bass shockingly committed suicide.

Bass tried to join another team, but with no luck. The owner of the Seibu Lions reportedly urged that no team hire Bass after all the trouble he had caused.

Isao Harimoto, the 3,000-hit man, added his opinion that Bass should never be allowed to come back. "How could they possibly let him play baseball," he said on a TV sports program "when there is a chance that the wife and family of the late Tigers' official might be watching."

At age 33, Bass's baseball career was over.

It was funny how, of the four *gaijin* who hung around together—Bass, Oglivie, Davis, and me—I would be the only one left. I stayed in Japan that fall. Toshiba-EMI released my record and threw a big bash for me at the ANA Hotel in central Tokyo. About three hundred people showed up, including Oh. Our group, Climb, was subsequently invited to appear on all the big TV music shows, with me playing the drums.

I was on the "Yoru no Hitto Sutadzio," a popular hour-long song show, and was a guest star on the comedy program "Tonneruzu" where I played the part of a *samurai* in a skit. They dressed me up in an old eighteenth-century *kimono*, complete with fake topknot and sword. As this *samurai*, I was supposed to protect a family that was being victimized by a mean *homozaimo*, a homosexual lord.

I was great, everyone said.

Also, the Japanese monthly version of *Playboy* did a long interview with me. But only after Wakabayashi approved the questions.

Then reality set in. The album did fairly well, selling about 25,000 copies, but the Giants made it clear they would re-sign me only on the condition that I not perform or record or have anything to do with music during my next year in Japan. The choice was between a million-and-a-half dollars and a fraction of that figure from music. It wasn't a hard to make a decision.

1989

THE SWEET SWING OF SUCCESS

I announced my retirement—for the fourth time—at the beginning of the 1989 season. It was getting to be a habit. I gave this important scoop to a *Hochi Shimbun* reporter in March, and then I repeated my intention to quit during a subsequent speech I'd been invited to deliver at the Foreign Correspondents' Club of Japan in Tokyo, attended by newspapermen from all over the world. "This is definitely my last year," I told them with conviction. "There are other things I want to do with my life."

How was I to know the kind of crazy year I'd have? That by the end of the season, a huge photo of me would be plastered on the left-field wall in the Dome and that all of Japan would be at my feet?

If I'd known, of course, I would have kept my big mouth shut. Instead, I began the season telling anyone who would listen that come October, I was gone, outta here. I would have my alimony paid off. I would be free. Et cetera, et cetera. Blah, Blah, Blah.

I should give part of the credit for the strange turn in

events to our new manager, Motoshi Fujita. It was hard to believe that a manager could make such a difference in a team. But Fujita did. He was a medium-sized man in his late fifties, who wore large horn-rimmed glasses and looked more like a school teacher than the ex-pitcher he was. In his playing days he'd been nicknamed "The Kettle," because he had such a low boiling point. Once, during a practice session, he'd gone up in the stands and personally removed a drunken heckler from the park. But as a manager, he was one laid-back dude. With Oh it was always "We've got to win, we've got to win, we've got to win." With Fujita, it was simply, "Play it cool." He never criticized the players. He constantly encouraged them. And I never once heard a reference to Shoriki's deathbed wish.

As a result, we got off to a terrific start, and I went absolutely berserk at the plate. I had 22 hits in my first 44 at-bats, and my average hovered around .450 until the beginning of June. I was several kilometers ahead of anybody else in either league.

I hit a *sayonara* home run one game to beat the Whales, which caused their young catcher Ichikawa to burst into tears on the bench afterwards and our normally sedate infield stands, usually occupied by stoic business types, to burst into choruses of *banzai!* during my postgame home plate TV interview.

What madness could this be?

At first, the Japanese press couldn't come to grips with the fact that I was doing so well. It couldn't be just because of the change in managers, the reporters thought. There had to be some other reason. Was it because I was single again, asked one reporter, loose, on the prowl, free of marital constraints? Had being divorced made me a more patient hitter? Had I had a religious experience during the off-season? Or was it all just a big accident?

A famous TV sportscaster by the name of Shinya Sasaki seemed the most disturbed. He turned to his viewers one night and said, "How long before we see the real Cromartie?"

Frankly, I wasn't sure what was going on either. I'd compacted my swing just a little bit more. I'd stopped going for the home run and was spraying the ball instead of trying to kill it. But that was mainly because the pitchers were throwing extra carefully to me for some reason; I saw more outside pitches, which I, in turn, was forced to slap to the opposite field.

Also I was feeling relaxed and having fun. That was partly due to the influence of Fujita. But I'd had fun before, and I'd never hit this well. Hell, I didn't know. Maybe somebody had sprinkled salt in my locker.

A reporter buttonholed me one day. "Why are you batting so well?" he demanded to know, in English. He seemed almost indignant.

"I'm just playing it cool, man," I said.

He looked at me quizzically.

"I'm mellowed out," I said, "having a ball."

He scratched his head. "Having a ball?"

"It's American Zen," I told him. "Think about it."

Then I walked off.

THE MARIONETTE

I picked up the *Sports Nippon* one morning in May and was surprised to see my picture on page one. I had my fist balled up, an angry expression on my face. I looked as if I was ready to punch someone.

The headline read, "Cro Attacks Hara!"

The photo had been taken during a practice session when I was giving a young Giant named Suguro a lecture about concentration and heart. "You've got to give it everything you've got," I'd said, shaking my fist for emphasis. But the front page story was about an article *Sports Illustrated* had published on Japanese baseball.

The *SI* piece talked about Japanese-style training and group philosophy. One of the players featured was Hara. The author of the article had written that Hara was overcoached, that every time he fell into a slump, Giants' coaches and former Giants' stars like Kawakami would try to correct his form. Accompanying the story was an illustration of Hara as a marionette, swinging a bat, an unseen puppeteer pulling the strings. There was a quote from me: "I'd try to tell Hara not to listen to the coaches, to play his own game, but he couldn't do that."

My point was that Hara had to contend with social pressures that American athletes didn't. If an American major leaguer didn't want to be bothered by a coach, he could say so. But in Japan, you couldn't because the coaches were considered as important to the team as the players. More so, perhaps. The reasoning was, you could always get players, but good coaches were hard to come by. You had to show them more respect than they sometimes deserved.

The newspapers, however, smelling blood, had twisted it all around. I was leading the league in batting at the time with an average of .443—43 hits in 97 at-bats. Hara was leading in home runs, 10, and RBIs, 26, and was also fifth in the league in batting at about .340. We were also in first place by a comfortable margin. Things couldn't have better; yet one glance at the front page, and you'd think I was ready to slug Hara.

The previous day's game had been rained out, and I guess the *Sports Nippon* was desperate for a story. But I wondered about the press in Japan sometimes. I really did. Some papers, like the *Sports Nippon* and the *Nikkan Gendai*, were like poisonous snakes. If you spent enough time around them, you'd get bit sooner or later. That happened to all of us. But it just seemed they went after me more than others.

The *SI* story caused quite a stir in the Yomiuri Giants' clubhouse. Guys would come to me, holding up the magazine, aghast. "Did you see this?" they'd say, indignantly. They thought it was an big insult that Hara was portrayed as a marionette. But it was the truth, even though I wasn't the one who said it. And they knew it was true. That's why they didn't like it. Sometimes the truth hurt.

Hirano and I once had a discussion about the $50 billion trade deficit between the U.S. and Japan. I told him I couldn't understand Japan. They owned half of Hawaii, yet they still kept their country closed to trade.

He really got his red flag up. He was pissed. He couldn't take criticism of his own country. Most Japanese couldn't. When you got on the subject of trade with them, there was the

Japanese side, which was right, and the U.S. side, which was wrong. And that's just the way they reacted to the *SI* story, too.

The article aside, Hara was, in fact, getting harder and harder to take. In camp, Fujita had shifted him from third to left field to improve our infield defense. It had been a wise move, but at first Hara expressed misgivings about it to a TV interviewer. He said that becoming an outfielder would reduce the amount of time he would be in front of the cameras, because he'd be involved in fewer plays.

But then in the opening weekend of play, he hit three big home runs, which were replayed endlessly on the evening sports news, and his misgivings disappeared. He was the league leader in homers, and he was on top of the world.

On defense, Hara would stand in left field, next to me in center, tipping his cap to the fans. He'd practice his batting form over there too, showing off for everyone. Perhaps he was trying to get the cameras to zero in on him. I couldn't believe it. I'd yell over to Komada in right field. "Hey, look at this shit, Komada," I'd say, pointing at Hara. Komada would laugh and shake his head. He thought Hara was a bit much, too.

Hara's attitude bothered me more than anything else. He was caught up in all this business about himself—Mr. Giants, Prince Charming, and all—but he wasn't doing jackshit about his game. He didn't try to make himself better. He didn't lift weights, which would have given him more home run power. He just did what the coaches told him and looked in the mirror a lot.

But I suppose what really bothered me about Hara was that he was always more popular than I was. He was always the idol, and I was just the *gaijin*.

THE NEW REGIME

If Fujita was loose, our new head coach Akihito Kondo, who'd come to us from Seibu, could not have been more careful. Kondo kept detailed notes on our games and used them to conduct the meetings—pre-practice, pregame, mid-game, postgame and day-off.

He was smart, he knew baseball in and out, and, though

strict, he had a congenial attitude toward the players. He wasn't full of himself, and I thought he was one of the best coaches I had ever seen.

But I had my doubts about another new coach named Matsubara, our hitting instructor, a big, stern-looking former first baseman. It was hard to believe he had once been a home run star for the Taiyo Whales because he didn't seem to know anything about batting. He had Roh so confused that Roh didn't know which end of the bat was up.

Then there was our new pitching coach Nakamura, a former Giants' ace. Nakamura knew pitching, like Fujita, and the players respected him for that, but he was very nervous. Kuwata was 5–0, but with an ERA of 4.08—and Nakamura kept changing his form. He had changed it six times since autumn training the previous year. Now he had him out in a "mini-camp" working his ass off.

Moreover, Nakamura seemed to take the blood-type bullshit seriously. He explained to the press that Kuwata's blood type was AB, and AB types, as everyone knew, learned faster than others but also forgot quicker. That was why Kuwata needed to practice harder than anyone else.

It was voodoo coaching. The Giants employed sophisticated computer readouts which covered every conceivable aspect of a player's performance, and then diluted it with quack psychology—like Reagan and astrology.

My teammates were still overcoached, but I was subject to less control than ever. The other guys had to learn an enormous number of signs—about ten times as many as we had in the States. I don't know how they remembered them all. Me, I only had two signs. One wink meant that I could steal. Two winks meant hit and run. It wasn't real sophisticated. But nobody ever caught on.

Gullickson told me one day how sorry he felt for Roh, who was stuck on the farm even though he had the ability to play on the first team. He couldn't understand why there had to be a limit on foreigners. In the States, you can have black, white, Latino, Chinese, Japanese, Martian, anything you want. If you can play the game, then they let you play. If you're good, they want you, no matter what color you were. It's that simple.

I couldn't understand it, either. Maybe it was because *gaijin* couldn't remember the signs. But after a while, I stopped questioning the institutional racism. The slave mentality took over.

"Listen up, boy. We only have two *gaijin* per team around here! You got that?"

"Yas, massah."

"And there's a limit for the all-star game, too!"

"Yassah, yassah."

Actually, the U.S. has limits too. There's a U.S. labor law that says only 10 percent or so of all professional baseball players can be foreigners. That's supposedly to keep a lid on Latins. Still, the U.S. government issues 500 visas or more every year, which is enough to have the entire starting lineup of every big league team be foreign.

Never happen in Japan.

No sah.

Mother's Day

The thing that gets you about living alone is living alone. There's nobody to talk to. I tried to call home on Mother's Day, but the overseas lines were all busy. So I sat in my apartment, staring at CNN with the sound turned down. Then I stared out the window. It was an extremely windy day. The wind had blown away the clouds, and you could see Mt. Fuji off in the distance. So I pulled out my video camera, and I took some video. That was fun. Then I fooled around with my drums, and after that, I sat sat down and watched some more TV, sound off. I was having a ball.

Time passed. I tried to call again. Same answer, pre-recorded message in English and Japanese: "Sorry, but the lines are all busy now. Please hang up and call again." I stared out the window some more. This was becoming addictive.

I started thinking about the home run I'd hit in little league when I forgot to touch third base and was called out. I don't know why that popped into my head. I was hitting .400, and there I was thinking about a little league screw-up twenty-five years ago and remembering how unhappy my father had been. It wasn't even Father's Day.

My kids would be coming over in the summer with my mother. Until then, I guessed I'd be doing a lot of staring out the window and watching CNN.

I tried to call again from the park. Both Gully and I did. But the lines were still busy. A guy on our team said, "What do you mean you want to call home? They have Mother's Day in the States?" The Japanese think they invented Mother's Day, as well as baseball.

I'd just given my talk at the Foreign Correspondents' Press Club, about baseball in Japan, which was reported widely in the Japanese papers. I got a lot of praise in the clubhouse for that. "Good talk, good speak...," said Yamakura. Okazaki, Hara, the front office people, they all chimed in too. Even the batting practice pitcher complimented me. They praised my speaking more than they ever had my ballplaying.

After the game, I decided to go home and think about what that meant. Maybe I'd stare out the window at the same time. Or perhaps I'd watch some more CNN. The possibilities were endless.

THE GAIJIN WHO MASTERED JAPANESE BASEBALL

Hara went out with a pulled muscle. Gullickson had a bad knee and was on the DL. Yoshimura was out for the season. And Egawa had retired. But we kept rolling right along anyway. The way we usually scored runs was unreal. Bloop singles, ground balls that just found the hole. If we got behind, we'd come back. We were unbeatable. Credit for most of that went to Fujita. He had completely changed the mood on the team. People *wanted* to play for him.

One of the secrets of our success, according to the reporters, was the way that Fujita combined the candy and the whip, as the Japanese say. There was a midnight curfew, which was tough, but Fujita had set up a mahjong room for the players on the road, which was stocked with beer and various brands of whiskey. The players could use it as they wished until curfew (ten o'clock if there was an afternoon game the next day).

Some of our coaches were even inviting the players out to dinner, which was rare. Usually coaches and players in Japan stayed as separate as officers and noncoms in the army.

There were other factors too. One was Nakao, a new catcher from the Dragons, obtained in a trade for Nishimoto, who had worn out his welcome with the Giants. It turned out to be a great deal. Nishimoto was enjoying a revival with the Dragons, and we had a catcher with vitality.

Another was that we were now a healthy mix of veterans and young players. Fujita had been using young kids fresh off the farm. Our new shortstop, Kawai, a nobody the year before, had come through with several key hits. Inoue, another young outfielder, was hitting .330, with 12 home runs, by the all-star break. Still another youngster, Okazaki, was playing third base and stinging the ball all over the place. Komada was hitting .300 with power, while Shino was his normal steady self.

We were solid down the order, and with Hara not playing third base anymore, our infield defense had strengthened greatly. But it was our pitching that deserved the most praise. It was awesome. When Gully went on the DL, the team didn't even miss him.

Makihara was 12–4 with four key saves in the first three months. Kuwata had ten wins. But the big surprise was Saito. He'd developed a great curve ball that nobody could hit, to go along with a 93-mile-per-hour fastball. Fujita put him in the starting rotation and left him there, and Saito repaid him by racking up eleven consecutive complete victories, a new Japan record. His comments in one interview were vintage Japanese: "I feel I've done something wrong by getting my name in the record book, as I'm not an established pitcher."

The rap on Saito had always been that he was weakhearted. Well, hell. The difference was that Fujita showed confidence in him. If Saito got into trouble, Fujita left him in to work out of the jam, whereas Oh would yank him.

I was hitting .452 on May 25. No one in the history of Japanese baseball had ever had a start like that. A few nights later, I met Oh for dinner at a *sushi* bar in Roppongi to celebrate.

Oh was taking a whole year off from baseball. He wasn't

doing any TV commentary, no play-by-play, no newspaper columns. The game had been his whole life for thirty-two years, he said, and he needed a rest and time to spend with his wife and kids. He wanted to get as far away from it as he could. Oh certainly looked a lot more relaxed than I'd ever seen him.

We sat at a shiny oak table in the back of a brightly lit room, talking like old friends, eating raw tuna slices and drinking *sake* out of small porcelain cups. Oh praised my batting, and at one point, he reached across the table, poured more *sake* for me, then lifted his own cup in a toast.

"Congratulations, Cro," he said, breaking into a wide grin, "You've mastered Japanese baseball."

Oh didn't make statements like that lightly, and for me, it was the ultimate compliment. It ranked with what Phil Collins and Geddy Lee had said to me.

I wondered how he felt, seeing the team he had managed for five years doing so well. I was sure that part of him was happy for the Giants, because that's the way Oh was. But I'm sure another part of him wondered how things would have turned out if the Giants had given him another year.

I stayed at .400 until the end of June, and we kept our big lead, which had ballooned to eight games. In early July, Naka-hata conducted a poll about my future. I don't know where I was, but I wasn't there when he interrupted a team mahjong session at a hotel in Ashiya. "How many guys here want Cro-martie to come back next year?" he asked.

According to him, the results were a unanimous "Yes."

"So what do you say?" Nakahata asked me later. "How about playing one more year?"

I smiled and said, "We'll see."

After that a different player would come up to me every day and say, "We want you to stay."

Now, when you're dealing with an ego like mine, flattery will get you everywhere. So I began thinking in earnest about playing yet another season. I'd just finished doing a major endorsement for Kirin Lager Beer which would be shown on prime-time TV, with an accompanying billboard to be put up in the Dome in September. Christ! A big time commercial! And pennant fever to boot. This was serious stuff. I was succeeding beyond my wildest dreams, and if the Giants wanted to blind me with a big check, well, OK. I could be blinded, as well as flattered.

THE GOOD, THE BAD, AND THE UGLY

Black clouds hit the horizon in the beginning of August. Makihara totaled his knee and would be out for the rest of the season. Then Kuwata was fined three million yen, about $24,000, the highest fine in the history of the Giants, for taking some money—fifty million yen—to be an "adviser" for a sports promotion firm. Kuwata said he hadn't solicited the money. It had just been given to him. But he'd accepted it without the Giants' knowledge and permission, and since the Giants insisted on controlling everything, and taking their commission, Kuwata's conduct was treated as a major offense.

The morning newspapers, in covering Kuwata's scandal, listed other great Giants' crimes of the past:

> CRIME: Shinozuka, December 1980, calling off his wedding shortly before it was scheduled to take place.
> PUNISHMENT: Confinement to quarters for a month.
> CRIME: Cromartie, October 1984, leaving the team without permission two games before end of the season.
> PUNISHMENT: ¥1,250,000 fine.
> CRIME: Pitching coach Horiuchi, June 1985, punching the equipment manager.
> PUNISHMENT: Severe warning.
> CRIME: Mizuno, May 1985, breaking curfew, drinking alcohol while still a minor.
> PUNISHMENT: ¥1,000,000 fine, confinement to quarters for one month.
> CRIME: Nishimoto, March, 1987, criticizing management.
> PUNISHMENT: ¥2,000,000 fine.

When you came right down to it, the Yomiuri Giants were a regular rogues' gallery.

We began to show signs of folding. We lost five in a row in late July, and the Dragons beat us six times in the span of two weeks. I was ready to give some of the credit for that to our pitching coach.

Take a game at Nagoya, in which Saito almost pitched a no-hitter. He had gotten as far as the ninth inning with one out, protecting a 3–0 lead, and Nakamura was having a nervous fit on the bench. He was sitting there, his leg going up and down a mile a minute, chain-smoking. He must have smoked two packs that game.

"Cool it, man," I told him. "You're making Saito nervous."

Then Saito gave up a hit. Nakamura immediately ran out to the mound to "calm" Saito down, which only made matters worse.

Saito walked the next batter, then gave up another single to let in a run. With runners at first and third and the score 3–1, Ochiai stepped up to bat. The crowd was going wild. Nakamura was about to pee his pants. Nobody was warming up in the bullpen.

Saito wound up and fired a pitch down the middle, which Ochiai hit into the right-field stands. It was sickening. Saito's face turned white. He went into shock. Dead shock. Nakamura turned his back and headed for the clubhouse, but Fujita, to his everlasting credit, went straight out to Saito who was moving numbly off the mound, to console him. He put his arm around Saito and walked him back to the dugout. That was class. Usually in Japan, if you lost like that, they'd treat you like dogshit. But Fujita, he was all right.

I blamed that loss on Nakamura. It wasn't just his nervousness; it was also the speech he had given us before the game. He talked about the time he played for the Giants and they were on a roll just like we were, then they went into a tailspin. That was real inspiring.

We lost the next night too, as Gully, back from the DL, got bombed, 5–1. Nakamura's speech had cursed us. I'd gone 2-for-3 with a home run. But I'd also made a bad throw in the seventh inning which allowed the go-ahead run to score, thereby contributing to Gully's defeat. I twisted my ankle on the play, and Fujita took me out for a pinch hitter in the ninth. After the game, a reporter inquired if my removal from the game was punishment for making the bum throw. My average stood at .404.

We were playing like shit. We were sluggish, balls were not being caught, errors and mental mistakes were being made everywhere. Bad throws by Nakao and Shinozuka handed a game to the Whales. I sat out that one, but stayed on the bench to cheer my teammates on. I wound up yelling at them instead.

"You bunch of pussies," I screamed. "You're like high school students."

Nakamura kept staring at me as if I had popped out of a bottle.

They were dead tired, of course. But no one would think to give them a rest. Not in Japan. No. We had more practice instead.

We had an injury list as long as the trade demands being submitted by the U.S. government to Japan. In addition to Makihara, Nakahata got hurt, then Inoue, who'd been really hitting the ball, and then Gully again, among others. Even our interpreter, Ichi Tanuma, was out of action. He suffered a stroke in Nagoya and had to have an operation to remove a clot on his brain. He'd be out of action for many, many months.

Despite all this, we somehow held on to our lead. Fujita kept plucking some young untried kid off the farm, and the kid would do the job. Fujita was a wizard that way. In fact, his Young Turks were edging some of the veterans out of their jobs. Nakahata, a sure .300 hitter, our captain, found himself warming the bench on his return from the injured list, and, at 35, began contemplating retirement.

Hara returned to the lineup in August, after being out for a month, to deliver a tenth-inning bases-loaded *sayonara* drive to the Dome wall that beat the Carp. On the interview stand after the game, he actually cried. I guess the emotion of being on the sidelines for so long caught up with him. I was surprised, and touched. I didn't think that Hara was capable of something like that.

I'd dipped below .400 twice, falling all the way back down

to .379 at one point, but both times I climbed back up to that magic mark. On August 11, I went 2-for-3 in our eighty-ninth game of the year to put my average at exactly .400. And it was a record. No one in Japan had ever been at .400 that late in the season.

It was also the quietest assault on .400 in the history of Japanese baseball. If it had been Shinozuka or Ochiai instead of me, you would have seen front page stories every day, with charts and graphs all over the place. But with Warren Cromartie, the papers usually found other topics to headline.

NTV was giving me a decent buildup. If I got a hit, they'd flash my updated batting average on the screen, and the great Shigeo Nagashima announced on nationwide TV that he was rooting for me to make it. But I could tell there were a lot of people who didn't want me to do it because a Japanese hadn't done it; they didn't want a *gaijin* to be the first. People were getting nervous about it. I could feel it. In fact, some coach in Hiroshima said that if the Carp, in second place, couldn't win the pennant, well then the very least they could do was stop me from hitting .400. Hearing that just made me want to try even harder to do it.

THE FALL OF GULLY

Gully was about as dejected as I'd ever seen him. In August, he'd been put on the DL for the second time that season, and when I went to visit him, he was "caving it," as we liked to say. His family had gone back to the States, and he was in his apartment alone, lying on the floor in a pair of jeans and a T-shirt, watching a video. *Lethal Weapon*, I think. The windows were closed. The curtains were pulled. He had shut out the outside world.

The Giants, with so many other pitchers doing well, had given up on him. His record stood at 7–5 with an ERA of 3.65, and a pulled groin muscle had sidelined him. Gully had been too heavy when he arrived in camp, which was his fault. Then he'd hurt his knee trying to get into shape too fast, and he never regained his sharpness of a year before.

Gully confessed that he just couldn't figure out the

Japanese batters. He had a curve ball and a slider, while most other guys in Japan had about five or six different pitches—curve, slider, *shooto*, fork ball, fastball. In truth, he needed another pitch. The batters were used to seeing what he had. He couldn't throw inside every time.

But also, he only got to start every nine days or so, while Saito and the others went every five or six days. You had to pitch regularly to be sharp.

The Giants' players had been supportive. So had Fujita. But the coaches were very cold. Especially Nakamura. None of them wanted to talk to him. They would talk to me, all the time, but not to him. In early August, at the Dome, Gully had pitched a victory over the Carp, 2–1, going six innings and allowing four hits. But Nakamura didn't even congratulate him. If it had been Saito or Makihara, Nakamura would have been all over the guy. It was irritating, so I went over and grabbed Nakamura by the arms.

"You go and say, 'Nice pitching,'" I told him.

He went, but he didn't like it.

Gully was so depressed. We sat there in his darkened apartment and talked for a long time, Mel Gibson firing away in the background. And I stayed to hear it all. I was his counselor, therapist, and friend.

After loving Japan in the beginning, Gully was now thoroughly down on the country, Tokyo in particular. He thought it was too crowded. He had a wife and three young children. Tokyo was no place for a family like that, he said. The language barrier also bothered him, and he did not like the way Japanese treated *gaijin*—like the cab drivers who frequently refused to pick us up.

Now, Tokyo cabs were nice. They were spotless, immaculate. Not like some of the garbage cans you have to ride in New York City. The drivers would usually have an air freshener installed and, quite often, a little vase with a flower in it, stuck in the rearview mirror.

Generally, the cabbies were polite, but the bad thing about them was they wouldn't always stop for *gaijin*. Maybe they remembered the war, or maybe they thought we'd cause trouble, or maybe it was just the language barrier.

We were in Osaka one night, trying to get a taxi, standing on the street. But the cabs ignored us. They were only stopping for Japanese, so we literally forced one driver to take us. He had pulled over to let a passenger out and we hopped in before he had a chance to leave. Was he pissed. His neck was straight as an arrow. Smoke was coming out of his ears. He wouldn't speak to us at all. He took us to the wrong place. I finally blew up. When we got out, I wasn't going to pay him. I was yelling, "*Wagamama!*" You selfish you-know-what. The cab driver got out and grabbed Gully's arm.

A crowd gathered around because they had recognized us. So we finally paid him. We were afraid somebody would take our photo and publish it in the scandal magazines. "Giants' *Gaijin* Start Brawl in Osaka!" the headlines would read.

Then there was the night Gully took his wife and sister out on the Ginza, Tokyo's most expensive area. They tried to enter a restaurant, but the doorman blocked their way and told them to leave.

"Japanese only," he said.

That devastated Gully. For him, that was the clincher.

So now, he had gotten the ass for Japan—and for the Giants. He'd come to the conclusion that Japan was a very prejudiced country, and getting worse. He was ready to hang it up.

"I'm done, Cro," he said, "I'm not coming back."

He'd said the same thing before, but this time he was serious. He also didn't have much choice, because the Giants didn't seem to want him anymore.

Well, I felt for Gully. But he had a couple million dollars in the bank, courtesy of Japan. That could make up for a lot. And he could still go back to the big leagues—which is what he eventually did, signing on with Houston the following season.

BLACK, IN JAPAN

Newsweek, the international edition, interviewed me in late August, and the finished product received wide attention in Japan because of some controversial remarks I made. Some examples:

> ...The money is good. That's exactly why we're all here. We're not over here to make friends. The Japanese are already jealous because we *gaijin* make so much money. So you're expected to do everything: hit the ball over the fence, catch the ball, whatever. When you don't do it, you're criticized. Every once in a while, they give you a little pat on the back. Very seldom.... You have to swallow your pride and be able to withstand some unusual elements that are put before you.
>
> Was there prejudice in Japan?
>
> —Sure, there's a bias against *gaijin*. The Japanese don't want to be outshined. They'd rather see their boys do it. They'll walk me to save face.
>
> Did I face racial prejudice as a black?
>
> —Of course. There is prejudice all over the world. And it is certainly here in Japan. I'd been called names in the outfield in Japan, just like when I was playing in the States.

Perhaps I overdid it. After all, Kirin Lager was putting my photo up in the Dome posing with a glass of beer, and the TV version of my new beer commercial was being aired every night. How could I claim prejudice when they did things like that?

But prejudice did exist. Boomer, Fielder, and the rest of us felt it. We couldn't count the times we saw a cartoon of a black in some ad or magazine drawing, showing the big eyes, the fat lips, exaggerating our features. Little Black Sambo was a popular doll in Japan. The Japanese said these caricatures were "cute." But how would they like it if they saw yellow "Jap" dolls with slanted eyes and big buck teeth for sale in the States. To us, it was demeaning. So was the Japanese politician who suggested that blacks in America seldom paid their bills.

I knew a black ball player who once tried to give blood in Japan but was refused. They were probably afraid he had AIDS. It was insulting. We didn't want to make a big deal out of it, but there was no question that prejudice was there.

We considered ourselves round-eyes first, blacks second. The prejudice was there because of our race, but there was also prejudice because we were *gaijin*. Black or white, we were excluded. Hell, just being non-Japanese did the trick.

Bass was one of the all-time greats of the game in Japan. But when he left, nobody cared. To most Japanese, he was a novelty, and somebody else would take his place. The Japanese liked fresh new *gaijin* faces, and if you hung around too long they usually got sick of looking at you. All in all, they preferred their own stars.

Someone once wrote that if white Americans wanted to understand the black experience in the U.S., they should try living in Japan. I think he knew what he was writing about.

FAME

I'd always had a pretty big ego, and I'd always wanted more attention than I got—from a father who never gave it to me, from managers and coaches who underrated my abilities, and, in Japan, from fans and sportswriters who thought I was overpaid and underproductive. I felt deprived and ignored.

Until this year, that is. Now, suddenly, everything was different, my comments to *Newsweek* notwithstanding. I was leading the league in batting—.393 as of September 3. We had an eight-game lead, and people like Nagashima were saying that I was key to the Giants' drive for the pennant, that without me, the Giants couldn't do it. What's more, the sports media were singing my praises almost every day—which was definitely a new experience.

I loved it.

But the funny thing was, I discovered I couldn't handle it. I found out that being the object of everyone's affection unnerved me, that it put a kind of reverse pressure on me. I was a huge success; and everyone wanted *me*. And finding myself in that position for the first time in my life, I became something of a bastard. Maybe I was punishing people for the ways I'd been slighted in the past. But instead of easing up and being happy about it all, I became moody as hell. I became grumpy and mean.

I was being swamped with interview requests, and I took a perverse glee in wringing as much money as I possibly could out of them. It was the custom in Japan to charge for press interviews—a custom not shared by American big leaguers, who considered interviews PR—but the Giants encouraged us in this regard.

One hundred thousand yen, about $800, for thirty minutes was the norm, and now that I was a big hero, I charged even more—several times more. I didn't make any bones about it. Guys wanted to talk to me on the field? "How much you pay?" was my response. Hell, I'd even charge magazines who wanted to write *about* me a fee just for the privilege of using my name. People were trying to take advantage of me, so I would do the same to them.

It was idiotic when you stopped to think about it—the idea that people had to pay for what was essentially a promotion for the *Yomiuri Shimbun*. But I didn't mind at all. My attitude, combined with some of the things I'd said in the *Newsweek* interview, was enough to make people keep their distance, which was perhaps what part of me, deep inside, wanted. Old patterns were more comfortable. Even if it meant alienating people I really didn't mean to alienate.

How Much Doggu?

Still, we had a pennant to win and many games left to play. So I tried not to dwell too much on my own psychological problems. Baseball needed my more immediate attention.

On September 11, Miyamoto pitched a 4–0 shutout over the Carp which put us eight-and-a-half games in front. We had 19 games left, the Carp, 26. I hit my thirteenth homer of the year to spark the win, although my batting average was slipping; it was down to .385.

A week later, our lead stood at seven games, with 14 games left for us, 22 for the Carp. But Hara, with 22 home runs, had choked so much as we headed down the stretch, that Fujita saw fit to mention it in a pregame meeting when we got back to the Dome.

"If the third, fourth, and fifth batters don't hit," he said, "we lose." Then he pointed right at Tatsu and said, "Right Hara?"

Well, Hara was more than a little embarrassed by that. And

wouldn't you know it, in the bottom of the ninth inning of a scoreless tie that night against the Whales, with runners on second and third, and one out, it was Hara's turn to bat. He wasn't about to be walked, even with first base open, because I was in the on-deck circle.

Hara was scared. Flat scared. His eyes were as big as silver dollars. Somebody had to try to calm him down, so I went over and called his name, trying to make myself heard over the din of the fans at the Dome.

Now, I knew that Hara's hobby was dogs, that he knew about breeding and raising them and what the prices were for different types of dogs. So I decided to try that tack. "Tatsu," I yelled, "My friend bought boxer dog. He pay ¥100,000—*ju man yen.* You think too high? *Takai?*"

Hara stared at me and blinked. I might just as well have asked him a question about rocket science. His mind was in the twilight zone.

"Hara," I tried again. *Ju man yen. Bokusa doggu.*"

"Eh, *doggu?*"

I'd made contact.

"Right. *Doggu. Inu.* Bow wow. *Bokusa. Ju man yen. Takai?*"

Hara focused on me. He had returned to earth.

"*Takai,*" he said, shaking his head at the ridiculous price.

It was only for a second. But it had taken his mind off the situation he was in. It had relieved some of the pressure. And when he finally stepped up to bat, he had relaxed just a shade. He swung at the first pitch and lined a *sayonara* single into left field.

After the game, Hara told Hirano that he really appreciated what I had done. But of course, he didn't appreciate it enough to tell anyone in the press.

DONTO MOOBU!

It was finger-pointing time again in Japan. Gully had gone back to the States for medical treatment, but there were plenty of other candidates left. There were stories in the press that Larry Parrish was going to get fired. He was on his way to hitting 40 homers for the Swallows, but management's rap against him was that he only batted .260, that he struck out too much, and that he couldn't play defense. What was worse, he couldn't bunt.

The same things were being said about Boomer, who was leading the Pacific League in batting average and RBIs, and Jim Paciorek of the Whales, who was hitting about .341 and would be winning the Central League batting title if it weren't for me. The Whales' owner declared to reporters that Paciorek didn't hit enough home runs—he only had 8, with 49 RBIs—and issued a public warning to Paciorek to shape up. He also blasted Carlos Ponce, who was hitting .274 with 19 homers and 66 RBIs.

Cecil Fielder's season was over. He had broken a bone in his hand and was gone for the rest of the year. Although he had 38 homers, his manager's complaint was that he didn't hit enough with men on base. I wonder what the manager thinks of Fielder now.

That sort of thing happened every year, of course. It was a way of taking the heat off some of the Japanese who weren't doing well, and, at the same time, it was a way to scare the *gaijin* into putting on a last-ditch job-saving spurt. But nobody was saying negative things about me for a change. I was the apple of everyone's eye. A Giants' executive was quoted as saying I should play in Japan until I was 40.

I had been seeing a lot of left-handed pitchers down the stretch, especially versus the Carp who were loaded with them, which helped lower my average to .382 by September 21.

We were edging closer to the pennant, stumbling all the while. On September 23, we beat the Dragons 8–3 in Nagoya. Our magic number stood at eight, with 13 games left. During that contest, a ball was lined to me in left center. I made a diving catch and landed on my shoulder, nearly knocking myself out in the process. I laid there in a haze of pain, then I heard words in English.

"*Donto moobu!*"

"*Kuro, justo mineeto.*"

I looked up and saw a half dozen pairs of eyes peering down at me. The eyes seemed to be getting rounder and rounder, the faces paler and paler.

"*Donto moobu!*"

I recognized the voice. It was Kondo, our head coach. His face was white.

A number of things went through my head at the time:

1. My shoulder was starting to hurt like hell.

2. The team would have to finish off the pennant without me.

3. I had lost my shot at .400.

4. I had lost my shot at Bass's single-season record of .389.

5. I still had a shot at getting the last bullet train back to Tokyo.

I didn't make the train. I had to stay over and see a doctor who told me that I had ligament and muscle problems, and that I should not play any baseball for a while.

And so I sat on the bench and watched my teammates lose three in a row, including the first two games of a three-game series with the Carp at the Dome. Hara was not the only one with a tight ass. Everyone had a case of nerves. Our lead dropped to four-and-a-half games over the Carp, with 8 games left to play for us and 13 for them. The Carp had won seven in a row. They were even with us in the loss column. And our magic number had disappeared. If they moved to within one-and-a-half games of us, they would go into first place, given the weird mathematics of baseball standings in Japan.

It was panic time.

At least we had a good excuse, which was always useful in Japan. We'd had more injuries than all the other teams in the league combined. And they kept piling up. We were playing our farm team, basically. It was a miracle we were still in first place. It was a miracle Fujita could field a lineup from the walking wounded. The soreness in my shoulder had diminished and I thought I'd better play. If I didn't, they might start blaming me if we blew the pennant.

It was Saito who saved our ass in that final game with the Carp, just like he had all year. Saito and the Japanese Shinto gods, that is. Give credit where credit is due. Saito pitched a two-hit shutout for eleven innings. But we were also lucky. In the eleventh, with two out and a runner on second, Hara hit an ordinary fly ball to center which miraculously turned into a double. The Carp center fielder, one of the best outfielders in Japan, lost sight of the ball in the lights, and it went over his head. Nine-hundred-ninety-nine times out of a thousand, he would have caught the ball. But tonight he couldn't see it. That had to be the work of the gods.

ICHIBAN

We clinched our pennant on a rainy early October night in Yokohama, which was also so foggy you could barely see the lights of the ships in the harbor just down the street. Miyamoto shut out the Whales, 5–0, and Hara hit a big home run in the seventh inning—his first in over a month.

When we trotted out to our positions in the bottom half of the inning, a huge roar greeted Hara in left field. TV helicopters hovered overhead. Hara doffed his cap. The stands exploded. Tatsu was in his element.

For the *doage* victory toss, Fujita went first. Then Nakahata, who had announced his retirement. Then they came for me. I can't say I minded the order. They lifted me up, tossed me in the air, legs and arms akimbo. Once, twice, three times. It was my first *doage*, ever. Then they went for Kondo, our head coach.

Then I did a *banzai* in front of the stands, three times in a row, and I trotted down to left field, to our cheering section, for more. Now *I* was in my element.

We had our celebration in a Yokohama parking lot, of all places, surrounded by huge plastic curtains that had been put up just for the event.

I was wearing my victory headband with "*Yusho!*" written on it and my blue sunglasses, the better to keep the Yokohama evening fog out of my eyes. Fujita made a short speech. It was his third pennant in four years as a manager, counting a stint in the early eighties, so he had to be doing something right. No manager ever deserved more credit for winning a flag than he did. His handling of his players, especially Saito, and the youngsters from the farm, had been superb. He would have been voted MVP if managers had been eligible for the award.

This being Japan, there were even more speeches to listen to, Shoriki and others, before we could get to the alcohol. Finally, Hara, Nakahata, and Shinozuka, the players with the most seniority, broke open a huge *sake* barrel with baseball bats. And then they turned us loose.

I spotted Nakahata across the way. I ran over and embraced him. He poured beer down the back of my uniform shirt. Then I saw Kuwata standing alone, over in the corner, pouring beer on himself. The others had been avoiding him since his money scandal and his interests in real estate had come to light. I went over to him, put my arm around him, and spilled some beer in his jersey. I didn't care what anyone else said. I liked the hell out of him.

Fujita had already asked me to return to Japan for 1990. I had gone into his office for a talk, three weeks earlier.

"You come back here next year?" he asked me.

"Yes," I replied.

He became very excited. He grabbed my hand and cried, "Good!"

"Next year, you make big money," he said.

Then he gestured, putting his hand in his jacket as if stuffing some cash into it.

I could relate to that.

My final record was .378, with 15 home runs and 72 RBIs. I won the batting crown and was a leading candidate for MVP, along with Saito, who finished with a 20–7 record and an ERA of 1.62, topping the league in just about every pitching category.

Kawakami, the godfather of Japanese baseball, and a man not known for his love of American baseball or American baseball players, wrote the following in a newspaper column:

> The Cromartie of this year makes your eyes go round. You get the impression he is a different person.
> Cromartie challenged .400. For 58 consecutive games to June 24, he did it. Then, after the All-Star break, he climbed back up, going 2-for-3 against Kawaguchi of

Hiroshima, reviving the possibility of the miracle.

In his 89th game, he finally fell off and never made it back, but his contributions were obvious to all, even opposing teams. Carp manager Koji Yamamoto said, "If we'd had Cromartie, we would have won the championship."

The thing about this year's Cromartie is he gave up home runs and concentrated on sure hits. No one kept the batting order going like Cromartie did. He was indeed a "hit maker."

From being a typical *gaijin*-style "first pitch" hitter, he became a batter who slowly and surely read the opposing pitcher. From a psychological point of view, he upset the opposition.

"Cromartie is there. If I get on base, he'll get me home...." That's the effect Cromartie had on the team as a whole.

I'm not saying Cromartie did it all alone, but he was an indispensable player for the Giants.

Fujita wanted Hara in the #4 spot. In order to do that, he put Cromartie in the fifth spot in the batting order. And Cromartie became the guy who drove the runner home or created a new change.

Fujita talked to Cromartie thoroughly about the formation of the batting order and got Cromartie's approval and understanding. From the moment Cromartie said, "OK, boss," his work was assured.

Asahi Evening News reporter Gene Saltzgaver wrote:

> When Cromartie missed games because of injuries, the Giants looked pathetic at best. He was the team leader and its inspiration. He batted .400 for a record number of games, then when his average started to slip, he was still the most dangerous hitter in the lineup, delivering clutch hits that kept the Giants in the thick of things. For his efforts and especially for his batting, he should be named the league's most valuable player.

RONALD REAGAN AND THE KINTETSU BUFFALOES

Nobody expected us to win the Japan Series. Our opponents weren't the Lions but the Kintetsu Buffaloes, an Osaka-based railway-owned team that had aced the Braves and the Lions out on the last day of the season. Three percentage points had separated these teams in the final standings.

The Buffaloes had an awesome batting lineup, led by Ralph Bryant, a former Dodger, who'd hit 49 home runs that season. Bryant had struck out 187 times, a new Japan record, but he'd also hit .283 with 121 RBIs. He'd smacked 4 homers in a final week doubleheader against the Lions. The Buffaloes also had a tough young pitching staff, led by a kid named Awano, who'd won 19 games.

We were the underdogs, primarily because we were still the walking wounded, without Makihara and a number of other players. The Giants ordered Gully back from the States, took one look at him in practice, then told him they couldn't use him—which was something he already knew. Roh, who had played the final month of the season with the first team, would be the other *gaijin*.

A famous Japanese fortune teller had studied the astrological charts of Fujita and Kintetsu manager Ogi and predicted that Kintetsu would take the series in five games.

Well, he was almost right.

We dropped the first two, 4–3 and 6–3, playing at Kintetsu's home park, Fujidera stadium, a drab, aging structure with no infield grass.

The place was jammed to the gills, with a standing-room-only crowd of 45,000. Hundreds of them had spent the night outside the stadium. The seats at Fujidera were extremely close to the field, and its hat-box shape helped keep the noise bottled up inside. We could all hear very clearly the insults the Buffalo fans were yelling at us.

"*Bakayaro!*"—the old favorite, "Go back to Tokyo!" and so forth. Osakans hated Tokyo. The press had predicted their jeering would unnerve us. And it must have, because we really stunk. Errors, mental mishaps, you name it, we did it. Saito and Kuwata got kayoed. Hara went 0-for-8, and in the fourth inning of game two, Fujita ordered him to sacrifice bunt. He couldn't even do that right, and popped out instead.

Game three at the Dome was even worse. Ronald Reagan, who was in Japan (collecting two million dollars from the Fuji-

Sankei media group for a series of public appearances), showed up to throw out the first ball and shake all our hands. Then a cocky, wiry young pitcher named Kato, who wore a gold chain around his neck and tried hard to look tough, shut us out, 3–0. Hara, shoved down to seventh in the lineup, went hitless again.

It was humiliating. We looked so bad that Reagan left early. In the postgame interview, Kato told a nationwide TV audience that even the worst team in the Pacific League was better than we were.

We'd stopped trying, I thought, even me. Although I'd had five hits thus far, I felt lethargic too. Something had to be done.

The next day I sat in front of my locker, thumbing through *Drummer* magazine, trying to look as angry as possible. As the guys came filing through, one by one, they called out "*Ooos.*" But I didn't answer. I wanted to make it clear how totally unhappy I was with our situation.

It suddenly became very quiet in the clubhouse. When they had all changed into their uniforms, I called a meeting. I wasn't the captain, but I was playing and Nakahata wasn't, so I felt I had the right.

"We've given up," I told my teammates, as Hirano translated. "We just gave three games to Kintetsu, flat gave it to them. If we're going to lose, we got to put up a fight first. Right now, your faces are no good. You look like losers. You've got no fight. What's the matter with you guys?"

Nakahata nodded and so did Shinozuka and some of the others.

"I don't live here," I went on, "so it's no big deal for me. I can go home when it's over. But you have to stay and you're only embarrassing yourselves playing the way you are. You owe it to yourselves and to the fans to go out fighting!"

Nakahata stood up, raising his fist, and said, "*Yosh!*" in agreement. All right!

"*Yosh!*" cried the others.

Then I walked out and headed for the field.

It wasn't exactly Knute Rockne, but it seemed to help.

That day one of our young pitchers, Kohda, shut the Buffaloes down, 5–0.

In game five, we beat their ace lefty Awano. With the Giants ahead 2–1 in the eighth inning, I came up to bat with two out and runners on second and third. They walked me to get to Hara who was, by this time, 0-for-14 in the series. He had looked so bad that it was painful to watch him. Then, on a count of two and two, the Buffaloes' reliever threw a fastball down the pipe, and Hara smashed it into the stands for a grand slam!

Even if you weren't particularly crazy about Hara, you had to be happy for him at that moment. He'd redeemed himself, just when we needed it. It was like a movie script.

On TV, all you saw for the next two days was Hara's home run, of course. NTV must have set a new record for replaying the same scene. The final score was 6–1, Saito pitching a four-hitter, with the Buffaloes' only run coming on a homer by Bryant.

Then we headed back to Kintetsu. I knew then we were going to win. We had the momentum. We had Kuwata rested. They were losing their composure. You could feel it.

In Fujidera, after a day of travel, we beat them 3–1, behind Kuwata, with Miyamoto and Mizuno in relief. The big blow was a two-run homer by Okazaki in the eighth inning.

Then came game seven, in which Kohda went against big-mouth Kato. In the second inning, Komada, who was the first baseman, smashed a huge home run to give us a 1–0 lead. As Komada rounded third, he looked over at Kato standing on the mound and yelled, "*Baka!*" as loud as he could. Suddenly the kid didn't look so cocky amymore.

In the fourth inning, we struck for three more runs and sent Kato to the clubhouse bath. In the sixth, Hara hit a two-run homer to give us a 6–2 lead.

Then Nakahata was sent in to pinch-hit. Nakahata, who had spent most of the series on the bench, walloped an enormous home run to center field. I don't think anyone was more surprised than he was. He had tears in his eyes when he crossed home plate. Then he went in back of the dugout and really started to cry. It was the last swing he ever took as a professional player.

We really creamed them. I added a home run in the seventh, and going into the bottom of the ninth, we led 8–3. The final score was 8–5, as Miyamoto came in to mop up.

And we were Japan champions.

It was storybook. It was what baseball fans, and baseball players, lived for.

At the final out, as we *doage*'d and hugged each other, it seemed that everyone was crying. Nakahata was sobbing openly. Komada too. Hara. Our coaches. Shit, even I had tears rolling down my cheeks.

THE CELEBRATION

The twenty-four hours following our big win in Osaka were among the weirdest and most exhausting I had ever experienced. We celebrated at the team's hotel, the Takezono Inn in Ashiya, all night, and most of us didn't get to sleep until 5:00 A.M.

Then we got up to catch the 10:00 A.M. bullet train back to Tokyo. We sat like zombies all the way back, too hung over to even sleep or eat breakfast, reeking of alcohol and cigarette smoke.

Arriving at Tokyo station, we sped directly to the Dome, where we changed into our home uniforms. From there we drove to the Yomiuri newspaper building and filed into a second floor conference room where the big brass had assembled, including the honorary chairman of the board of Yomiuri, Mutai.

We stood there puffy-faced, red-eyed, and unshaven, as all the executives made speeches. First Fujita, then Shoriki, then some others, and finally Mutai.

They had served us drinks, a glass of beer each, but we weren't allowed to take even a sip until the speeches had all ended, which wasn't to come for quite some time. We shifted wearily on our feet, holding our glasses, nauseated by the smell of beer. Mutai took the floor and talked for what seemed an eternity. He was like some ancient *daimyo*, reading a rescript to his subjects.

He thanked everyone personally, except me. He mentioned each player's name on the Giants, including Hara's several times, but the name *Kuromatei* never passed his lips.

His speech lasted for a solid hour. I know because I timed it. When he was finally finished, and we were ready for the toast, the head on my beer was gone. Flat beer. It seemed to suit the occasion.

When Mutai had finished with us, we were paraded through each floor of the building, to be greeted by all the Yomiuri employees. They were lined up at their desks like members of a clan army, applauding as we passed by.

Following our salute by the House of Yomiuri, we embarked on a two-hour ticker tape parade through Tokyo.

We sat in open cars, the first occupied by Fujita and Shoriki, who was sitting up ramrod straight, like a wooden Indian. I rode in the second car with Hara and Nakahata. Office workers opened their windows and showered bits of paper down on us.

It was almost 5:00 P.M., the most crowded time of day in Tokyo, rush hour, twilight approaching, and we snarled traffic everywhere we went. But nobody seemed to care, least of all the police, who couldn't stop smiling at us. People would stop their cars, get out and come over to shake our hands. There were fans hanging from trees, girls were screaming, and huge congratulatory signs were plastered all over the place. There must have been 300,000 people along the way. It was absolutely insane.

My left arm soon became sore from people grabbing it. I looked over to see Nakahata cringing in fear next to me, trying to keep away from the fans who were clawing at him in delirium.

Later that night, we appeared on NTV, in a one-hour special aired nationwide. During the show, Nakahata confirmed his retirement. In a recent poll, he had been chosen as one of the ten all-time best Yomiuri Giants and also one of the ten most popular.

He'd appeared in only fifty games this year, partly because of injuries and partly because Fujita was going for younger blood. He was only 35, and he could have continued to play if he had really wanted. But he was moving on. It was said he'd be getting ¥100,000,000 the next year, as a TV commentator, which was about three-to-four times what he had been making as a player.

In the middle of the program, we were all asked to say something about Nakahata. When they came to me, I discovered, to my shock, that I was all choked up.

"*Saiko no tomodachi.*" He was a great friend, I said, speaking in broken Japanese. Tears filled my eyes. "*Sabishi ne.*" I'll miss him terribly.

I meant every word of it.

All in all, it had been quite a day. Three hours on the bullet train, three hours at the head office, two hours on parade, then NTV in the evening to cap it off. I was more exhausted than I'd ever been in Miyazaki.

I went home to Miami to rest. The Giants, predictably, went to Palm Springs for a special two-week training camp.

The MVPs were announced in November, and lo and behold, it was Bryant in the Pacific League and Warren Cromartie in the Central League.

Saito could just as easily have been chosen. So could Awano. In fact, a newspaper article suggested that the Foreign Ministry had applied pressure on the sportswriters to cast their ballots for the *gaijin* because of deteriorating relations between Japan and America.

The mood between our two countries then was as poisoned as I'd ever seen it. We were having arguments over trade, and Japanese companies were buying up choice U.S. real estate like Rockefeller Center. A best-selling book in Japan entitled *The Japan That Can Say No* accused Americans of racism and branded Americans workers as lazy. In parts of the U.S., "Remember Pearl Harbor" bumper stickers were appearing. A survey taken that winter asked Americans to rank the countries they trusted; Japan finished eleventh.

With all that coming down, perhaps the Foreign Ministry really did feel compelled to act, lest Japan itself be accused of racism.

A famous sportswriter known for his bluntness later said:

Not every Japanese is happy about two Americans winning the MVP. Many older Giants fans, for example, do
not like the idea of foreigners, especially black foreigners, playing for their team. They may cheer Cromartie if
he hits a home run and do a *banzai* along with him, but
in their hearts, they despise him. They are secretly glad
that the South African government had granted
Japanese "honorary white status."

Although Gully and Fielder returned to the major leagues,
Parrish, the home run king of the Central League, was
released. He then accepted an offer of about a million dollars
to take Fielder's place on the Tigers.

Me? I was expecting twice that. $2,000,000. All I needed to
know was where to sign.

1990

MUTAI

I sat there in the all-too-familiar banquet hall with its brilliant white tablecloths, glistening china, and red carpets, as Mutai rambled on. I had taken my wristwatch off and laid it on the table, timing the speech to see if Mutai would break his own record. The longest talk he'd ever given us was one hour and fifteen minutes, according to my statistics. But today, he looked like he would go on forever. Many of my teammates were eyeing my watch, smirking and giggling at my insolence, covering their mouths with their hands. But I didn't care.

I felt like walking out. I really did. Once again, this 90-year-old man had insulted me by saying he was looking forward to the day when Giants didn't need *gaijin* anymore.

I was sitting right there, not forty feet away from him, when he said it. Everyone was calling me the leader of the team, saying the Giants would never have won without me. I was the MVP, for Chrissake. But Mutai acted as if I didn't exist. All he could talk about was Hara—who was eating it up.

There were other players that Mutai didn't seem to like. He had insulted Egawa too, at our 1986 preseason dinner. He'd said that Egawa should have won more games, that he didn't show enough guts. But at least he had mentioned Egawa's name. Right out loud. In all my years on the team he'd never once uttered the words "*Uoren Kuromatei*." And he'd never once spoken to me personally. Maybe he still remembered the war or something.

I'd had major contract problems over the winter. In response to my demand for a two-million-dollar one-year deal, Mutai had said, "The day we have to pay a *gaijin* two million dollars is the day we don't need him."

His attitude was one reason I hadn't flown back to Tokyo to pick up my MVP. "Send it UPS," I told Hirano. So Nakahata attended the awards ceremony to accept the trophy for me.

Mutai finally relented on the two mill, but only after Hirano made two trips to Miami try to talk me down, and only after Fujita had strongly interceded on my behalf—or so I was told. But I'm sure having to pay the money stuck in Mutai's craw. I had a bad taste in my mouth too.

Now Mutai was zeroing in on Kuwata, who was involved in yet another scandal. A new book entitled *Goodbye Masumi Kuwata, Goodbye Professional Baseball* insinuated that Kuwata had at one time associated with a suspected gambler and that he had even revealed the days he would be pitching—something that Central League teams kept a closely guarded secret until game time.

Kuwata vigorously denied the charges, and Giants' general manager Takeshi Yuasa, after investigating the matter, cleared Kuwata of any wrongdoing. But a second investigation, conducted later by higher-ups, revealed that Kuwata had accepted cash and an expensive wristwatch from the guy, although no evidence was found that Kuwata leaked his pitching dates. Kuwata said he thought the man was just an enthusiastic, wealthy fan—a business type.

It was not the first time that the image of the Japanese game had been so besmirched. In 1969, two players had been banned for life in the so-called "black mist" game-fixing scandals. In 1988, a Seibu Lions' coach named Doi was fired after he was arrested for gambling at mahjong, an illegal activity in Japan but one which is prevalent anyway. To repent, Doi shaved his head and entered a Buddhist monastery.

However, this was the first time that a member of the Giants had been so tainted. The sports dailies were having a field day. "The Lie!" screamed the *Sports Nippon*. "Guilty! Lie Exposed!" went a headline in the *Sankei Sports*.

By April, there were four different lawsuits underway involving the Giants, Kuwata, and the author of *Goodbye*.

I truly felt for Kuwata. In my opinion, he was a little naive, but he was a nice kid who had gotten bit by a snake. Fujita was really upset about what happened. He thought Kuwata got a raw deal, too.

If those were the kind of standards you were going to apply, why single out Kuwata when everyone else was just as bad? The sports manufacturing companies, for example, would come around and service the players with gloves and shoes. And the all guys would take them. The media were always pressing cash into the players' hands—interview fees, or money for some award or another. And private companies sponsored most of the cash prizes for the all-star games, the Japan Series, and the league titles, which ran into millions of yen. That was why we were professionals—to make money.

Hell, if it was the Giants' policy to charge money every time a player said two words to a reporter, what was so illogical or inconsistent about taking gifts from anyone else?

Gamblers were everywhere. You didn't know who you were talking to half the time. Guys would show up at the park, be introduced as a friend of a friend, shake your hand, ask for autographs, and leave. You'd see the guy again in the hotel bar on the road and he'd buy you a drink. Just another fan. A businessman. You have no idea he's a gambler. And you get sucked in. Veteran ballplayers developed a nose for such things, but for the younger ones it was the harder to tell. If a gambler wanted to get to you, he usually could.

Konishiki, the popular Hawaiian *sumo* wrestler, once posed for a photo with two visitors at the *sumo* stable. They turned out to be gangsters, and the photo was published in a magazine. Suddenly, Konishiki was "associating" with organized crime figures.

Kuwata screwed up because he lied about the money. He tried to hide it from the tax people. But I still thought Kuwata was fundamentally a decent kid. Christ, how many other players on the Giants had tried to conceal some of their side income from the government at one time or another? All of them? I knew of one ex-Giant star who made personal appearances and got most of his fee under the table. It was almost a national pastime in Japan to cheat on your income tax.

Mutai was still sputtering on. I suppressed another yawn and looked around the room. How the faces had changed since I first joined the team. Nakahata—gone, Egawa—gone, Nishimoto—gone, Oh—gone; even Sudo, our gruff farm team manager had left—to manage the Taiyo Whales. All the people I'd been closest to. Junki Kono was still there, but he was spending more and more time on the farm. Yamakura and Shinozuka were in the process of being eased out.

There was still Hara, of course, who would have another typical Hara year—.300, with 20 homers, a month on the disabled list, and a photograph of him visiting his Ginza mistress's apartment published in a scandal magazine. But Hara and I had always kept our distance from each other. We'd never gone out together, never had a down-to-earth talk. He'd come around once in a while and ask me about the major leagues, how they hit and how they fielded, and so forth. But heart-to-heart? No. I think jealousy kept us apart. Mutual jealousy, I might add.

Komada and Okazaki were on the verge of becoming the new team leaders. An American named Mike Brown had been signed up. And a whole new cast of characters was stepping on the Giants' center stage. I'd only just begun to make friends with them. I'd bring my CD to the clubhouse and put them on the player Shino kept in his locker. I'd rap with them about music and different performers—trying to get their minds off of baseball, if only briefly.

Mutai finally finished talking—I'd clocked him at one hour and ten minutes—and our reception broke up. I felt a sudden twinge of sympathy for the new faces on the team. Think of all the speeches that lay ahead of them.

SONNABEECHI!

"Hey! SONNABEECHI!"
  "NEE-GAAHH!!"
  "BAKA!!!"
The man sitting in the middle of the center field stands in Nagoya was yelling at me again.
  "NEE-GAHH!"
  "BAKAYARO!"
  "MAZZAFUKKING KURO!"
From my position in the outfield, I couldn't see him, but I could hear, and recognize, his voice. It was the same old guy, drunk as always, who always came to the park just for me. He'd started making his appearances after I'd punched that Dragons' pitcher, and he was still p.o.'d about it. How could I tell?
  "NEE-GAHHH!"
  "SONNABEECHI!"
I'd actually started to get used to him. There was something about his consistency, about the way he never failed to show up, that I admired. I respected persistence. The guy was always there, just like the *oba-san,* the old woman who was inevitably waiting when our bus pulled into the stadium parking lot to scream out at me, "Yankee Go Home."

The old man had extra reason to be mad today. We were kicking the Dragons all over the place. The final score was 12'-4, to complete a three-game sweep. We were in first and the Dragons were in the cellar, in the middle of a five-game losing streak.

My friend wasn't the only fan in the stadium to be upset. When the game was over and we'd hurried onto the bus, Dragons' fans were milling outside screaming insults and throwing things at us—lit cigarettes, empty beer cans, rocks, and what have you. Like I said, without them, it didn't feel like Nagoya.

In a way, I didn't mind so much. I'd grown used to it. I could even smile about it. What had bothered me more was the behavior of some American fans in Hiroshima, where we'd played a few days earlier. They were U.S. military guys from a nearby base or ship in the harbor, whatever. They were out of uniform, but they were skinheads, so it wasn't hard to tell. There had been a whole group of them there in the center field stands.

They were throwing ice at Brown and me in the outfield. Yelling obscenities and calling me nigger. They were trying to show the fans in Hiroshima that they were anti-*gaijin* or whatever, because Hiroshimans are notorious for not liking Americans—Americans, of course, being the ones who dropped the A-bomb on them. You could walk into a bar in Hiroshima, and the first words you might hear would be "Japanese only." And you'd be walking out again. That happened to me more than once there.

Why these *gaijin* thought that they could win the hearts and minds of Hiroshimans when they obviously represented the institution that bombed them in the first place remained a mystery to me. But there they were, trying their damnedest anyway.

One fellow, wearing a Carp cap, had his shirt off and was running up and down the aisle, screaming his head off.

"Cromartie, you suck!" he yelled, trying to coax the other Japanese fans into following his lead.

"Cromartie, kiss my ass!"

His friends were trying to start the wave.

It was interesting. I'd heard this kind of racist bullshit before, both in Japan and in the States. And those words certainly weren't new to my teammates either. But it was the first time they'd heard them coming out of the mouth of whites. It unnerved them. It made them feel uncomfortable, worried —for *my* sake. They looked at each other, suddenly alert, and you could sense a kind of protectiveness there, like they wanted to be sure *I* was OK.

I was OK, just irritated as all hell. I finally turned and yelled at the guy with no shirt.

"Hey, asshole. Get a real job!"

That stopped him—momentarily.

But it was nice to be able to respond in English for a change.

Back in Tokyo at the Dome, Gully called the clubhouse

from Houston. He'd just beaten the Mets, 10–5, for his first major league win in over two years. But he was more interested in the scoop on Kuwata. So I told him. And I told him about Sudo too, and how the Whales had kicked our asses twice in a row at home (in fact, they gave us trouble all season).

Gully loved it. So did I. Mutai had stuck it to Sudo more than once. He had fired Sudo once in 1975 and Sudo wound up working in a steel factory for a while. Sudo had been brought back under Fujita, and his success with the young players on the farm was one of the reasons we won the pennant. It was easy to understand why the Whales had wanted to hire him.

Sudo had wanted to take a couple of coaches with him. Mutai said no. So now Sudo was sticking it back to Mutai.

Gully was overjoyed at being back in the major leagues —back where real baseball was played. "Cro," he said, "It's great here. But you forget how big these guys really are."

I asked myself would I feel the same if I were in his position? Times had changed so much—I had changed so much —how *would* I like it?

THE LIGHTS OF TOKYO

I had a dinner appointment that night with some publishing people in connection with this book. We met at my apartment, then got into my Mercedes, and drove through the nighttime traffic to Roppongi, the roads a swirl of headlights and neon signs. It was something a lot of *gaijin* chose not to do—drive in Tokyo, that is—but I'd become expert at it, weaving in and out of the narrow lanes of cars. All the activity turned me on.

I couldn't believe how Tokyo was changing. It seemed that every other day a new building went up. This city was growing so fast you couldn't keep up with it. Ten percent of all the companies in Japan were construction firms, I was told, and they had to be kept busy—even if it meant covering all of Tokyo with cement, which is what they had a good head start on doing.

I parked in front of a no-parking sign about ten feet from

the Roppongi intersection, the heart of Tokyo. There was a huge campaign in progress against illegal parking. But what the hell, if they gave me a ticket, the front office would take care of it. It was one of the perks that came from being a star with the Tokyo Giants.

I walked into the Hard Rock Cafe, and many people stopped to gawk. It seemed that everyone knew who I was —which separated them from Mutai.

The Hard Rock Cafe was perhaps the most popular night spot in Roppongi, perhaps in the entire city. Half of it was a bar, the old-fashioned type bar with foot rails; the other half was a restaurant with smooth wooden tables about twice the size of what you'd get in an ordinary Japanese restaurant. Normally, the place was so crowded there was barely room to stand.

The American-style size of the place is what brought the crowds in, that and the decor—electric guitars hanging on the walls, photos of rock stars everywhere, a big luminescent clock at one end that gave you "Hard Rock Time." There were a lot of *gaijin* there, but a lot more Japanese—most of them young, all of them mingling.

I sat down with my friends, ordered barbecued chicken and cranberry juice, and we talked about the upcoming project, shouting over the roar of hard rock music and the din of a hundred different conversations. Three young ladies came up to our table to ask for my autograph, wish me well, and swear their undying devotion to the Giants. "*Gambatte*," they squealed, as they left. Girls kept walking by and giving me the eye, sending out vibes. But I tried hard to ignore them. After all, this was business.

I always got my share of invitations. Women would send me flowers, presents. This past trip to Nagoya, a young Japanese girl got in the hotel elevator with me. She couldn't have been much more than 18. She handed me a letter, in Japanese. When the elevator opened on the first floor, two reporters were there waiting for me. She didn't want them to talk to me. She had something more important on her mind. But I stayed away from that sort of thing pretty much. You never knew what kind of scandal it might turn into if the press found out.

I tried to be discreet.

The relationships I'd had with Japanese women—and there were a couple whose names I can't reveal—were real relationships, not one-night stands. These women became friends. What I liked about them was that they were so well-mannered, with a kind of shy innocence that was very different from the tough aggressiveness of some women I'd met in America. They were also incredibly clean. Their skin smelled sweet, like honey—with a touch of soy sauce—and tasted great. Most Japanese women had lithe bodies, with small hips and compact breasts, which to me only enhanced their appeal.

In bed, because they were on the shy side, they were a little inhibited. You didn't see as many moaners and screamers as you did in the States. When they talked, they'd say things like "*kimochi ii,*" feels good, or "*ookii,*" big, or "*saiko,*" great. At the crucial moment, they'd say, "*Aah iku wa,*" which meant "I'm going." You didn't have to understand Japanese; the meaning was clear enough.

Japanese women seemed just as dedicated to form as the players were in baseball. They worried about the right body movement and proper position. There had to be a harmony to it all. If something wasn't right, or you had trouble coming, the girl would usually apologize.

"I'm sorry my technique is so bad," she might say. "I'll try harder."

And when it was over, the girl would turn and say, "I'm sorry it took so long. Thank you for your patience."

That was the kind of dedication I liked.

But back to the Hard Rock—it was a slice of the new Japan. The young people you saw in there were not going to live life like their parents did. They weren't putting up with that nonsense about hard work and self-sacrifice and being chained to a dull job all your life. They were loaded with cash. They had poise and savvy. And they were out to have a good time. Our ballplayers must have envied them. I'm sure the average salaryman did too.

After dinner, I paid the check, said goodbye to my friends, and went outside. The temperature had dropped, and I shivered in the cool night wind as I made my way back to my car. I hadn't even gotten a ticket, it turned out. I unlocked the door, got in, and turned on the heat. A small crowd gathered to watch. They were smiling, friendly, shouting words of encouragement, still basking in the glow of our championship year.

Well, they really did like me, I thought—just like Sally Field at the Academy Awards. And that was just fine with me.

On the way back, I stopped off at Wave, Roppongi's big swinging record–video store to check out the new CDs. It occurred to me, as I wandered through that amazing high-tech setup, how much at home I had come to feel in Tokyo. It wasn't so much being famous—that would change, I knew. It was the feeling of being accepted. I got the impression that now that I had endured six years in Japan, taking everything that had been thrown my way, the Japanese had finally decided to adopt me. In a way, I really belonged.

It wasn't the first time I'd had that feeling. The winter of the previous year, I'd been sitting in my new living room in Miami, a stone's throw from where my wife and kids were living, watching the Emperor Hirohito's funeral on TV. All these scenes of downtown Tokyo appeared on the screen. There was Roppongi, the Hard Rock Cafe, a *sushi* shop I frequently went to, a *yakitori* place I knew. It was all so familiar.

It was the strangest, most unexpected sensation. I felt like getting on a plane and flying back to Tokyo. I was startled by my reaction, but I suddenly realized I was *homesick* for Japan! I sat bolt upright in my easy chair and thought, "God damn! The place has really gotten under my skin." That year I returned to Japan a little early.

I drove home slowly, parked the car out in front of my apartment building, and took the elevator upstairs. I stuck the key in the door, switched on the lights and surveyed my empty living room—dining table, sofa, TV, and new state-of-the-art CD player, courtesy of Aiwa.

I couldn't count the number of hours I'd spent alone in Japan—in this apartment, in hotel rooms all over the country. So much time to think about myself and the life I'd made. I remembered the times when I actually cried—coming to Miyazaki for another year, getting up at five the first morning, jetlagged out. It would all hit me, and I'd asked myself what I was doing here, again, separated from my family, far far away from home. One evening, I opened the window and screamed out at the mountain across the way. I swore to myself that I'd never return to Japan.

But I wasn't saying that now. No. Japan *had* changed me. I knew I wasn't the smartest guy in the world, but neither was I the dumbest. And if I wasn't the greatest player ever to put on a uniform, I'd worked hard and I'd learned to persevere. This country had helped teach me how—to no small extent. I'd made the most out what I had, and what I had now in my seventh year in Japan was not bad at all.

I pulled a coke out of the refrigerator and put on a Phil Collins CD—"In The Air Tonight."

"I'm home," I said to no one in particular.

Then I walked over to the window and stared out at the flickering lights of Tokyo for a long time.

Another season had begun in Japan.

And it was all right with me.

THE SUMMING UP

I don't regret leaving the big leagues or the U.S. I could have played there for a number of years more, but then I wouldn't have had the Japan experience. And playing in Japan has been one hell of an experience, to say the least.

Coming here was the most difficult decision I'd ever made in my entire life. I'm glad I did it. As a result, I've found that it has been easy to make other bold moves too, like starting a rock band.

It is also the one thing that I can really talk about.

The Japanese have taught me a lot in the seven years here. I gained another outlook on life. I learned to cope with a different style of living and with different ways of communicating, like relating to the unspoken word. Living in Japan, you develop a special antenna for the feelings of others.

Most of all I learned the meaning of being a team player in Japan, of being a Group Person. I've come to understand the value of togetherness, which is something that Americans need to realize, especially American big league stars.

Patience is a great virtue where the Japanese are concerned. They don't seem to get upset or show their emotions a lot because it upsets group harmony. Granted, that has its positive and negative sides, but Japanese-style patience has rubbed off on me.

People back home have told me that I have a different attitude than I used to. Mind you, I'm still not the type of person to hold everything in. I express emotions. I bitch a lot. I say it like I see it. And I'll still tell the next guy to fuck off if the urge strikes me, which is something the Japanese never do. But living in Japan, I have tried to tone it down.

Japan can be a very peaceful place. You don't have guys at each other's throats all the time like you do in the States. But it can also be stressful, because you constantly have to worry about the feelings of others around you. Or what they *really* think and aren't telling you. You just can't say the first thing that pops into your mind.

Sometimes I think the Japanese carry their love for harmony a bit too far. You could throw up on the table in the middle of a dinner party and the Japanese would do their best to ignore it. They'd pretend it never happened. They do that a lot in Japan. If they don't like something, they pretend it doesn't exist. That's got its good points, but it's also a kind of refusal to accept difference or failure or how life really is.

Basically the Japanese are a very honest people. You leave your wallet in the taxi, the next day the guy delivers it to your door. Somehow they find where you live. In New York, you would never see the guy again in a million years. In New York, they are always looking for some way to rip you off. I flew into JFK one year and hopped in a cab for LaGuardia. The ride cost me forty bucks. The driver kept going around in circles. He claimed he got lost. Welcome to the U.S.A. Well, that sort of thing doesn't happen in Japan.

But the Japanese are just as arrogant and self-centered as Americans. They think they are god's gift to the world, just like a lot of Americans do. The Japanese are very rich and successful now, and they feel they don't have to cater to anybody else. You see that more and more.

At the same time, a lot of Japanese are traveling abroad these days. They see how prices are cheaper in other countries and how living conditions are better—more outdoor space, bigger houses and apartments, much less crowded. Now you might find that about 20 percent of the people who've gone abroad don't like Japan when they get back. They feel confined—physically and mentally.

But the ways in which Japanese differ from Americans are far more than those in which they are similar. The Japanese stick together. They believe in following a leader. They are quite fixed in their own ways. There's absolutely no element of surprise to their life. Nobody—or almost nobody—is going to buck the system. It's safe, secure, and always the same. Just like in baseball, everybody knows that if the leadoff batter gets a hit there is a 99 percent chance that the next batter will bunt.

In general, the Japanese are fairly nice to foreigners, at least on the surface. Of course, there are many who don't like *gaijin,* but at least they leave you alone. They don't speak to you, that's all. They don't beat you up on the street like they do in some parts of the U.S.

It is not easy to bridge the gap between Japan and America. A Japanese and an American can look at exactly the same object and see two different things. Examples: *Gaijin* will say Ochiai gets grooved. Japanese will say the pitchers jam him all the time. Americans will say Japanese work too hard and wear themselves out. Japanese will say *gaijin* are lazy. Americans will say the Japanese game is too slow. Japanese will say the American game is too fast. Americans say that the Japanese don't have the guts to stand up for what they believe in. Japanese say that Americans are selfish and greedy. It goes on and on.

But there are times when I feel that it actually works, this business of hands across the sea. As a foreigner in Japan I have had experiences that have changed my life. It's been unbelievable. My Japanese friends have shown me decency and kindness. So have my teammates. There isn't one of them who wouldn't be welcome in my home, and I mean that. I've made all kinds of noise about them, but all in all I have great respect and affection for them. We've been through a hell of a lot together. Some people have been amazing. They know when it's my kids' birthdays, and they send presents.

And I think that's in part because I tried to fit in. I worked hard and kept in shape. I always went to camp in top condition. I gave my all as much as I could. And in that way, I showed respect for the job we had to do and for my teammates and for my hosts. I had my own ideas about doing things, but I also tried hard to fit in. And although it wasn't easy, in the end I was able to do it.

I've learned that attitude plays an important part in whatever you do in life. You've got to be able to adjust to succeed, to ride the waves, to smooth out the bumps in the roads. Some people can't do it. Other people won't do it. I learned that I could do it. And it was Japan that taught me that.

THE LAST OF CRO

In 1990, I got off to the worst start of my career. I was in the low .200s for all of April, with one lousy home run. Even in little league I was never that bad. In frustration, I turned for help to the best batting coach I knew.

I called Oh one rainy evening in May. He was at his new office, a sports promotion company in Toranomon, just off the Ginza. The time was 6:30. At 7:15 he walked into my Hiroo apartment, dripping wet.

Oh removed his coat, and after exchanging a few words of greeting, he took off his suit coat too. And there, in my living room, he demonstrated what I was doing wrong.

"You're dropping your shoulder again," he said, in excellent English—he'd been studying the language in connection with a plan he had to hold charity sports events for underprivileged children around the world. Then he went through the lesson he'd given me years before in the *yakitori* shop in Aoyama.

We talked for an hour about my form, our lives together, our mutual experiences, and then he reviewed my batting flaws once more. When he was satisfied he'd solved the problem, we hugged and he left.

It made for a nice story, but, unfortunately, it didn't do much good this time. I continued to struggle all year. I eventually finished at .295 with 14 home runs and only 55 RBIs.

We won the pennant again, easily, but we got blown away by Seibu in the Japan Series in four games.

At the end of the year, I announced my retirement.

And this time I kept my word.

(Editor's Note: Warren Cromartie's batting average stood at .278 with 5 home runs at the all-star break, and yet he led all outfielders in the all-star fan voting. It was one of the highest vote tallies an American player had ever received.)